The
World's
Largest
Man

HARPER

An Imprint of HarperCollins*Publishers*

The World's Largest Man

A MEMOIR

Harrison Scott Key

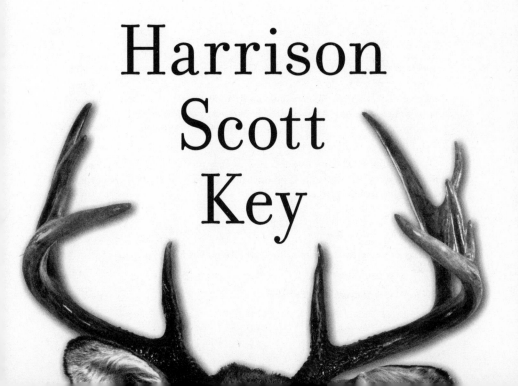

HarperCollins books may be purchased for educational, business, or sales promotional use. For information, please e-mail the Special Markets Department at SPsales@harpercollins.com.

FIRST EDITION

Designed by William Ruoto

Library of Congress Cataloging-in-Publication Data has been applied for.

ISBN: 978-0-06-235149-4

15 16 17 18 19 ov/RRD 10 9 8 7 6 5 4 3 2 1

—❧ ⁜ ❧—

For my wife and also my lover, who have the pleasure of being the exact same person, and who hates
it when I call her "my lover," so I do it a lot, because
I have a disease that makes me say it.

Note to the Reader

—✹ ⊹ ⊹ ✹—

I have changed the names of many characters in this book, because most of those people own guns.

The
World's
Largest
Man

—❊ ✦ ✦ ❊—

·

A Conversation with My Mother About This Book

—❊ ✦ ✦ ❊—

When I left Mississippi many years ago, I would sometimes come back to visit my parents, and at some point, my mother and I would end up in the kitchen, while my father sat in the living room watching *America's Most Wanted* and trying to decide which of his neighbors were lying about their identities.

She would be cooking, and I would be watching her cook, and she would ask me this Very Important Question. She started asking it about twenty years ago, and has never really stopped. I still remember the first time.

"Did you have a happy childhood?" she asked.

She is a needy woman, but when you're married for forty years to a man who has the emotional tenderness of a Soviet farm tractor, it's easy to be needy.

"I need to know," she said. "I need to be validated."

I bought her a Deepak Chopra book once, and this is how she started talking.

"Don't worry," I said. "I have no memories of being molested."

"Molested?" she said. "What are you talking about? By who?"

"By anyone."

"I want to know. Who didn't molest you?"

"Many people."

"Why didn't you ever say anything?"

"Because it never happened."

"Are you hearing this?" she said in the direction of my father, who now slept soundly in his big chair, dreaming of home invasions.

—❦ ✦ ✦ ❧—

CHAPTER 1

·

Don't Tell Me a Love Story

—❦ ✦ ✦ ❧—

They say the South is full of storytellers, but I am unconvinced. It seems more accurate to say that it is full of people who are very, very tired. At least this was my childhood experience in Mississippi, where there was very little to do but shoot things or get them pregnant. After a full day of killing and fornicating, it was only natural that everyone grew weary. So we sat around. Some would sit and nap, others would sit and drink. Frequently, there was drinking and then napping. The pious would read their Bibles, while their children would find a shady spot to know one another biblically, or perhaps give birth to a child from a previous knowing. Eventually, though, all the sitting led to talking, which supposedly led to all the stories, or at least the beginnings of stories.

In my family, we were unable to finish any. Until now.

Back then, most of our stories were told at the dinner table, after the meal, by my father, Pop, and his father, known to his peers as Monk. These men, to whom I am deeply grateful for giving me life and a name and any remnant of virility that might linger in my fragile and bookish bones, could not get to the end of a story if you gave them a map and a footpath lined with Nilla Wafers. In their storytelling, they went back and forth, like Vladimir and Estragon, in a slow and maddening game of interrogatory squash played by men with no arms.

"Well," Monk would say, from one end of the table.

"Well," my father would say, from the other end.

This is how all their stories began. I'd be sitting there, waiting for a story, a tale, something.

"You ever speak to old Lamar Bibbs?" Pop would say.

"Not since him and Gola Mae went down yonder after the thing up at the place," Monk would say.

The younger me would perk up, eager to hear some gothic fable drawn from the mists of Mississippi Hill Country lore. Perhaps a story about a mule trampling a baby, or the time when everyone got the yellow fever and died.

But all was quiet. Monk would be leaning over and staring at his folded hands, as though he had been bludgeoned with a skillet, while Pop would be studying his dentures, which he held in his palm like a small, wounded vole. Then he would place them back into his mouth, having divested them of any lingering corn.

We were in Coldwater, Mississippi. Ronald Reagan was president, spacecraft were shuttling in the space over our heads, and the homes of American children were filled with Atari consoles. But here in Coldwater, it might as well have been 1850.

"Whatever happened to old Billy Bridgewater?" Pop said.

"Pulled a tumor out his head."

"Out his head?"

"Cracked him open like they might would a coconut."

"Seem like it would change a man."

"He got to cussing awful bad is how they knew."

"At his wife?"

"At everybody."

"Church, too?"

"Sad to say."

"Was it him got his ear chewed up over in Hernando?"

"Naw, that was fellow name a Gentry."

"Jim Gentry?"

"Luther."

"Luther Hines, you mean."

"Grassley."

"Old Luther Grassley!"

"He's the one got him a dog looks like a wolf."

"And the one ear."

I was eager for them to finish the story about whatever bad thing happened to Lamar and Gola Mae Bibbs, or how Mr. Grassley lost his ear and how that affected his ability to find happiness or wear eyeglasses. Really, I just wanted to hear any story that didn't compel me to wonder if these people really were my people, or if they'd found me in the back of a dead gypsy's wagon. I was sort of starting to feel like they had.

"Papa fought in the Spanish-American War," my grandfather said, looking down at the brass zipper of his coveralls.

Finally, a story about our family. War. Honor. Death.

"Did he kill any Spaniards?" I asked.

Ah yes, I would hear how my father's father's father climbed San Juan Hill, flanked by Teddy Roosevelt and General Calixto Garcia, to impale some gallant Basque with a bayonet glinting in the Cuban sun. Did he die? Did he win glory? Did he slink into Havana under an alias and take up with a mulatto woman and make a Cuban baby that he remained in contact with for the rest of his days, sending letters downriver to New Orleans and eventually paying for the child's first trumpet?

"Shoot, boy, I don't know," my grandfather said. "He got tired and stole him a horse and come home."

It didn't bother me that one cannot actually ride a horse from Cuba to Mississippi, unless that horse is either magical or inflatable. What bothered me was that the story offered so little information. Perhaps they were trying to protect me from the truth: that our family was born in dishonor and wickedness, rife with ancient malefactors, Chekhovian job-lots, con men, Marxists, crooked preachers, barn-burners, possibly union bosses from the fiendish land of Cleveland. Or, worse, that our family was uninteresting.

We lived in Memphis, but Pop insisted we play baseball just over the state line in Mississippi, where the game retained its purer, more barbaric qualities. My rural teammates had fascinating lives. Many of them lived in trailers and other sorts of homes capable of being rolled down a hill, which had a real sense of adventure to it, while others had metal teeth and chewed tobacco. Here we were, barely eight years old, and one of them was already an uncle, while another teammate came to practice one day carrying a giant dirty baby.

"I wish I had a little sister," I said.

"Shoot, this here's my aunt," he said, carrying her like a sack of Ol' Roy dog food.

I was sure such family arrangements must violate some important commandment or at the very least demonstrated what sorts of accidents can happen in homes capable of interstate travel. Still, those boys had interesting families, with what I imagined to be shirtless parolees and tattooed cousins in bikinis and knife fights around the dinner table. Why couldn't I have a family like that?

I secretly hoped my people were hiding something, some story that would illuminate the dark underneaths of our beds. But my parents were not even divorced. Pop was a devoted father, a large and powerful man who showered us with guns and love. He did not drink, or hit our mother; his only luxury the occasional heart attack. And Mom was a saint, a gentle schoolteacher who believed in the inherent goodness of all creatures, unimpeachable in her love for others, a woman who seemed to believe that the source of all human pain was merely a misunderstanding or an accident, never intentional, and whose greatest sin was smoking cigarettes in the bathtub, where she believed we could not smell them, and which made us believe she was trying to set the house on fire.

Of course, even in our serene, sidewalked neighborhood, there was trouble, families who were dismembered and flailing. I had seen under those families' beds, had found all sorts of secrets, mostly in the form of magazines filled with naked women. These women had breasts the size and shape of experimental weather balloons, and looking at them made my pants hurt. Perhaps my own parents hid things under their bed, too?

One day, I ran home, reached my arm into the dark horizontal crevasse, and felt something: a secret magazine! When I pulled it out, my fears were not allayed. For there in my hands curled the glossy evidence of dark family secrets: an old copy of *Mississippi Game & Fish*. I could only pray that my father had no sexual feelings for the eastern wild turkey.

Here's what I knew about my family:

Our people were originally from somewhere between Scotland and the Holy Land. They were poor and downtrodden and forced to eat their children. They sold their uneaten children onto a boat that debarked somewhere between Baltimore and Charleston, so that those children could learn to be poor and downtrodden in a whole different place. Eventually, these children fled the Atlantic seaboard for the fertile lands between Memphis and New Orleans, where they were promised the opportunity to starve to death under more democratic forms of government that only occasionally enslaved people. In time, some took to preaching, others to cattle and cotton, and they entertained themselves on Saturday nights by hitting one another with a razor strop until the sun rose and it was time for church. With hard work, my grandfather obtained a cow and sold its milk. When the teat ran dry, he trapped mink, which he took to Memphis to trade.

"Who'd you sell them to?" I asked.

"The Jews," he said.

"Like in the Bible?"

"I reckon."

Also, I knew, had heard whispered, that my mother had once been married to a man named Gene and my father had once been married to a teenager.

Who was a hussy, they said.

There was quite possibly a gun involved, the first gun I would ever shoot. A .410.

Had the gun been stolen? Won in a duel? Or had I made this up? Dreamt it? Hoping it would be true?

And who was Gene?

"Gene is gone," Mom said.

"Tell me about the hussy," I said.

"There's nothing to know."

Perhaps Gene and the hussy were part of the same story?

I was still a child but wanted to know so much, about the past and the hussy and Gene and the history that seemed to hold secrets of lust and calamity, but whom could I ask? Monk was interested only in stories that took place before the discovery of penicillin, and Pop was too busy with his demanding coronary condition. Mom was the obvious one, but she seemed too fragile.

Best to wait.

One problem was that, in my family, stories were not good things.

"Don't you tell me a story," Grandmother Key would say upon asking one of us if we had done something unspeakable, such as desire food when hungry. She said the word *story* as my father did, the first syllable rhyming with *low* or *row* or *no*.

A sto-ree.

"I seen you take a biscuit," she would say.

"No, ma'am," I would say, dropping the delicious greasy puck into a back pocket. She was a good-hearted woman, but she believed that eating between meals led to terrible things like miscegenation and the use of microwave ovens.

"What would Jesus do if he thought you was telling me a story?" she'd say.

What I thought was, Jesus would like me to have a biscuit, because he loved me and did not want me to suffer. Eventually, though, I would surrender and hand over the puck, covered in fuzz, and go outside for a switching.

"This is what happens when you tell me a story," she'd say, peeling a thin, leafy shaft from the hedge. From a very young age, I learned that stories were fraught with sin, never true, and that if you told them, somebody would start hitting you with the shrubs.

But maybe they hit you because the stories were true. Everybody I knew, it seemed, had disturbing true stories to tell about their family arrangements, and I wanted a story or two of my own, wanted it fiercely, a story that would tell our story, that might involve some secret sin, a gun, fisticuffs in a baptismal, something.

"Our family is boring," I told my brother, Bird, one cold workday, as we were burning more garbage.

"Boring, hell," Bird said. "Fucked-up is what it is."

He had a look on his face that suggested he knew things I did not. I pressed him, but he said nothing. Later, while scavenging for clean socks in his room, I came across a scrapbook, mostly chronicling Bird's early attempts at art and athletics, but with something else, too: a very old news clipping about an agent of Mississippi's Alcohol and Beverage Control dying in an automobile accident. The date was August 1977. The agent's name was Gene.

Here's what I gathered:

Gene was Bird's biological father.

Gene had died, tragically, suddenly, leaving Mom and Bird. Then Mom, bereft of a husband and someone to cook for, had married my father, a union that eventually produced me.

But the date on the article was 1977.

And I was born in 1975.

So Gene died when I was two?

No, that wasn't right.

And odder still was that, when he'd died, Gene had been married to a woman named Faye. Which was strange, because that was my father's sister's name. My aunt. Aunt Faye.

What did it all mean?

The upshot was that Gene and the woman who'd soon be my mother had divorced and then in the span of a year had each remarried, and their new spouses, Faye and Pop, respectively, happened to be siblings, which meant Gene had to watch his new brother-in-law father a child with his ex-wife.

Wait, what?

Had this Gene really divorced my sweet mother and married my sweet aunt Faye, the sisters-in-law who now seemed to get along famously, smoking cigarettes out back after Sunday dinner? And why had my father married his new brother-in-law's ex-wife? And wasn't it wrong to have a cousin who was also your stepsister and an aunt who was also your stepmother, as Bird must have had? I needed help figuring it out—maybe a compass, some graph paper, a eugenicist. I had enough knowledge of human biology to know that such rambunctious behavior could lead to birth defects, or at least a great deal of confusion at family dinners.

I confronted Mom with Exhibit A, the newspaper article.

"Why was Gene married to Aunt Faye?" I said.

She took a great deal of time to fold her dishrag into a pleasant, limp quadrangle over the edge of the sink she'd just emptied.

"Why do you want to know?" she said.

"Do I have all my chromosomes?"

"Good Lord."

Something happened in that moment. The woman, Our Mother of Perpetual Hope, this gentle, beatific fifth-grade schoolteacher with the little Santa Claus brooch, she of the perennial smile and the everlasting faith and the lovely cloud of permed hair that could have snared a passing brace of mallards, crumbled like a biscuit in a boy's back pocket, and then told me everything.

How she and Gene had lived next door to Aunt Faye in the small town just up the road from my grandfather, the latter a widow herself by that time, with two children who would eventually be my older cousins. How Faye had invited my not-yet mother and Gene and little Baby Bird for Fourth of July down at Monk's farm. How Mom had met Pop there, him with a precious little kindergartenish daughter and married to a whole other woman who was always napping in some other room. How Pop and Gene had quickly become hunting buddies, enjoyed killing things together, deer, ducks, time. How

Pop and Gene had gone to the Liberty Bowl one cold winter night and then sat in the truck afterward, watching their breath.

"I'm going to leave her," Gene had said to Pop.

And Pop thought Gene was crazy, and said so, and Gene left her anyway.

And the reason Pop thought Gene was crazy was that the woman was a good woman, the kind you don't leave. The kind you marry.

And so Gene had left my future mother and the Little Baby Bird, had just up and disappeared, then reappeared, with the neighbor, Faye, Pop's sister.

If you feel that this arrangement requires a diagram, you are not alone.

And so Mom left town, putting herself and her boy away quietly in shame, and how Gene's old hunting buddy, this swaggering talker with the giant head, had shown up on her doorstep with a hanging-clothes bag over his shoulder and a burning fire in his heart.

"Go away," Mom had said.

"I've come for you," Pop said.

"You're married," she said.

"Not no more," he said, the napper having walked out for a quieter bed.

And Mom told it all to me, how she let him inside, and he told her what he wanted: a good wife. He'd had two bad ones, he said. Also, he needed a son of his own. And she figured, well, she could probably see to that. Pop was right: She was a good woman.

"We both needed to start over," she said.

And so my mother and father were married, and Gene and Faye were married, and Mom and her former husband were once again in the same family, married to a brother and a sister, and it was unclear how this would ever be normal and who should bring the coconut cake on Christmas.

It was around this time, I believe, that Mom took to locking herself in bathrooms with cartons of Winston Lights and mystery novels.

And then I was born, making the whole situation terminally irreversible, son of a son of a son, to carry on the family name, with what was said to be a giant head, like the fruit of a gourd, like my father's before me, a great big gourd-head baby.

I had to sit down to take it all in, and use a pencil and pad to work it out, trying to see that my older brother, really a half brother, had once been my stepcousin, if such a thing even existed, and that my mother and aunt had been married to the same man in the span of a year. Finally, I had my story, and I wanted to unhear it. Bird was right. Fucked-up is what it was.

Which is what makes it such a good story, and probably why I just told it to you now, more than thirty years later. I am in a new place, a new home, far from Memphis and the Mississippi that would make me into the man I am, whatever kind of man that is. Skittish. Prone to sweating and stories. These days, I find myself wondering what sort of story I should tell my own children.

"Tell us a story!" my oldest daughter, eight, asked before bed one night. She and her sisters were on the top bunk, where my enormous boulder of a head rose like a moon over the horizon of their bedclothes. It was a new century.

"A story?" I said.

"One from when you were little, like us!"

I have told many stories since leaving Mississippi, at comedy clubs and in black boxes and on Greyhound buses and inside Waffle Houses bathed in oleo and yellow light, where I deployed pink and blue packets of artificial sweetener as visual aids. I would write their names on the packets, blue for Gene and Bird and Pop, pink for Faye and Mom and the other women who starred in what had come to seem, in the intervening years, a sort of Old Testamentish farce.

It is a sad story, and a funny story, and our story.

"What kind of story do you want?" I asked my daughters, in their nightgowns.

There were so many to tell, and to finish. The farmhouse in Coldwater is empty now, and so many of my people are dead and buried on the greenest hills I've ever had the pleasure of crying on, and Faye is dead, too, and so is Gene, him buried in a double plot that will be forever single, because Faye married again and is buried elsewhere. And Ronald Reagan is in the earth, and the space shuttles are forever grounded, and Atari is gone.

"Tell us a Mississippi story!" one of my daughters said.

We live in Savannah now, a city with sidewalks and art galleries and things to do besides kill and fornicate, and the South is dying, maybe dead, driven from the earth by progress and the demand for affordable chinos. Nobody is ever bored anymore, and Mississippi is terra incognita to my children, a place at the far end of the map where dragons be.

I looked into their eyes and remembered wanting to hear, to know, so desperately. Were they old enough to hear the story of our family?

"Hurry it up in there," my wife said from the other side of the house. It was bedtime.

"Tell us a story about when you killed some deers!" they said.

Should I tell them a hunting story, I wondered, or the story of how my great-grandfather was a horse thief, or the story of the boy who was older than his very own uncle, or all the stories of my father and the things he showed me and did to me and with me and for me, and how I came to be a part of this world, fathered through what seems like sin and defilement, but was really just the human heart behaving as it will, when set loose?

"Well," I said.

And they leaned forward.

This is how all my stories begin.

CHAPTER 2

·

The Imaginary Farm

—≼ ✦ ✦ ≽—

This funny thing happens when people ask where I'm from, especially when I'm at academic conferences, where people are so often from uninteresting places.

"Mississippi," I say.

"Oh, wow!" they say.

I can tell they've never seen a real live racist before, or at the very least someone who's related to a racist, or has seen one in the wild. It's exciting for them. They want to tweet it. They want to write a memoir about it.

"So," they say. "What's Mississippi really like?"

I can tell what they really want to ask is, What was it like to grow up around crazy people who believe that whatever can't be shot should be baptized? But they are afraid to ask, because they are not yet sure if I am one of those people.

I am.

Kind of.

Not really.

Sometimes.

I do believe in the power of Jesus and rifles, but to keep things interesting, I also believe in the power of NPR and the scientific method. It is not easy explaining all this to educated people at cocktail parties, so instead I tell them that it was basically just like Faulkner described it, meaning that my state is too impoverished to afford punctuation, that I have seen children go without a comma for years, that I've seen some families save their whole lives for a semicolon.

My father believed a lot of crazy things: that men with earrings were queer, that the pope got to pick the Notre Dame football coach, that we couldn't possibly have made all those expensive calls on the telephone bill. He would sit in his recliner and review the bill like some Old Testament scholar with a gift for high blood pressure.

"Who called 734-908-4560?" he would say. "Who *is* that?"

"Who knows?" Mom would say.

"Somebody knows! And I aim to find out!"

"Why does everything have to be a conspiracy?" Mom said.

"Where the hell is 734?" he said. "Sounds Canadian."

"What about that number sounds Canadian?" Mom said.

"Who in this family thinks we can afford to talk to Canada? This ain't the League of Nations here! Where the boys at? Go get the boys."

"We're right here," we said. "We've been sitting here the whole time."

"Godalmighty, boys, which one a you is calling Alaska here?"

"I thought it was Canada," I said.

"How expensive of a call was it?" Mom said.

"A dollar fifteen," he said, his face expanding, reddening, his heart preparing to outgrow the Saskatchewan province and explode.

Sometimes his illusions were as big as his head, massive fantasies with gravitas, hallucinations with enough mass to reroute rivers and change lives forever.

I was born in Memphis, Tennessee, but Pop did not like it there. It was too progressive. The public schools were too clean. The hospitals were too well equipped. Sure, they had jobs there, but they also had sidewalks, for Godsakes. Pop was a country boy and did not know what to think about sidewalks. And Godalmighty, all the boys did was ride bikes and play video games and sit around getting sissified. If you wanted to toughen up your kid, teach him about knives and woods and whatnot, your only resource was the goddang Boy Scouts.

Pop especially hated the Boy Scouts.

"Why they gotta make them boys wear them damn neckerchiefs?" he said. "It's sissy enough as it is, I mean, a pine-box derby? They make them little boys play with toys and play campout in the middle of the city, and then go and make them wear a dang lady's scarf. It ain't right. You too old for silliness such as that."

I was six.

But no, it's okay. I'm not bitter. I understand: He wanted something more for us. He wanted to take us to Paradise. A place where we could grow to be real men. A land of werewolves and tooth decay, where sidewalks and neckerchiefs had no quarter.

Mississippi, he said. We had family down there. We played ball down there. We ate most Sunday dinners down there, but we always had to leave, come back to the city, and stare at the goddang sidewalks until it made Pop's soul hurt.

And then he got him a job down there, only he didn't say "down there," like us city people. What he said was "down yonder."

"Down yonder," he said. "It's different."

Yonder. Strange word. I'd heard it used before, but never really knew what it meant.

"What's a yonder?" I asked Mom.

"It's a place."

"What kind of place?"

"A place not like the one you're at."

Permanent residence in Mississippi was going to be very different, it was explained to me. In Memphis, for example, a trailer was a thing you saw in a parade, while in Mississippi, it was where you got your mail. In Memphis, you went to church to hear about the dangers of premarital sex. In Mississippi, I would learn, you could go to church to have it.

I guess the city just crowded Pop, like a tight collar on a shirt that shouldn't have been dried so hot, and he had to go.

"These houses is too close together," he would say, of our little Memphis neighborhood. "It ain't right."

His only real belief about urban design was that houses should be far enough apart to let a man stand in his own front yard and relieve himself in relative privacy. At our suburban home, this was not possible. My older brother, Bird, and I made it a practice to urinate on all four sides of the house, under the judging eyes of neighbors who did not share our wonderment at the joys of urethral art.

"These boys need space," Pop said.

"They need to stop doing number one on my pansies," said Mom.

"Boys need to be raised in the country," Pop said. "Where you can run and jump and play and work and farm and hunt and fish and those kinda sorta things. Where you can learn to work like a man. Shoot, I grew up on a dairy. You want to talk about work, son. Shoooooot. I worked."

"Are we going to have cows?" I said.

"Maybe."

"And horses?"

"I like me a good horse," he said.

"And chickens and turkeys?"

"You boys is going to like the country," he said. "Work and whatnot, that's how ye learn about life and stuff." Pop was raised in a home where he rose at four in the morning to milk. "Don't you want to milk cows?" he said.

"Not really," I said.

"All you got to do is pull the teat down hard," he said, and yanked my arm.

I was not an animal lover, and did not like the idea of going around in the dark, tugging on animal parts. I could barely find my own parts with the light on.

Did they even have lights in Mississippi?

We're almost there!" Pop said. We'd driven about two hundred miles, long past communities with appropriate tax bases and school systems. There was nothing out there. After a long while, Pop explained: "There's a store up the road a stretch. They got candy, food, ammo, block cheese, ice-cold Co-Cola—heck, man, they even got clothes!"

What was this store called, we wanted to know.

"A general store," he said.

I had always preferred my stores to be as specific as possible. And hadn't we seen one of those in a movie? Perhaps with cowboys and excessive scalping?

Driving on, we sprang forth from the dark womb of pines and into a cleared valley of green, and there, glowing in unsullied puritan white, we beheld a Currier & Ives farmhouse with a real Thomas Kinkade–Painter of Light

sort of magnificence. Something in me, some ancient long-
ing, awoke.

All these years, here I was, going to malls, Skee-Balling in
the Chuck E. Cheese, curdling my brain in a chilling vat of
HBO and MTV and Nickelodeon. Who knew I would experience such overwhelming love at the sight of a new home? I
had visions: overalls and rubber boots. Chickens and turkeys.
Horses and mules. I would name them. They would be mine.
We would be the best of friends. The sort of friends you milk.

"Wow," Mom said. "Pretty."

Behind and around the house were a warren of rough-
hewn, but handsome, tin-roofed barns, and dozens of pictur-
esque cattle scattered hither and yon.

"Is that really our farm?" I said.

"Not really," Pop said. "It's just yonder."

The car was slowing, but not stopping, and the full-orbed
American pastoral skidded by us, slowly, slowly.

"There," Pop said. "That's our house."

We were at the bottom of the hill now, pulling into a gravel
driveway. Our home was a low-slung, brick ranch with a bad
roof and a gravity problem. No barns, no gardens, no signs
of animal life, save what appeared to be a cat carcass in the
driveway, supine, as though it had been murdered in the act of
sunbathing.

When I walked into my new bedroom and looked out the
dusty venetian blinds, I finally saw some live animals: a lazy
clot of black cows not ten feet from my window. I liked the
idea of cows, but this was a bit much. How could I sleep at
night, knowing they were right there? I opened the window
and discovered the ripe, invasive smell of live beef. In one great
olfactory flush, I lost whatever verve I had for Pop's farm. I did
not like animals so much, I remembered. They could eat you
before you had the chance to eat them.

Mom came in. "What do you think?" she said.

"The cows seem a little close."

She looked out the window. "Oh, look, how cute!"

"Are these our cows?" I asked.

"I'm not sure," she said. "Just don't touch them."

"I'm not touching anything."

In the coming years, this woman, my mother, would become my ally. We shared so much in common, such as our love of baths, and our belief that cows should not be touched. She had grown up in Greenwood, Mississippi, a little town in the Delta that, while isolated and surrounded by a cottony expanse that extended a hundred miles in every direction, was still a town, with the sorts of things that towns have, such as libraries and streetlights, but I'd seen no libraries on our way here, and the sun was gone now, and it was dark. So dark. Out the window, all I could see were stars, and the real farmhouse we had passed back up the hill, high and imposing and proud.

Pop began to speak about our new home in strange ways. Besides "the Farm," he called it "the Hacienda" and sometimes "the Plantation." Would our new plantation have slaves, we wondered? Yes, was Pop's answer. We would be its slaves, and he our master.

He bought tools, saws, axes, mauls. He took the watercolor brush from my hand and stuck a shovel in it.

"What do I do with this?" I said.

"Work," he said.

"Like how?"

"Shovel something."

"What do you want me to shovel?"

"It don't matter. Go."

And so there I'd be, digging holes in the backyard, the

judgmental cows on the other side of the fence, eyeballing me like I was about to steal something.

On real farms, there is always work to do, always something to be fed, led, slain, rode, fertilized, prayed for, fought for, and mortgaged until you can't hardly keep your pants up. That's the reality of farms. But Pop didn't let reality get in the way of his dreams, and so he invented new tasks every afternoon, every weekend, waking us at the red light of day to do some new work on our imaginary farm, like scrubbing utility poles and trying to milk the dogs. He could fill whole mornings with tasks worthy of inclusion in the medieval trivium. For example, picking up sticks. For an acre of yard covered in trees, this was no brief task.

"I mean even the little sticks," Pop said. "Them that's no bigger than your tallywhacker."

A few minutes later, my brother, already having launched into the vulgarity of rural puberty, turned to me. "Sticks no bigger than a pecker?" he said. "Shoot, he must be talking about you. My sausage is huge." Bird was adapting so well to the country. It suited him: the language, the work, the emphasis on sausage.

Bird and I burned, raked, washed, held secret discussions about the possibility of Pop not knowing what century we were in.

"Time to clean out the barn," Pop would say.

"But we don't have a barn," we would say.

"I mean the shed," he said, swatting a fly that wasn't there and staring off toward horizons of land he didn't own.

Where had he brought us? What mysteries would this place reveal? In those first days, it revealed mostly ticks. But there would be more. Pop had plans, you could tell. The look in his eye. He looked at Mississippi the way he looked at telephone bills: fiercely, ready to blow. He knew the secrets of this place.

"You ready to learn?" he would always say, before showing us how to do something important, like sawing the head off a tiny squirrel he'd instructed us to shoot.

I was not ready. I would never be ready. I wanted to go home, back to a place where they had malls and ice cream trucks and all the squirrels still had their heads.

"This is home," he said, on that first day in Mississippi.

We were standing on the back porch, and briefly, I allowed myself to be impressed by the vastness of pasture off to my right, big as ten Superdomes.

Okay, I thought, that part is kind of pretty. Maybe, a little.

It had been a long drive from Memphis, and we hadn't even stopped once for gas, and so it seemed the most natural thing in the world to unzip my tiny little Toughskins jeans and urinate.

"The heck you doing, boy?" Pop said.

"Using the bathroom."

"That ain't a bad idea," he said.

"I got to drain my lizard, too," Bird said, and joined us.

I couldn't have known that everything was about to change, that unholy phantasms of agricultural posturing were gunning for us, that Mississippi was going to have its way with me. All I cared about right then was draining my lizard, watering the grass of our new farm, while Mom watched from the back door and remembered wanting daughters.

CHAPTER 3

·

A Secret Race of Giants

—⚜ ✦ ✦ ⚜—

Where are we going to go to school?" I asked Mom.

We had moved in September, and so far had seen nothing resembling a school, or really any buildings besides our house that were not intended for the worship of God or the slaughter of livestock. I am sure my father hadn't given much thought to the school system where he'd bought our new home. To him, school was school. You went to the one closest to your mailbox, whichever one that was. There was no talk of private schools, of test scores and rankings. His thinking was, Why in the hell would you pay to go to a school where everyone was probably a pussy?

My thinking was: because I am pretty sure I am a pussy.

"You boys going to Puckett," Pop finally said, a few days after we settled in.

Puckett. Strange name. It sounded like a curse word, or the sound you'd make if you were stabbed underwater. I stood in front of the mirror and said the name aloud three times, to see if a demon appeared.

Puckett. Puckett. Puckett.

No demon.

I felt better.

The long trip there was filled with hope, through miles of verdant glens smelling of chlorophyll and Christian charity. I ignored the occasional sign of economic hardship, the homes and trailers where there appeared to be an excess of chickens roosting in derelict sedans. Ten miles later, we saw it: low and flat like a military barracks, its bleached brick the color of creamed corn. It looked like a dystopian outpost, the sort of place where one might see a wild dog in the road, eating a baby.

In the office, we waited while a pleasant woman with a golden bouffant the shape and luminescence of a Fabergé egg clutched a Smith Corona at her desk. Hers was old hair, harking back to a more innocent time, before Nixon and low ceilings, when women had been forced to use their hairdos for the ensnaring of moths and small birds.

The door opened and in walked a tall boy, tall as a man, sinewy and lean with scabs across his dirty, streaked arms, followed by a teacher.

"Sit!" the teacher said, and walked out.

"Sit down, Willie," the hair lady said.

Willie sat.

A sour stink suffused the room. Sort of like garbage, if it was wrapped in a decorative sack made from the soiled underwear of lumberjacks. My nose shuddered. I would come to know it as the odor of poverty, a new sensation to my delicate suburban nostrils, a tangy olfactory assault wrought by those whose homes did not have running water. I tried, briefly, to pity this large student, but found that his odor had incapacitated the parts of my brain that controlled both language and compassion.

Another woman entered, smiling, a mannish lady with thick forearms and short gray hair. The principal. She looked at Willie.

"I hope you're not still stabbing people with your pencil, son. I thought we talked about that. What are pencils for?"

"Eating," he said.

She turned to us, introduced herself.

I could not take my eyes off Willie, who could not take his eyes off my pants. I'd worn parachute pants, snug nylon trousers appropriated from distant breakdancing cultures, with many zippers, designed to make one look as much as possible like a duffel bag.

I shouldn't have worn those pants.

"Let's find you a class," the principal said, leading me to the door. I clutched Mom's hand and performed a quick mental calculation concerning the difficulty of reattaching myself to the wall of her uterus.

"Remember," Mom said. "You're very special. You have talent."

The only talent I needed, in a school full of Willies, apparently, was the ability to digest my school supplies.

I met my teacher and my new fourth-grade class, and noted with concern that many students were dressed like Native Americans. I was instructed to sit behind a child in the back wearing an actual headdress. I searched for clues that I had accidentally been enrolled in the Mississippi Sanatorium for Children Who Must Wear Costumes to Feel Not Crazy or perhaps that I had died and was now in hell.

Recess came quickly.

In Memphis, recess took place in a canopied glen, the centerpiece a playground constructed of artisanal hardware and swarthy timbers salvaged from a sunken colonial schooner. This new playground was rather Dalíesque, though, a grassless pasture of hard dirt, its sparse equipment of weathered iron apparently welded on-site from the remains of expired locomotives.

Many of the students were enormous, tall, thick, with long orangutan arms and sideburns, and this included many of the girls, who, in a far corner of the playground, appeared to be stoning a boy roughly my size.

"I got a gun," said a voice behind me.

I turned around and there stood a young man wearing no costume at all, save the badge on his flannel shirt.

"Today's Western Day," he said. "Then it's Nerd Day." A Surrealist nightmare unspooled in my imagination: Cat Day, Vegetable Day, Infectious Disease Day.

It was homecoming week, he explained.

"You and me should be friends," he said. "You could come over to my house and watch my brother soup up his car. He can soup up all kinds a shit."

"Soup?" I said.

"Ain't you ever souped up nothing?"

This boy was Tom, my first friend. He was short and stumpy, like me.

"Where you from?" he said.

"Memphis."

"Never heard of it."

"Everybody here is really big."

"See that dude?" he said, nodding toward Willie, who was now lurching around and menacing classmates. "He's seventeen. He's been in sixth grade for like a million years. He's poor as shit and has a huge pecker."

I wondered if I should say anything about Willie's odor.

I zipped and unzipped one of the many pockets on my

trousers. They were expensive pants. I'd cried many tears to convince Mom to buy them. Her reluctance had troubled me, made me think we might be poor.

But we had water, and a phone, and regular penises, like normal people.

"He sort of smells funny," I said.

"Yeah, I know. He had sex with a horse."

I knew it was wrong to be cruel to the poor. I'd learned this in Vacation Bible School. I wanted to pity Willie and the others who had no phones and lived in barns and might actually have no parents, but I found it hard to have compassion on someone who touched innocent farm animals with his penis.

"Hey, you got a gun?"

"Oh, sure," I said. "Lots."

Technically, it was true. My father had guns. It was understood that, one day, he would put them in my hands.

That fall, others wanted to know, too. Did I have a gun? What kind? Was mine as big as theirs? What had I killed with it? Did I want to see their bruises, caused by their guns, because they were so big?

"Ain't you ever hunt doves?" they said.

"No."

They explained that basically, a dove was a grayish bird that flew real fast and tasted like chicken but was smaller, and more delicious, because you had killed it with your own hands.

"With your hands?" I said.

"With a gun," they said.

I missed my old school, where all we did was watch television and then talk about it.

If things were strange at school, they were stranger at home.

For one, my toys began to vanish. The stuffed animals, the

Hot Wheels, the Darth Vader Carry Case with its army of figurines. I searched the house for these items, but casually, as though I were dusting. For every toy that disappeared, Pop was close behind with something that had recently been bleeding. A duck here, a fish there, the head of a noble whitetail extending from the wall as though stuck between this and some happier dimension. Soon, there was a new animal on my wall: a mallard that Pop had plucked from the sky.

"Why is there a duck in my room?" I asked Mom.

"Your father thought you would want it," she said.

My parachute pants were getting tighter, and beside them in the closet appeared a number of strange new garments that can best be described as "army issue." For Christmas that year, I received gloves, boots, overalls, a floppy green hat, a bandolier.

"What's this for?" I said to Bird.

"Shotgun shells," he said.

"For why?"

"For killing shit."

Bird seemed pretty excited about killing shit. He had never had the chance to kill much shit in the city.

In the city, I had been my best self. I had done many things well. I sent and received many love notes, for example, asking girls to "go with me," and they agreed, and we went. Where? Technically, nowhere. What was important was that we had agreed to go nowhere together, which was a testament to the strength of our love. But in Puckett, it was not so easy. Many of the girls in my new school were very pretty. After a few months, I got up enough courage to hand one a note.

"What's this?" she said. She was blond, small.

"It's a note," I said, and hustled off. The next day, at recess, I found her waiting for me.

"Hi," I said.

She grabbed where she must have thought my nipple was and twisted with great power. Immediately, my areola sent a distress signal to the prefrontal cortex along the lines of "Go on without me" and "Tell my family I love them."

"We don't go with boys like you," she said, and ran off, disappeared behind a tree, presumably to feed on small woodland creatures.

Boys like me? What did she mean?

In Memphis, I had been praised for my intelligence, my mastery of facts and spelling, but in Puckett new kinds of intelligence were desired, involving gunpowder and animal husbandry and the books of the King James Bible. Everything I'd done well before didn't matter.

There, I'd been a rider of BMX, a winner of trophies, unafraid to wreck and bleed. Here, everybody had scabs and scars and wounds far greater than mine. There were boys with leg braces, missing teeth, rickets, broken hands from animal attacks. There was a boy with a dent in his head deep enough to catch rainwater.

"What happened to him?" I asked Tom.

Tom didn't even look up.

"Hatchet fight."

A year after starting at the new school, I had my first real chance to show these classmates that I was as tough as them, or could at least fake it. It was Labor Day weekend, the opening day of dove season.

I had never really given much thought to what it might be like to kill a thing. Unlike most men in my family, I found it quite easy to romanticize animals, attributing to them deep human feeling. At the grocery store, I felt a strong desire to pray for the lobsters in the tank. I worried about them. At the very least, I felt, they must be extremely bored.

The day before the hunt, Pop came home from work bearing gifts, handing Bird and me each a camouflage vest with a tag that read, "Now with deeper, spill-proof game pouch to prevent seepage."

I had no desire to be around the seeping of things and could not imagine wearing clothing that promoted it. Dead things were one thing, but wearing dead things that had the potential to seep their deadness onto you was something new.

Pop took us into the pasture to practice shooting. To me, he gave a 12-gauge, a large gun for a boy my size. I did not know what gauges were, but felt 12 might be too many.

Pop hurled clay doves in low arcs, instructed us to shoot at them. I aimed, pulled the trigger. The kick was unexpected. I fell down, and my eye started bleeding, as did my nose.

Bird was better. He was very committed to the warrior lifestyle, and he hated himself for not having enlisted to fight in Vietnam, despite the fact that he was a newborn at the time. His gift for weaponry, unlike mine, neared the level of art and would have won him respect from any number of warring Native American peoples, whereas I tended to shoot more creatively, like an enraged Hells Angel at an Oakland riot.

"Good," Pop said.

When we woke up the next morning, it was still dark, because, according to Pop, the early bird really did get the worm, although in this instance he also got murdered. I dressed in clothes Pop laid out for me, camouflage everything: pants and a T-shirt and cowboy boots and the anti-seepage vest. I looked like a shrub with a head.

So much had changed. I had come to Mississippi in clothing designed primarily for dancing, and now was wearing clothing engineered for the transport of dead birds.

We loaded up, and many miles later came to rest at the tail of a queue of trucks that wormed off the blacktop and into a wide, flat glen where two men stood with a bucket apiece, doing head counts and taking money.

"Watch out for the crazies," Pop said.

"Who are the crazies?" I asked.

"Anybody I shoot with this here," he said, and fingered the small pistol on his hip. It was, as I recall, exactly the kind of thing a crazy would do.

I noticed in the glare of headlights a handful of grown men drinking what appeared to be toxic levels of beer.

Pop rolled down his window, stuck a few bills out.

"We don't want to hunt around no drunks," Pop said to the man, who cracked open a container of beer so tall that I briefly mistook it for a can of Rust-Oleum.

"Only rules is," he said, "don't be shooting nobody in the face."

"This doesn't seem very safe," I whispered to Bird, who was now applying black greasepaint to his face.

"You think 'Nam was safe?" Bird said.

On some level, we were all playing supporting roles in my brother's larger Vietnam fantasy.

Have you ever seen a wedding in an exotic place, like Palestine or Juarez, where there's a lot of drinking and the shooting of guns wildly into the air in joyous celebration? That's what dove hunting is like. It's fun for most people. For me, it was more like the first ten minutes of *Saving Private Ryan*, the part when Tom Hanks is trying not to die.

Detonations of smoke and light rippled down whole ranks of shooters, thundering across the pasture and down into my groin like a herd of angry horses intent on flushing the kidneys. When for a brief instant the din halted, I heard a dry rain in the branches overhead and found myself pelted in the face by what felt like handfuls of dry rice hurled through a particle accelerator.

I was going to die.

But I did not die. Instead, I missed. Many birds. Thousands, it seemed, while my father and brother slayed them with upsetting speed. Eventually, it got quiet. The birds were all dead or gone, the hunters blacked out from medical emergencies involving acute alcohol poisoning. All that was left was us and the heat and the late summer sun. Body fluids pooled in my boots. My pants, once so large, now seemed so tight. I was sweating in places where I didn't even know I had skin.

Tight pants always made me angry.

I was angry at Bird, for believing he was in Cambodia, and I was angry at Pop, who insisted that we spend holidays shooting things, and I was angry at my classmates, who seemed to know more about the diameter of pellet spread at thirty yards while using a modified choke for upland bird hunting than, perhaps, how to spell the word *diameter*.

Mostly I was angry at me, for not having killed anything. I wanted to kill. I wanted to be liked. And then, something happened.

A cote of doves was crossing the pasture, flying fast and low through heat vapors right at me. Bird aimed, but waited. Pop held his hand up: Wait. Let your brother.

They were mine.

I aimed, and pulled the trigger, and one bird hit the dirt.

"You got him!" Pop said.

I got him.

I walked out into the sea of clods and looked down at my tiny dead chicken. Shit, I thought. I had never thought "shit" before that moment. But shit was easy to think now.

What was I supposed to do with it?

"Put it in your sack!" Bird yelled across the vapors of noon.

But the bird was not dead.

This is the story of my hunting life, one that would unfurl over the next decade: the thing killed from afar is not killed and must be killed again, at close range, where you can see the opal wetness of its eyes seeing you back, close enough to feel you could learn something of the animal's personality, take it home, give it a name, feed it, love it.

"Just whop its head real hard," Pop said.

I picked up the bird as instructed, the small gray package of feathers and meat. Yet the dove was not gray, not at all, but many colors: clusters of white, pale yellow, black feathers, its head nearly pink under the sun, its chest mother-of-pearl, glinting dark purple if you let it catch the light. The dying animal looked at me.

It quivered in my hand, shuddered, its head darting. Pop suggested I knock it against the tree, but how? Just throw it, like a ball? That's the thing they never tell you about killing: It's not easy. You have to commit.

So I threw it at the tree, and the bird landed and flapped its wings as if to say, Try again, please. I hit it against the stock of my gun, and it flapped some more. Finally, I laid the dove across a root, pushed aside any lingering shame, said a prayer, and stepped on its little skull.

It was my first time to kill a thing.

Nobody even asked me how it felt.

I'll tell you how it felt: Go outside and shoot the first bird you see, but shoot it in the wrong place, so it's not dead, and then go pick it up and throw it at the side of your house a few times until every happy thought dies inside of you, and then crush its tiny head with your shoe. How does that feel?

We gathered on the sidewalk in front of our classrooms, and there was much talk of the weekend's hunting. The boys pulled their shirtsleeves up, revealing their bruises, purple and pink and yellow, a visible record of conquest. The bigger the gun, the wider the bruise, the better the hunting, the better the huntsman.

"Mine's bigger," one said.

"That's a girl one."

"Mine's as big as a hamburger."

"A hamburger for babies."

Tom and all the other boys, the boys I would come to know and be deeply fond of in those distant years, they were all showing their proud new tattooed contusions, and they turned to me.

Had I hunted, they wanted to know.

I had, sure.

Had I killed anything?

Sure, yes.

I stood on the sidewalk waiting for our teacher to let us in the classroom and every eye in the fourth and fifth and sixth grades, it seemed, was on me. My black eye intrigued them, the scar on my nose.

"You been in a fight," they said.

I said nothing. I let them think it.

"Let's see your bruise," they said.

There had been a small one yesterday. Surely it was gone now. I looked down, lifted the sleeve on my little polo. Nothing. Tender flesh.

So I lifted higher, and there it was, yellow and red and purple and six inches across and spreading to my chest, mostly as a result of my wild and reckless shooting. A bruise the color of the bird itself, and just as big.

"Dang," they said. "What kind of gun you got?"

"A twelve-gauge."

"Must be like a bazooka," said another.

"That's some Rambo shit right there."

"Hell yeah," I said, like it was something I said all the time.

I stayed at Puckett for several more years, made friends, felt very much at home.

The boys, they invited me to their farms to kill shit with them.

The girls, they agreed to go with me, and we went nowhere together, in love.

The teachers were kind, even though they occasionally hit us with what I assumed were canoe oars.

I went to Puckett, and then to another school up the road, and almost died only a handful of times. Eventually, I was allowed to graduate, when I delivered what is still largely regarded as the worst speech ever made in the state of Mississippi by someone who was not visibly drunk. I was salutatorian. This, in a state that consistently ranks lowest in test scores, where children have frequently mastered childbirth before long division, and where the ability to read often gets one labeled as "uppity" or "probably an exchange student," was no real feat.

But I was proud. I had done it. And they had taught me so many lessons, things you can't learn in the city, like how to kill shit, and what happens if you don't get baptized, and how to love the sinner but not the sin, and how you even have to love the people who love the horses. Every child deserves an education like that.

—⚞ ✦ ✦ ⚟—

CHAPTER 4

·

Monsters We Met in the Forest

—⚞ ✦ ✦ ⚟—

Killing birds, that was easy. Birds were small, and only the beginning of a campaign of slaughter through the animal kingdom that would come to define my new life. The woods held creatures larger than birds, such as turkeys, for example, which many considered a bird, and which I considered a friend, but which I was told should be considered an enemy.

"When are the turkeys killed?" I asked, hoping I could make plans to have liver failure on that day.

"That's a long way off," Pop said.

What about all the guns, I wondered, and all the camouflage he'd laid out for us to wear?

"Tomorrow's Doe Day, boy," he said, holding up my gun for inspection. "You best get ready to kill something got more legs than a dang turkey."

"Okay," I said, lying.

I had hoped my butchery of the dove would have filled my quota for ritual murder, but it was explained that anybody can kill a stupid bird. If you wanted to be a man, they said, you had to kill something that could kill you, if it got angry enough. I was ten years old now and preferred to focus on hunting more acceptable wildlife, such as Twinkies. I did not feel equipped to hunt things with fur, which, unlike Hostess products, can become enraged when shot.

My brother and I were told to lay out our clothes and gear for Pop's review, which, as I would soon learn, we would be doing every Friday night between the airing of *A Charlie Brown Thanksgiving* and the Martin Luther King Jr. Day parade. While our nation celebrated the season of all things holy and bright, my brother and I were forced to continue waking up before dawn, dress up like a pair of Japanese yew trees, and hide in the woods until we lost all feeling in our extremities, at which time we were instructed to start shooting things.

Bird was very much looking forward to it.

"It's gonna be some monsters out there," he said.

"Monsters?"

"Great big ones."

Pop inspected the blade of my small knife, my box of shotgun shells. He plunged his hands into the bulging pockets of my coat.

"What's this?" he said, pulling out a handful of candy.

Candy, I thought, would help the time pass, and might bring me some small happiness in the dark. The woods, before dawn, were a terrifying place.

"Those are Jolly Ranchers, sir," I said.

"Jolly *what*?" he said. He did not like the idea of things being jolly.

I explained that it was a delicious fruit-flavored candy.

"Gimme one," he said. I did. "These wrappers make too much noise," he said, fingering the clear plastic wrapping. "Out there tomorrow, you just need to open it in your pants. So you don't cause a racket. Can't kill nothing with a racket."

I did not understand how to open candy in my pants. It

seemed like it would take more dexterity than I possessed and possibly a third hand located in the crotch area.

In my family, every little boy dreamed of Doe Day, the one day every year when the Mississippi Legislature invited children under the age of sixteen to shoot females of the cagey and elusive whitetail. As such, Doe Day had religious import for the rural youth of our land, affording as it did a sort of swinging door into the halls of manhood. It was a provincial rite, like the Poy Sang Long of Myanmar, the Vision Quest of the Lakota Sioux, the Bar Mitzvah of Long Island. Like the Quinceañera, Doe Day involved colorful costumes and a great deal of knifing things. Like the deb balls taking place that same month in Jackson, it involved a great deal of pageantry, blood, and weeping.

It was explained to us, as children, that it was not generally chivalrous to kill female deer, but that it was required once a year as a population management tool. There was simply not enough food for all the deer, our fathers explained. They painted horrid pictures of maddened whitetail hordes—hungry, desperate, overrunning villages, stealing and eating children like Bavarian gypsies. It would not be pretty, and it was up to the children of Mississippi to thin out the growing herds in a single day, lest our state suffer a catastrophe of Malthusian dimension.

Why females, you ask. They were easier to kill than males, the spikes and bucks, and the sooner a boy killed a large animal, the closer he got to taking on all the glorious accouterments of rural manhood, such as joining the volunteer fire department and, after a long hard fight, graduating from high school. It was a lot to live up to.

If I can just shoot one of these things, I thought to myself, I will be a hero.

This ambition, though, was complicated.
By fear.
Of the woods.
And the monsters who lived there.

Pop woke us at approximately 4:30 a.m. These were the unhappiest moments of my childhood. The hour seemed excessive for a year as progressive as 1985. We did not live in a developing nation, where rebel armies and tribal carnage might necessitate getting up so early, say, to keep your sister from getting assaulted. My half sister did not even live with us. She lived in Memphis, which no longer had a rebel army.

We dressed and drove a few miles to borrowed land on which we'd been given special dispensation to hunt, a dark and forgotten corner of the legendary Alton's Creek Hunting Club.

All of us had heard stories of the monster bucks on Alton's Creek land. It was run by a syndicate of farming brothers who had several manly sons, and also several manly daughters. The deer of Alton's Creek, like the hunters themselves, were monstrous. Pop had seen this for himself on slow drives down silty and cool dirt roads that ran through club property like seams on an old, fine coat. We'd stepped out of the truck and seen the tracks of more than one buck, the loveliest impression a man can find in the earth, in the shape of an inverted heart, cloven in two.

These tracks had a phantasmal quality, as though they mapped the trail of a ghost, had heard the sibilance of some forest secret. Pop saw enough tracks to convince him that we should make friends with the family of farming brothers, and we did, and they allotted us hunting rights on a small tract on the northernmost edge of their club. We suspected this was not the best hunting parcel in their portfolio, but at the very least,

Pop was sure there'd be females there, something for his boys to shoot on Doe Day.

We pulled off the blacktop onto a sunken dirt track and set out on foot, walking through the cold November dark until our heads steamed in the ray of Pop's old chrome flashlight.

"Here," Pop said, stopping.

This is where Bird would be hunting.

Woods as dark and old as those could be full of all kinds of violence: cougars, wild hogs, Independent Baptists. Oh, I knew it was possible. I knew *Bulfinch's Mythology* and Edith Hamilton's oeuvre like the books of the Bible and was still young enough to cling to threads of hope with regard to St. Nicholas and leprechauns. When St. Peter said the Devil prowled like a lion, seeking whom he may devour, I believed him. And now I was in the woods, dark and wild, triangulated between Satan the jungle cat and any other feral thing that might come ambling along. This corner of Rankin County was not heavily populated. We had moved here only a year before, and who knew what creatures called this place home? It might be a goblin, or a basilisk, or some kind of temperate leviathan, or simply a cabin-dwelling libertarian who did not believe in dentistry.

I waited, in the black cold, for Pop to get Bird settled and come back to me. The canopy of trees disallowed moonlight and stars, and it was just me and my gun. Something up the trail caterwauled. An owl hooted. The woods were a gaping maw.

Pop emerged from the dark, and we walked on. After a time, we came to a bend in the trail and Pop led me off the path and down a thickly wooded hill. "Right here," he said. "Clear them leaves, sit up against this tree, and don't get up till I come for you."

"When?"

"Later."

Later, of course, meant lunch. We would eat bologna and cheddar cut with our hunting knives and sit on the side of the road for an hour or so, then come right back out here until dark. I would be out here all day, sitting, waiting, vegetating, turning numb with cold, losing the higher faculties of language, doing my best to imitate the world's most apathetic tree fungus. The sitting was bad enough, but the thought of eating bologna was enough to stick the barrel of the gun in my mouth. It was a hellish meat, the flesh of Satan's horses, a sausage infused with alien gases and the tears of abandoned children.

Pop walked away, and I turned to see the cold firefly of his flashlight bounce up the hill, through the trees, into the black hole of woods. I was alone, in the dark, so small, so young, and carrying a firearm. This did not seem wise. According to my mother, I could barely keep my penis from urinating all over the toilet seat. It troubled her, and she complained to my father.

"You got bad aim, boy," Pop said. "Piss goes in the commode."

"If he can't hit the toilet," she said, "Lord knows he won't know where to point a gun."

"It's different," Pop said.

"He'll shoot himself in the head," Mom said.

"Maybe so, but it's different."

I cannot explain my general fear of the woods. When you sit there, in the dark, you hear things. The distant crack of twig and trunk, body and bone. The flittering of unseen wings. The nasty lamentations of bipedal creatures that defy taxonomy. A couple of years before, one of my uncles had fooled me into staying up with him one night to watch *American Werewolf in London*, a picture guaranteed to make any child fear dogs, Europe, and the sudden appearance of unwanted back hair. I was not happy about it.

"Why aren't you laughing?" he said.

"Because I'm over here pooping on myself," I wanted to say.

For a young boy sitting in an empty deciduous vale as old as myth and cloaked in nothing but gray moonlight, werewolves did not seem out of the question.

Also, Sasquatches.

When I was four, one of my aunts had forced me to sit on her lap while listening to the soundtrack of *Sasquatch: The Legend of Bigfoot* on a record player. This classic seventies film was groundbreaking in its portrayal of the inner lives of large, West Coast–based primates, but I was not a fan. Bigfoot's personal soundtrack was a symphonic blend of a rehashed *Jaws* theme mashed up with the terrifying call of Sasquatch himself, which sounded like a tornado siren mating with a box fan.

"Do you hear the Bigfoot?" my aunt would say.

"That's the sound of my urine pooling on the floor," I wanted to say.

These and related torments made me skittish and liable to shoot anything. Every distant howl was a werewolf. Every thud, a lumbering Sasquatch, on his way to disembowel me before his next recording session. Is this how I'd have to spend every weekend from now until adulthood, when I could escape to somewhere safer and more fun, such as college, or prison? That morning, Mom had said something about going to town, to the library, while we were out hunting. She was a teacher at a different school, but she taught children my age. She must have understood my brain and heart and developmental condition much more profoundly than Pop did, and which sorts of activities could help me be successful at life, such as reading, perhaps in a library, surrounded by books and warm chairs and no trace of werewolves or bologna.

Oh, to be with Mom. We would have a quiet breakfast of something that did not need to be murdered, and then we would go to town, where I could check out mystery books and would have the option of soiling, or not soiling, myself, depending on my mood.

But I had a penis, and that meant I had to be out here, with the monsters.

Finally, the void of Genesis divided itself into the black of the trees and the chrome of a clear dawn. I could finally see the gun in my lap, my only defense against the creeping things of the earth. For some reason, Pop had not let me take the 12-gauge of our dove hunt and instead equipped me with a .410 single-shot, technically the weakest shotgun in the history of gunpowder. The largest thing it could kill was an adult field mouse, and only if the mouse was very close and very still: duct-taped, for example, to a nearby tree. The gun's only real purpose was to give the mothers of very young boys something to pray about on the weekends. Which is to say, if handled with care, a .410 could blow just enough brains out one side of your head to make it uncomfortable. Mom voiced concern about my handling this gun, or any gun, but Pop always explained that being accidentally shot in the face was just a part of growing up in the country.

The night before Doe Day, Pop had shown me photographs of deer.

"Behind and above the shoulder," he said, pointing with a finger as thick as the barrel of a real man's gun.

"I say shoot it in the head," Bird said.

"Shut up, boy," Pop said.

I liked Bird's idea. In movies about Vietnam and cocaine, which were the only kinds of movies Pop would let us watch, people were always getting shot in the head, and it seemed pretty effective.

"The head seems pretty good," I said.

"No, look here," he said. "Shoot the heart. Behind the shoulder, and above."

"But the head seems good, too."

"That's where the brains is," Bird said.

"The head ain't no count," Pop said. "It's too small. Hard to hit."

"I still think the head is where the brains is," Bird said, as though it were a revelation, a bit of news.

I sat in my little dirt nest like a timid ovenbird. The sky was bright now, but the woods were still woods, still full of Minotaurs, and me, forced to wait on Pop, without even a bit of string to get back to the truck. All morning, I heard the distant, deep boom of rifle and shotgun, miles away in every direction, the sounds of late autumn. These were the men of Alton's Creek, harvesting their game.

The first growl I heard was not from the foul gullet of a Cyclops or a Mothman. The low, visceral gurgling sounded like the rooting of some giant Calydonian Boar up the hill, behind me, the horrid scourge of Artemis, come to eat me.

Just my stomach. Clearly, I was hungry. It was time to go. The only way to make that happen was to fake a shooting—into the trees, perhaps—and send Pop running. I would say I missed. We would poke around in the leaves, dry as tinder, loud as fire, for blood. We would not find it, and given the lateness of the morning, we would leave the woods early. But as soon as I cocked the hammer of the world's smallest shotgun,

I realized I was not the only large mammal in the immediate vicinity. Something was just to my left and behind me, a haloed mass of fur on the edge of my vision. I stiffened like a cat. It was Sasquatch, come at last.

The beast came into view, without my having to turn. It was a very small doe, smaller than some dogs. Strangest of all, she was so close, nearly close enough to touch with my gun. She did not see me. My visible parts had become of a piece with the tree, my smells had become the smells of the earth. I was invisible.

Her head was down. She was a pretty animal, her features as delicate and lithe as a girl's. Her elegant legs, thin as saplings. Her face, demure as a lady planting bougainvillea. The coat, as blond and sheen as the walnut stock of my gun. She rose up and stamped her hooves back down again as she inched forward, from the corner of my eye into full view.

What came to mind was not Bambi, but rather Clarice, the Claymation doe of *Rudolph, the Red-Nosed Reindeer*. Clarice was literate, lovely, an ingénue, the Mia Farrow of stop-motion wildlife. And here she was.

She looked up and saw me.

"Hello," I whispered.

I saw her, and she saw me see her, and she did not move.

I moved my gun a little, just to get it out of the way, so this natural communion might flower into something deeper, more memorable, and perhaps she noticed that I was holding, not an olive branch, but a machine designed for her destruction. After all, I was not Rudolph. If anything, I was the Abominable Snowman, the enemy, because my breeding suggested I was about to send Clarice way past the Island of Misfit Toys and on toward the Archipelago of Dead Things.

Still, she did not move, did not run, just lifted her head to look at the gun. She was comely enough to have stepped right out of Bulfinch. I knew this mythic wood was full of monsters, but it had never occurred to me that creatures of such precise symmetry, such unexpected grace and beneficence, might also be out here. What other Apollonian charms peopled this country, I could not guess. Fairies and wood nymphs, perhaps. Creek-bound mermaids. Junior high cheerleaders.

I raised my gun and cocked the heavy steel hammer without even remembering I'd done it. I knew: If I missed this deer, so close, a gift from the gods, then I would just have to go ahead and join the drill team and get a vagina. I brought the gun up to my face, set my eye down square with the barrel, like I'd been shown, looked down the polished blue-black steel of it to the end, to the bead, and through that to the animal itself. She looked right at me. Never before in the history of modern hunting had a game animal been so deserving of mercy and a happier life in a petting zoo.

You would be a lovely pet, I thought.

And then I aimed where the brains is, and pulled the trigger.

Smoke and fire inside my skull, and then: The doe was gone. The thin, dry air of November was all that was left of her. The last thing I'd seen on the other side of the gun's bead was her ear, like the petal of some candied flower.

I'd been taught to wait. If the deer was dead, she'd be twenty or thirty yards down the hollow. They can run a good piece when shot, a hole in their heads or hearts or lungs. After five minutes, I stood and looked. I stepped where she'd been, looked for blood, possibly an ear.

Then came Pop, down the hill.

"You get him?" he said.

"It was a her."

"Was she a big one?"

"Just kind of a normal-size one," I said. "Actually, real small."

"How small?"

"Pretty small."

"Was it a yearling?"

"You mean, a baby?"

"I mean, did it have spots," he said.

"Maybe."

"Well, shit."

Oh, no, I thought. I've killed a baby deer.

"Where was you when you shot it?"

"I was there and it was here," I said, pointing to two spots on the side of the hill, embarrassingly close. Pop studied the area. We enlarged our radius of ground. We came back together, quiet.

"I think you missed it," he said.

I was embarrassed, terribly, and relieved, terribly.

"You aim for the heart?" he said.

"It was kind of more the head area," I said. "She was up in my face."

"Boy," he said. "It don't get no easier than that."

I didn't tell Pop what I knew. That the deer had to be dead, that it had been close enough to suffocate with a plastic grocery sack, that I did not miss, could never have missed. I got on my hands and knees and looked for blood that might have dried into the colors of the hillside. It had vanished: a ghost.

I found a few pieces of short, stiff white hair, the kind you might find around a deer's eyes, in its ears.

"I think I shot off its ear," I said.

"Son, do you see an ear around here?"

The door into manhood had swung wide, and I had not gone through it.

"Let's go," Pop said.

On our way to the truck, the woods were a different place. The old ancient terror was gone now, as dissipated into the ether as the sound of a gunshot two counties over. It was just trees and hollows and leaves and mud. It no longer seemed appropriate to be afraid. After all, I had a gun. If anything, the werewolves and Sasquatches and deer should be afraid of me. Hell, I was shooting off their ears. With enough practice, I could eventually shoot them somewhere more vital, like the legs, so they couldn't run, or the face, so they couldn't see where they were going.

It was time to grow up, to see the woods not as the setting for some terrific malevolence, but home. These deer weren't made of clay. They were made of meat, and meat's what's for dinner, and I loved dinner very much, even more than candy.

We fetched Bird and slogged to the truck and headed out to Styron's General Store, to purchase ungodly amounts of bologna, which was unfortunately what was for lunch on that day.

On our way, we came to a knot of trucks on the side of the road, and Pop pulled over. It was the broad-shouldered brothers and sons of Alton's Creek Hunting Club. They were gathered around a pickup, looking down at something that lay hidden there. From my seat, I saw it: a buck of such heft, such immensity, with a rack of antlers as thick and tangled as briarroot. They held it up for us to see, and we admired it, the awful beauty of it.

"I told you they was monsters in here," Pop said, as we drove away.

CHAPTER 5

The Phantom Caprice Classic

Mississippi had its share of monsters, in its woods, and its waters, and its Walmarts, that much was clear, but what impoverished, war-ravaged land didn't? The land and its people held many secrets. Was that really an Indian mound? Was there really a secret cabin by that creek back there? How was the earth so fertile? How were the women so fertile? And also the girls? Since they seemed to get pregnant so young, and disappear? What had happened to them, and their babies, and their lovers?

There was one great mystery, more terrifying than Sasquatch, larger than the bulging Indian mounds, and right inside our house: my father. Who, it should be noted, was actually not larger than an Indian mound, but who, like many Native American burial sites, was rumored to contain bones. Who was this man, who'd dragged me away from all happy things?

The facts of him were unremarkable. He was a salesman. That was his job, the thing someone paid him to do. But he did not look like a salesman. He was not stooped and pathetic like Willy Loman, or toothy and garrulous like the men who sold cars and furniture on our television. He was more like a large granite slab with eyeglasses and a heart condition.

His gut was an oaken cask, his chest meaty and wide, like two Thanksgiving birds yoked together with chicken wire. The man had Popeye arms, and his head was large and round, hard enough to be its own helmet.

In his work, touring the villages of rural Mississippi to sling asphalt bids at county supervisors, he was tieless in his shirt-sleeves and brown Sansabelt slacks. Pop did not even need a belt. He was that much of a man.

He wore steel taps on the soles of his shoes, and every step he took across the linoleum had the grave sound of military judgment, like a man on a horse clopping up behind you with bad news. In the right pocket of his Sansabelts, next to the money clip, he carried a small pocketknife, as men of his generation often did. He did not carry it for show. I have stood by his side as he refused to pay certain prices for automotive repair and have heard him threaten to remove a mechanic's scrotum and testes and feed them to our dog.

I felt it was wrong to force our dog to consume the scrotums of the service industry, but I was too young to reason with my father. He was a fortress: You couldn't get in.

At Ole Miss football games, I watched him point a beastly finger, thick and square as a ham hock, at drunken rednecks and tell them to cease their tomfoolery, and then I watched them cease it, silenced like the raging waters of the Sea of Galilee.

How could you question a man who'd done such a thing, or who had threatened to engage in armed duels on bass boats?

"Good morning to you!" the other fisherman said, during one nice, serene Saturday morning on Pelahatchie Bay. "You all catching anything?"

"Why don't you move?" Pop said, as he believed this was our fishing hole.

"Pardon?"

"Why don't you scoot on out of here?"

"I believe I was here first, good sir," the cordial fisherman said.

"I got a twenty-two pistol says you ought to get your candy ass on up the river."

The man trolled away.

Pop pushed other men around, but he didn't speak like an angry man, which perhaps made him more frightening. He might say he was going to pull off your arm and beat you to death with it, but he'd say it in a charming way that made you want to let him. He spent his life crushing the souls of other men with this violent charm, me included. But there was one man Pop could not crush. That was Clyde, his boss.

I wanted to know why. One day, I decided to get a little closer to Pop, to see what I could see.

"Can I go to work with you tomorrow?"

Pop lowered his *Rankin County News,* a publication I would later value chiefly for its photographs of local virgins. Since 1848, the paper's motto has been "Fear No Man, and Render Justice to All."

"Work?" he said. "With me?"

I told him I was bored. It was summer. Even with baseball and the long lists of chores that ensnared one in a Kafkaesque nightmare of yard work, there was very little to do. Our summer days were languorous rural protractions, punctuated by moments of terror and death. We took guns into the woods and shot things to see if they were alive. We found cold creeks, built dams from Yazoo clay, and did our best to drown one another. I hadn't planned anything very interesting for the next day. I was going to spend the morning sharpening my hatchet, which I had planned to spend the afternoon throwing at feral cats. A ride in Pop's company car would mean, at the very least, a buffet lunch.

"I reckon," he said. "If you want to."

Pop worked for Southland Oil Company, a small Mississippi firm that had poked a few dubious holes in the Delta and earned most of its money by turning crude into molten blacktop for the long, hot roads of our state. Pop was a traveling salesman for Southland. He sold the same roads he drove.

In the Southland company car, always the latest model of a Caprice Classic, Pop drove from one small town to the next, meeting county supervisors to discuss asphalt prices by the ton. He came home each night with little to show for his work but brown paper sacks full of tomatoes he bought off the backs of trucks in counties with names like Neshoba, Choctaw, Jefferson Davis. In the sun of a windowsill, Mom set out sheets of newspaper and placed the tomatoes on them, to ripen. Pop ate them all.

Sometimes, along with the tomatoes, he brought home the great unseen burden of Clyde. Clyde was a loud man, a dervish with a voice like gravel and gasoline, one who, I deduced from the discussions in the living room, came at you with everything. He was older than Pop, but tall and lean and with a full head of speckled black hair and a push-broom mustache. If Pop was a government mule, Clyde was a wild Appaloosa.

I did not understand my father's quarrel with Clyde—he didn't share such things with his children. But after we'd gone to bed, or out to play ball in the yard, Pop lumbered into the kitchen to discuss the subject with Mom. On occasion, we listened at open windows, around paneled corners. I could understand very little of it, only that Clyde was a motherfucking sonofabitch who mocked and derogated Pop's lack of formal schooling, and more. This, as one could imagine, made Pop want to rip off Clyde's head and take a shit down the hole in his neck.

"I'll kill him," Pop said.

"Don't kill anybody," Mom said.

"I'll do it," he said. "I'll whip his ass. I'll knock that god-dang mustache right off his face."

"You'll be fired," Mom said.

"I'll be a hero," he said. "Then they'll make me the boss." Pop was under the impression that modern companies func-tioned much like the animal kingdom.

I worried something might happen. He would do some-thing rash. He'd been doing rash things for so long. It was his talent. His gift. He'd threaten to buy a new boat, and then bang: Evinrude shadows across the lawn. He'd threaten to whip one of us for asking too many questions about lunch, and so we'd ask a question about supper and he'd come out swinging.

Soon, he would do something to Clyde. I knew. I prayed. I wanted Jesus to help my father use the faculty of reason, or at least imagination, in dealing with this hateful man, or we'd all end up homeless, bereft of our baths and boats.

What would Pop do? A man of action always does some-thing.

We left the house right after sunrise. Fearing I would need a way to pass the time, I had strategically placed a book in my pants. Out there in the country, I was always putting things in my pants, sometimes to hide them, such as books, and sometimes to warm them, such as my hands, and some-times because I was bored. Boredom, I knew, was a dangerous thing. For some children, it led to experiments with sex, and drugs, and alcohol, and lighting one another on fire, some-times with the alcohol. For some of us, the never-ending rural ennui led to destructive habits with literature. And so I took books everywhere, to places where reading was discour-aged, such as church, and school, and I often found myself in the principal's office having to explain my fascination with knowledge.

I blame my mother, who introduced me to the perverse habit of reading through the gateway drug of encyclopedias, which she begged my father to purchase from a man at the door, hoping to counterbalance our growing knowledge of firearms and axes and tractors with more peaceful, productive knowledge that could be found in the *World Book*, such as a list of the major exports of Bolivia, which she felt would help us in our lives, should we end up in Bolivia at some point in the future and need to barter for tungsten, which is just one major export of Bolivia.

I loved those encyclopedias, the closest thing we had to the Internet, despite our not knowing what the Internet was. The *World Book* was our rabbit hole into the world of ideas, and I am grateful to Mom for convincing Pop to take out a second mortgage to buy them, which is likely what he had to do, given their size and weight and gold-leaf pages. The lot of them must've weighed as much as the gun cabinet, and their prominence in our living room meant a great deal to Mom, and to me.

They were not cheap, and did not go unused. A boy could get as lost in them as the woods. In its twenty-one volumes, I learned about clouds, trees, Dwight Eisenhower, and Vasco da Gama, spent rainy days absorbing facts that would come in useful much later in life, such as the estimated temperature of the surface of Mercury, or a visual chart with the comparative sizes of various deers of the world. The smallest? The Key deer. I still remember that. It felt significant, having a deer with my last name.

These encyclopedias led to literacy, which led to the frequenting of book fairs and libraries, which led to competitive reading for the March of Dimes, which led to the Hardy Boys, and to Jules Verne, and ultimately to more lurid fiction that I did not show to my mother.

On the day I went to work with Pop, the book in my pants was a short novel by Robert Heinlein that can perhaps still be found at bookshops under the banner of "science fantasy." If a book is a frigate, as Emily Dickinson says, then science fantasy is a castaway galleon for the freakish and diseased, and even as a boy, I always felt some measure of shame while reading books where the alien life-forms had large breasts. The *World Book* had no entries about such beings. I looked.

We drove and drove, into the morning sun, and then beside it, and then under it. We listened to FM country and AM talk. We did not speak, really. I couldn't think of anything to talk about. And then Pop launched into a declamation on fishing lures, his ideal topic for oral interchange.

"You seen that new Red Belly Devil Horse I got?" he said. "Now that's a jig, boy!"

I pretended to be asleep. I was unfamiliar with the new products of the freshwater fishing industry and found his fixation on largemouth bass upsetting.

Finally, I pretended to awaken and pulled the book from the warmth of my crotch.

"What you got there?" he said.

I was always coy about my books, afraid Pop would find them effeminate. In our family, the only books men read were in the Bible and you weren't supposed to do it for fun. You did it because Jesus would hurt you if you didn't. The only people I knew who read novels were women and girls. It was like being caught trying to put a sanitary napkin in my underwear. Only it was worse, because the name of the book was *The Star Beast*.

"What's it called?" he said.

"It's just a stupid book," I said.

"Reading's good, I reckon." He meant it in the same way that blood transfusions are good. They are necessary, perhaps, in times of great distress. "What's it about?"

It was difficult to share even the most basic narrative elements of the book without sounding like a girl, and I was not a girl. I was on the fence line of manhood. I was old enough to have already killed something that weighed more than me. A deer. A bear. A cousin. And I had failed. He was worried about me.

And now, the books.

I wanted to explain why I liked to read. How books helped me imagine realities alternative to this one, realities where children perhaps were allowed to read in peace. Imagination. Yes. That's why I read, surely. So I could imagine. Did Pop imagine? That's why I wanted inside of him. I had to know: Did he imagine me a disappointment? Was my apathy to the largemouth and large game and small game and ball games a sort of disease that he imagined he could cure?

"What's the book about?" Pop asked.

"It's just a stupid book about a star beast," I said.

"A who?"

I read from the back cover: "It's a sentient creature belonging to an advanced alien race, brought back to the earth many years ago," I said.

"Oh," he said.

We drove down the highway, chasing its hot, molten ripples across the distant edge of the blacktop. This was his asphalt.

We drove and drove. He said, did, nothing. He simply stared at the road ahead. The July afternoon was hot and bright and then hot and wet and then bright again. I asked if we could roll down the windows, but he refused. The jet wash of air would have upset the sculpted flap of hair on his great big marble-slab head, kept in place by half a bottle of Vitalis Maximum Hold and a great deal of prayer. The windows stayed up, the hair stayed down.

I tried asking Pop about his work, but he offered little ex-position. He asked even fewer questions of me. He was not a great fan of the interrogative sentence, unless it was some form of the question, "Did you see that deer?" We did not see any. It was hot. Deer don't like hot any more than we do.

We wheeled into the town squares of villages like Kosciusko, Philadelphia, Newton. Pop traveled to these rural seats of power to offer Southland's services in the building of roads and entreat public servants to buy his asphalt. I suppose they did. I do not know. He left me in the car, with the window cracked, like a dog.

"I used to read," he said, as he set his heft down in the seat of the car at one courthouse.

"What did you read about?" I said.

"Mussolini," he said. "He was an eye-talian. In the war."

This was encouraging. Up until then, I was pretty sure Pop only read the *Rankin County News* and telephone bills. I had never seen him read a real book. I had recently read *The Rise and Fall of Adolf Hitler,* and I saw the shimmer of a real conversation out there on the road ahead.

"Did you like it?" I said. "The book?"

"It wasn't one of them kind *you* read," he said.

"It was longer, you mean?" I said. "Like history?"

"No," he said. "I mean maybe it was a TV show."

I fell asleep against the car door. And, as I slept, I had a vision. I saw Pop, standing on the highway. He was in the Holy Land, but it was still Mississippi, but with a purple Syrian sky. And then Jesus came out of the air like a Shoney's Big Boy.

And as Pop journeyed, he came near Coldwater, Mississippi, on the road to Memphis: and suddenly there shined round about him a light from heaven. And Pop fell to the earth, and heard a voice saying unto him, "My son, my son, why dost thou persecute me?"

And Pop, squat and dwarflike, trembling and astonished, said, "Lord, what wilt thou have me to do?"

And the Lord said unto him, "Arise, and go to junior college, and drop out after the last football game. At the appointed time, it shall be told thee what thou must do. It will likely involve asphalt products. I knoweth it does not sound like promising work, but it may include a company car."

And just like that, the Big Boy Jesus went back to paradises yet unknown.

I woke up.

Pop had looked so alien in the dream, with hair and strange clothing, his pockets filled with papers and pencils. It was him, but different. Or perhaps it was me, but older. I rubbed my eyes. We were home. While I slept, he had purchased a sack of tomatoes.

I have little doubt that Pop could have hurled Clyde across the road like a broke-down lawn mower, but he did not. Pop had no education and had labored long and hard to a salaried position. If he tried to pull off Clyde's genitals with his bare hands, he would be shuffled back down the Great Chain of Being and end up shoveling rocks on a Department of Transportation road crew, where he'd started this long vocational march.

And he made very little money, but twice as much as he should have made, given his education, making him a gelding to Clyde, beholden and enslaved, as all working men one day become. Clyde, apparently, knew this. He did not like Pop. He needled and bedeviled and provoked my father. I do not know how he did this—only that he did it. I overheard my father narrating stories of things Clyde had said in the company of colleagues and clients, hurtful things that demanded vengeance. Maybe Clyde mocked Pop's rural laxity with forms of the verb *to be*. Maybe he mocked Pop's high scores at golf, a popular game in the asphalt industry, or mocked my father's bowlegged cowboy walk. I do not know.

But I know he did this at hotels and motels, during conventions of the Mississippi Road Builders' Association. And worst, at these conventions in midcentury Gulf Coast hotels, Clyde did this in the company of men. These men would ordinarily have shown Pop a great deal of respect, I am sure, knowing that at any moment he was prepared to coldcock them with a Gideon Bible. But with Clyde in the room, Pop was passive and sterile, the butt of the joke. I could see it in my mind. I could imagine it.

Clyde was the only man in the world, it seemed, who could hurt my father, and I gathered that Pop was only biding his time until he could return the favor.

It was still summer when Pop crawled under the company car with a pair of pliers and a roll of duct tape. "Fear No Man," the paper had said.

"Hand me that Phillips head," he said.

If he couldn't beat Clyde to death with a metal chair, as I was about to learn, he could at least detach the odometer from the Caprice Classic.

Pop wedged himself underneath the car, despite the fact that it was only a foot off the ground, and this was significantly less than the diameter of his head. What a glorious head! He could have stored all the Great Books of the Western World in that enormous fleshy Death Star head.

I asked him what we were doing.

"Fixing the car," he said.

"What's wrong with it?" I said.

"Nothing yet."

He invited me to crawl under the car and assist. I did, and my sensitive moral thermostat ticked this way, tocked the other. Pop did not fix cars. When he crawled under them, it was usually to extract a mangled cat from the fan belt housing. He used my small, bookish hands to find the odometer cable. It was black, and similar to a cable on the family's disabled exercise bike, purchased by Pop after his heart exploded during a duck-hunting trip a few years before, when he attempted to lift an aluminum boat over his head. The bike's cable ran from the front wheel to an odometer on the handlebars, where one could assess how many imaginary miles one had pedaled at that imaginary speed. The car's odometer cable, though, ran from the front wheel to somewhere underneath the dashboard.

"Yank it," he said.

"Yank what?" I said.

"The wire, boy. Don't be a dummy." My soft and uncalloused conscience understood now. Pop reached up, and with a bearish paw, pulled the cable from its housing. "Like that," he said.

Clyde would fire him if they found out, I knew. I prayed about it, there under the car. Should I say something? I should say something. I could not say something.

Pop crawled back out, stood up, satisfied.

I'd worried that Pop was going to take a tire iron to Clyde's face, but in the end, my father had surprised me. He had an imagination after all, and what he'd imagined was how to turn a company car into a family car without Clyde, his boss, the man who signed his checks, ever knowing.

Who was my father? I still did not know what was inside of him, but was starting to find out. He was my great Indian mound, full of bones and secrets. He could do things. Maybe one day, I'd learn to do those things, too. Maybe I had no interest in catching a bass and putting it on the wall, but maybe, just maybe, I could draw one, or write a story about one, and put it on the wall, or the shelf, or the dash of his car, for him to read, next to that sack of tomatoes.

"Thanks, boy," Pop said, handing me the tools to put up.

I took them from his impressive hands and wanted to reach out, to hold him, climb up to him, get inside, if not his head, at least his arms. Did I love him? I imagined him loving me, and it almost seemed real. You can be so close to a man for so many years, right there next to him in the car, and never know the worlds that turn inside him. You couldn't find Pop in my encyclopedias, I knew that much. He was my star beast, belonging to an alien race, brought to the earth many years ago.

Later that evening, we drove to Sunday night church. It was always a long, dreadful drive to evening worship, but these miles did not count. They were as imaginary as miles on that old exercise bike, as free as grace, a judgment to Clyde. He was behind us now, and we feared no man and rendered justice for all, rolling toward the house of God in our sedan of lies.

CHAPTER 6

•

The Boy Who Got Stuck in a Tree

—❧ ✦ ✦ ❧—

It was very exciting, learning that my father was a liar. At least, to his employer, which I understood to be a sin, but a special kind of sin that is required when your employer is a horse's ass. My father, I reasoned, must be more complex than previously believed. Perhaps there were "things" occurring in his head, such as "thoughts" and "ideas." I wished he'd share them, but he almost never did. He was a simple man who did not ask questions, which made him so complicated, whereas I often asked too many questions and felt very complicated, which I felt made me seem simple.

"Do you like your job?" I said, once.

"Like?" Pop said. The word seemed to disorient him.

"You'll go to college one day," he said. "And you can pick your own job."

"I will?"

"You got a head for it," he said. "But you got to get that paper."

"Paper?" I said.

"Diploma," he said.

"Yessir."

"Just keep reading them books," he said.

But books were full of stories and stories were full of lies and lies hurt Jesus's feelings, so I didn't know what to think. I blamed my family. They were the ones who taught me so much about telling stories, and how not to do it, and then, in inspired moments of surprise, how to tell one so good you forgot what day it was, and I liked forgetting what day it was, so I made certain life choices that would allow me to get paid to forget what day it was and teach others to forget what day it was, which is, after all, what I think heaven probably is: the whole world, forgetting what day it is. You have to, I bet, with an endless supply of them.

I especially love telling stories on holidays. It's a good time to remind myself of why I love my family, and why I live in another state. We told a lot of stories on a recent Thanksgiving, my father and me sitting at the table over breakfast, remembering what it was like back then, when I was so small and full of potential, and he was so large and full of ideas of how to shoot things.

"Morning," I said.

"Morning," he said.

We sat there in silence for a good five minutes. I had a book, just like in the old days, but I was no longer embarrassed and did not feel it necessary to carry it in my underwear.

But should I open it? Opening it would have been an admission of failure, evidence that nothing had changed, that We Could Not Communicate. He sat there and stared at the wall. He had a great talent for sitting and staring at nothing. I'd seen him stare like that so many times over the years—in church pews, bleachers, trucks, but mostly on deer stands.

"Be a good day to hunt," I said.

"Yep."

I enjoy talking about hunting about as much as I enjoy talking about new technologies in women's hosiery, but I have very few subjects that I can discuss with my father, and those subjects are: Football, Weather, Money, Children, Children Today, Beating Children Today, and Hunting. We had not hunted together with any regularity in twenty years, and this, I knew, was a hurtful thing to him. So we talked about hunting. And like a great big mossy boulder that had been given a good nudge, Pop came alive and rolled down a hill of stories.

We talked a good two hours. These were harmless stories, about cold days and elusive deer and the happy memories that I am sure Pop thinks we must share. But we do not share them, not really, largely as a result of something that happened in the woods on December 16, 1988. I made sure not to tell that story.

By midmorning, our storytelling had grown repetitive and the rolling boulder of my father came to a flat place and stopped. He stood up, and went into the living room, and turned on one of those hunting programs called *Buck Blasters* or *Chasing Tail* or *Ted Nugent's American Patriot Sasquatch Slaughter*. I sat there and read my book, but I couldn't stop thinking about all the slaughtering I'd seen over the years, and the last thing I'd seen slaughtered up close, back on that December day when I was thirteen.

Nobody wants to hear a hunting story that goes like this: "I went to the woods, and I saw a deer, and I shot him, and it was amazing." No, the best hunting stories are full of surprise twists and sudden reversals, such as, "I went into the woods and shot my brother, but then I learned that he was not my real brother."

The surprise twists in my stories mostly revolved around how I would shoot at things, and they would almost never die. This can be frustrating, not only to the hunter, but also to the animal, who might now be missing an essential part of its body. It may sound cruel and unfeeling and perhaps even upsetting to the reader. And to that, I would say: It is even more upsetting when it was you who did the maiming. You should try it sometime. It builds character, mostly through nightmares.

This was funny at first, my inability to kill anything very well, a sort of family joke. *Ha ha, the boy missed*, they would say, every Christmas. They laughed, I laughed. It was all good family fun. Occasionally, I prayed that God would send a gang of jackals into our Christmas dinner to murder them all, but mostly I just smiled.

Ha ha, you got me. And the jackals will get you.

Growing up in the country, it seemed like every little general store had Polaroids of slaughtered things over the register. Magazines and newspapers carried black-and-white photos of young boys posing with their very first slaughters. Most of these boys were in elementary school when they'd done it for the first time. And if you looked closely, you could tell: Some of them were girls.

Girls!

Who'd killed deer!

People like to say places like Mississippi are bad for girls. Oppressive, they say. But I've still never met a girl down here who wasn't encouraged to kill something, should she have a taste for it, as many did. All the feminists I knew as a child owned guns and knew how to remove the liver from an animal with a knife, which earned them a great deal of respect from men, since those men also had livers capable of being removed by those same knives.

If girls could do it, why couldn't I?

Other boys my age had done so much, already had wives and children of their own. Did I have a bad eye? Nerves? Palsy? Or worse, perhaps I was in possession of an overactive conscience or had some genetic defect that made me have emotions about animals?

"Don't worry, you'll get one," Pop said.

That's sort of what I was afraid of.

The day I finally got one, that cold December day, started at 4 a.m. When Pop turned on my light, I had been dreaming. Of what? Of a childhood that didn't involve waking at 4 a.m., mostly.

"Roll out," he said.

I had so many questions. What day was it? What time was it? Why couldn't I have been born with no arms? I knew, though, even if I had no arms, Pop would have found a way for me to hunt, rigging complicated pulley systems into trees and hoisting me up in a sack, then dropping me on the animals with a knife in each foot.

This day would be a cold one. "Arctic blasts," the weatherman had said, illustrated by what appeared to be an angry cloud vomiting ice crystals across the southern states. "Your plants will die," he said, and I briefly considered how great it might be to be a plant.

Should I play sick? I'd done it before. I'd faked fevers and nausea on many a brisk morning, but you can only fake illness for so long before your mother believes you've had a bad blood transfusion and are now dying of AIDS. Although the idea of spending a quiet, comfortable day in quarantine sounded nice. Sometimes, I claimed to have vertigo or ingrown toenails, and occasionally both at the same time, which I demonstrated, on the eve of a big hunt, by limping and running into walls. But

Pop wasn't fooled. He must have known what was in my heart, where I really wanted to be. It wasn't Disney World, or the zoo, or even a well-heated infectious disease facility. What I wanted was to be with my mother at our little sanctuary, a special place that none of the men in my family even knew existed. We even had a secret name for it. We called it the "grocery store." How shall I describe this Elysium of wondrous delights? Ours was called the Jitney Jungle—in Brandon, many miles away.

I was not encouraged, generally, to go grocery shopping with Mom, because Pop knew that if you sent your sons to the grocery store too much, they might learn how to locate water chestnuts, which could lead down a dark path toward vegetarian stir-fry and the wearing of aprons and eventually marrying someone named Cecil. What Pop couldn't have known is that my special time with Mom at the store was much like hunting, in that she allowed me to seek out items and bring them to her.

"Find me some Hershey's Syrup in a can," she'd say. "And some Borden's."

Borden's was our ice cream, and it came in a bucket the size of an aboveground pool. How could hunting deer ever compare to hunting vanilla ice cream, which is generally docile and will let you pour syrup on it without running away?

I hunted every item with the skill of a Choctaw huntsman with a taste for lists and couponing: Chef Boyardee, Pop-Tarts, Fritos, Hostess Frosted Donettes. I studied this place, learned its secrets, luxuriated in its odors, the brightly illuminated freezer section, the heavenly splendor of the candy aisle, where I crouched low and fondled engorged bags of M&Ms with erotic tenderness, and the metallic pungency of the butcher's counter, where the meat had been relieved of its more disturbing qualities, such as the eyes, which had a way of searching you out with pity.

"Let's go," Mom would say, and in minutes we'd be at another Promised Land, the Brandon Public Library, where Mom showed me how to obtain a library card and books on magic, which made her a kind of wizard. On the way home, she'd let me read aloud, especially when whatever I'd checked out was funny, and we'd laugh like drunk schoolteachers, and like Kafka says will happen, the sea inside me unfroze. I was the daughter she never had, and I knew it, and she knew it, and I was beginning to think Pop knew it, too. But I trusted him. I was his boy, and I knew that if he wanted me to do something, then it must be the right thing for me to be doing, and sometimes it meant work, and sometimes it meant play, and sometimes it meant bloodshed.

I would have to get up. On that day, my inner seas would remain frozen.

Pop turned on the light.

On my floor lay a host of flannel and chamois and canvas, my allies against the cold, but also the enemies of my dignity. By the time I got everything on, I would be prevented from performing necessary bodily functions, such as relieving my bladder, or actually being able to touch the place where I believed my bladder to be located.

First, the socks. Cotton. Why cotton? Because we did not understand what people who read *Outside* magazine understood, that cotton will absorb your sweat and then use it against you. Good socks cost good money, and Pop had more important things to spend our money on, such as prosthetic feet, since our original feet had frozen and fallen off.

Next, I pulled on a pair of waffled long underwear, also of cotton, and then a cotton union suit, and then two pairs of sweatpants with an excess of fabric in the groin region, so that it looked like I might be concealing a fruitcake near my genitals, followed by multiple sweatshirts and a chamois shirt that had once belonged to Pop and had been given to me because too many hot dryings had abbreviated its length and now it could only be tucked in with the aid of duct tape and bungee cords, thus compelling me to pull my sweats up even higher until my chin appeared to be wearing the pants.

Over these pants, of course, I wore more pants.

Then I stuffed the whole of myself inside a pair of hand-me-down coveralls, lined in a material resembling industrial furniture pads, so that when finished, I looked like the world's largest camouflage throw pillow. My boots were in the den, next to the woodstove. Putting them on would be difficult, now that I could no longer bend at the waist. Even walking to the den would be problematic. Rolling would be easier, or blacking out and having medical personnel drag me on a litter.

Bird was already in the den, sharpening his knife, while Pop danced and sang by the stove. Slaughtering always put him in the best mood. While singing, he would goose Mom in the bottom, and she would attempt to blind him with a spatula, and then he would sing some more. It was an odd thing to have to see at four in the morning, your mother defending herself against your father with baking utensils. But I couldn't look away, because I had lost the privilege of turning my head.

Mom presented me with a sausage biscuit in a napkin.

"What are you going to do today?" I asked.

"Oh, go to town, I guess, get some groceries."

I'm sure she could tell I wanted to go with her, and that I knew I couldn't. She knew I had to go.

"Don't forget the Hershey's," I said.

"My baby," she said.

But her baby would not be coming back.

The place we drove toward in the dark was County Line Hunting Club, at the edge of the Bienville National Forest, a camp we'd joined a year or two before. The camp house was no gentleman's hideaway. It was a double-wide trailer, dog pens, a grand old Confederate flag that looked like it had been chewed by aphids and a pack of abused coyotes, the smell of old blood and rotting carcasses; it might have been a kind of romantic hideaway, if you had kidnapped your lover and planned on turning her hide into a lamp. Yet its woods were lovely, nine square miles of hardwood bottomland and hillocks of pine. Men with names like Foots still trapped on this land, and shot muskets. It was unclear why some of these men used such primitive firearms, but my thinking was that anybody named after a body part could probably shoot any sort of gun he wanted.

In the front seat, Pop and Bird strategized about the day's hunt, while I attempted to sleep. "I believe you may get one today," Pop said to me.

The probability was high. It was Doe Day again, the annual day when I was statistically most likely to disappoint my father, and Pop expected fewer hunters in the woods today, even the grizzled musketeers who lived on the land. He didn't say why. Perhaps there was a Klan rally, or a Dentists Without Borders in the area. But yet again, I had legal sanction to shoot pretty much anything that moved.

"You know you'll have to drink its blood," Bird said. "Since it's your first."

Bird was always reminding me of this. We'd recently seen perhaps the most important film of our youth: *Red Dawn*, a coming-of-age tale about how Patrick Swayze fights communism with his hair. There's a scene where one of the young American guerilla fighters slays his first deer, and they sit around the dead thing.

"You've got to do it, it's the spirit of the deer," Swayze says, filling a mug with blood from somewhere deep in the carcass.

"When you drink it, you'll be a real hunter," says Charlie Sheen.

Swayze hands the mug of blood to the young deerslayer, and reluctantly, the boy drinks. It's important to remember, as they're doing this, that they've all got tree branches attached to their heads.

Then Sheen says, "You know, my dad said that once you do that, there's going to be something different about you. Always."

Yeah, what would be different was that he would never speak again, due to the thirty hours of uninterrupted vomiting.

In a film full of harrowing scenes, this was the one that kept me up at night. Would they really make me do it? Soon, our headlights illuminated a dark hole in the trees. We got out, loaded up, said goodbye in clouds of illuminated breath.

"See you boys back here at lunch," Pop said.

My stand was old, and its platform small: basically a kitchen chair nailed to a tree three stories up. I did not worry so much about falling, owing to the excess of padding around my internal organs. It was going to take something much more aggressive than gravity to penetrate my costume.

I put a round in the chamber, in the dark. My gun was a .30-30 lever-action, a short, sturdy rifle that held eight rounds. I had come so far from the .410 single-shot of my first days in the woods. Now I had the opportunity to miss eight times in a row.

I looked into the sky and could see nothing but Orion, my old hunting buddy, through striations of black canopy. We were doomed to hunt forever, he and I.

I sat there.

And I sat there.

And I sat there some more.

In one terrible instant, that terrible thing happened, the single most tragic experience of my, and just about any, childhood: boredom.

All childhoods are full of it. For some, it is the great crucible of imagination, those long, lonely days bereft of various entertainment technologies, freeing a youngster to wander in the undiscovered country of his own unfettered mind, where he can learn to enjoy reading and creativity while slowly going insane. They say going insane is fun, but they are lying. You hear things. You see things. You look at your watch. It is 6:45 a.m. It is dark. You decide to think. And you think some more. And then you think about what you thought, and then you think about looking at your watch, which you do, which still reads 6:45 a.m. Haven't you been thinking for longer than less than a minute?

What time is it?

6:46 a.m.

Only five more hours! Five hours was nothing. I was wearing so many clothes, it would likely take three hours just to take a bowel movement. Which left two hours, which seemed like about how long it would take to chew off my own tongue.

Finally, it was daylight.

Could I see anything? Brown trees. Orange leaves. Purple sky.

Did my father ever get bored? It was his greatest skill, this ability to sit and stare and wait. It wasn't a listless stare, pathetic and melancholy. He looked more like a farm animal in a pasture, just sort of existing, and it was hard to know what might be going on inside his large baseball cap. His brain must have been huge, or perhaps there were other items in there, such as an old tractor transmission. Did he have thoughts about his thoughts? Did he ever experience that moment where you realize you're you, and you're realizing you're exactly you and not anybody else? Or did he just think:

Tree. That is a tree.

Pie. I like pie.

Sit. I like to sit.

I wished I could think like that. My mind raced, ran off without me, looked around, saw that it was alone, returned to find me, but got lost, and we became separated for hours.

Time: 6:47 a.m.

It was officially day.

I was officially insane.

Still, there was something far more terrible about this whole enterprise, more tragic than boredom, and that was the horror of what we were actually expected to do to the animals.

Was I the only one who became unsettled and swoonish at the sight of a large, inverted carcass hanging from a tree, its vital organs strewn about like children's toys, the occasional pack of hunting dogs fighting over a lung, another one looking for a quiet place to enjoy the severed head? It happened all the time and nobody else seemed bothered. People just walked up to the bloody carcasses and carried on entirely normal conversations, as though a man wasn't standing there squeezing deer feces out of a large intestine and small children weren't playing football with a liver.

I knew Pop would make me do it one day, when it was time, even though the sight of blood gave me the vapors, especially when it was pouring out of things. And I had heard stories about deer who took too long to die, who'd been shot in the eye and blinded and run into barbed wire, or shot in the gut, the green pasta of intestine spilling out while they ran, wrapping around the hind legs, causing the creature to tumble into a creek and drown.

With my own eyes I'd seen a deer shot in the leg, stabbing at the earth with the other three like a hurt spider, and managing to get seventy-five yards in that condition, while my father offered to let me finish it off.

The deer was alive. It looked at me. What a crime to shoot it in the neck, when all it really needed was a cast, maybe a hug.

"Shoot it," said Pop.

But I didn't, and he put his gun to the animal's neck, while I pretended to see something of interest in the trees.

And I also didn't watch later, when we dressed it, which, if you've ever done it, you know, it's pretty much the opposite of dressing.

It hung by its hind legs, upside down, swinging by a thick cable as Bird cranked it higher and higher until its head was off the ground. Pop handed me his knife.

"What do we do first?" he said.

It had been drilled into me that the first and most important step in dressing a deer is to make sure it's dead, because nothing will ruin the meat like watching it run away. I surveyed the hanging carcass and reasoned that, yes, it must be dead, owing to the hole in its skull. Next, with an economy of nips and one long vertical slice, Pop showed me how to peel the deer like a banana.

"Like taking off a wet sock," he said.

Sure, I thought, if you had been born with the sock attached to your body.

"Now what do we do?" he said, while we looked at the skinless, dripping deer.

My first instinct was to suggest that I have a seizure and be hospitalized, but I thought, No, that's probably not what he's looking for. He handed me the knife, made a line with his finger, indicating that I should open up the body cavity so that its organs might spill out. The smell was hot and metallic and fecal.

I cut, and then Pop took a hatchet and cracked its sternum in two and opened the deer up like a valise, revealing the horror inside: pretty much every organ ever invented. Yellow fat, blue stomach, green gut, pink lung, purple liver, and that heart, that meaty red heart, big as a baby's head.

"Now we got to cut out its butthole," he said.

All around America, children were cutting out paper snowflakes. Here in Mississippi, I was cutting out anuses.

I was no man.

So I kept shooting. I kept shooting, because that's what Pop told me to do, and I kept missing, because something was wrong with me. It was like I didn't *want* to hit the deer. Sure, the idea of gutting another one by myself was horrible, but I thought it would be different if I'd done the killing.

But why did I keep missing, everybody wanted to know at every Thanksgiving and Christmas. And I explained: because it was dark, and the deer could not be seen, or it was raining, and the distance could not be known, or the deer had been running too fast.

Three or four weeks before that December day, I'd shot at something.

It had been run by a beagle. I'd heard the sound a mile off, grateful for the break in tedium. I was hunting a big wide-open swale of woods, a bank of fog over the whole little valley. The sound grew. The dog was coming this way.

Today would be the day.

Louder. Louder.

Where was the deer?

I watched, scanned, tried to pierce the fog, see through it. Then: There. Something.

The tiny beagle came into view.

Was it too late? Had the deer slipped by me undetected?

Then: a deer.

Six points.

Oh!

Oh!

Oh!

What do I do?

The primal urge to slaughter came alive. We were not hunting Little Debbie Snack Cakes here. I could feel my heart beating inside my eye sockets. The deer was running, sort of picking its way through scrub and over deadfall, not frantic. In three seconds, it would be gone.

Shell: Chambered.

Gun: Raised.

Safety: Off.

It was coming right toward my stand. Could it be any easier?

One hundred yards.

Seventy-five yards.

Fifty yards.

Ready.

Aim.

Breathe.

It dashed in a strange and unwelcome vector, toward a thicket to my right, and now it was running with every evolutionary advantage. There, in the moment between its gentle sauntering toward me and its startling rocketry away, I am not sure what happened. I fired wildly, desperately, and as soon as I pulled the trigger, I knew: It was gone.

The last thing I saw was its flag of white tail vanishing into the woods, bright and erect, a warning to others that if they didn't look now, they'd miss the idiot in the tree, who didn't know a good thing when it was coming right at him. That tail

I'd seen so many times, a friendly *au revoir* from the animal kingdom.

Goodbye, the tail said.

Goodbye, I said.

That was then, and this was now.

"Dear Jesus," I prayed. "Help me."

Let the nightmare be over, I prayed. Let me kill something, and gut something, and maybe it can be over, and Pop will let me alone, or a miracle will happen, and I will learn to like it, perchance love it. It was a fervent prayer, long and filled with laborious King James pronouns, to awaken a more ancient Lord who liked seeing things die.

I told God I would be willing to do anything to make it happen.

"Just give me a sign, dear Lord, that you heard me," I said.

And I said amen. And then he sent me something much bigger than a sign.

---✂ ✦ ✦ ✂---

CHAPTER 7

·

The Things They Slaughtered

---✂ ✦ ✦ ✂---

God sent me a sound.

It started as a faraway whisper, the crash of a distant wave, then grew to a lurid swish, perhaps something in the leaves, some lumberjack kicking his way through a pile. And it was getting closer. So close now that I was pretty sure it was a herd of deer being run by a mute hound, or a bear, or two bears, hungry bears, or a moonshiner dragging the corpse of his adversary, possibly being chased by the two hungry bears. Louder. So loud it was upsetting. Why could I not zero in on this sound? My chest was a tom-tom, my gun bounced in my hands.

The animal must be quite large.

It was right under my stand. I looked.

An armadillo.

The escape of butterflies into the bloodstream was at once electrifying, sickening. How had the armadillo gotten so close? I wanted to shoot it just for scaring me. If this was a sign, the sign said, "Pay better attention."

But wait. Another sound, more sinister, a sound that wanted to be heard, a stamping. Thunk. Bucks will do this during the rut, and it was the rut.

Thunk.

Behind me.

I turned off the safety, put finger to trigger, pivoted, and saw it.

A bird.

Not just any bird, but my brother: Bird. He was very close, twenty feet away, and not even wearing his orange. This was his way of showing me he was a Hunting Ninja. It was also his way of potentially becoming a Dead Hunting Ninja.

"I could've been a deer," he said.

"I could've shot you," I said.

"I'm sure you'd miss."

He was always doing this, sneaking up on me so he could insult me from close range. It was his primary way of communicating with those he loved. But that day his sudden appearance set in motion events that would change my life forever, and also change the life of at least one deer forever, a deer I would soon be shooting, which has a way of changing almost anything's life.

He said to get down.

"Why?" I said.

"It's something wrong," he said.

I did what my brother said and climbed down, because while he may have lacked the ability to conjugate verbs, he would've known how to kill those verbs if they had been running through the forest. He was sixteen now, and he'd already killed his first, and his second, and third. Actually, there was no telling how many he'd killed. He obeyed so few hunting laws, largely as a result of his believing that he had Native American blood, which he believed absolved him from all state and federal hunting and drug statutes.

"Cherokee didn't need no fucking hunting license," he'd say.

What was the Trail of Tears like, I wanted to ask. Had that been hard, watching all his people die of the measles? But also, I wanted to believe. It was a story our grandmother had told us about being descended from a Cherokee chieftain, a version of the same fairy tale told to most poor whites and blacks across the South, a way of making us feel better about genocide and gambling. I'd heard that such blood could earn me a college scholarship, which I believed was my passage out of this alien land, while Bird used this story to explain his preternatural desire to learn things about animals by smelling their feces.

"What are you doing?" he said, while I was still in the tree.

"Unloading my gun," I said. One did not merely shimmy down from three stories up with a loaded gun on his back. One took precautions.

We'd both attended a hunter's safety course that summer, mandated by law. Pop and Bird were nonplussed. What could some game warden with a college degree in wildlife management teach us about the sporting life? It was an insult to them. But I liked it. I was curious as to what other men might teach me, particularly men who may have written books on such matters, or at least men who had read those books, or perhaps any book.

I learned, for example, that it was preferable to shoot a deer in the heart, and not from a moving vehicle, or the window of one's home. I also learned first aid, in case the massive deer we'd just shot was actually a family member, and that it was best not to strap a dead deer to the hood of one's truck, a common sight at our club, as the heat of the engine had been known to cook the deer, which would bloat the carcass, which would prevent the hunter from actually seeing the road in front of him, which might result in the additional slaughter of animals and people.

I also learned about the horrors of hypothermia and how one might grow disoriented and fall into a river and never be heard from again, and how to build a fire so as not to die from exposure, and how, in order not to fall out of a tree, one might tie oneself to said tree with a rope or harness, as though one were about to be launched into space.

Pop nodded in general approval of these lessons, though I suspect that, to him, tying oneself to trees seemed a bit womanish.

"Let's *go*," Bird said.

"Where to?"

He turned and stared into the trees, as though he had heard something I didn't, perhaps deer, or distant gunfire, or merely the ancient spirits in his head.

He walked. I followed.

I was not to ask questions. We were still in the woods, still hunting. He crept forward noiselessly on the roadbed, gun drawn, while I trailed behind. This is what he called "stalking."

Pop did not approve of stalking, but Bird didn't care.

Stalking deer is not unlike stalking a human, in that both involve mobility, concealment, and a mild psychosis brought on by the inability to experience human love. I kept accidentally snapping twigs, making Bird turn and scowl.

"Watch where you step."

It was hard to explain that my excess of garments prevented me from actually controlling the movements of my legs.

"Don't be such an idiot," he said.

"Yes, okay, sorry."

He was fearless. He would just hit people. He would laugh big bellowing laughs that frightened small animals. He would blow a snot rocket right there in the middle of a baseball field, a jet of mucus erupting from a single nostril with enough force to clear his sinuses and disorient the batter. He was a badass. He had balls. Literally. He had shown them to me. They were enormous.

Would mine ever be that big, I wondered? What did it feel like to be a man?

He looked so good in his hunting outfit. Jeans. Field jacket. Tall. Thin. Like a J.Crew model, if they wore bowie knives. How could he get away with wearing so few clothes? Was he simply unafraid of the cold? Or did he lack the necessary nerve endings? And why did he insist on smelling everything?

Bird was led by native spirits, but what led me?

Suddenly, he pulled up his gun and shot into the woods. But I had seen nothing.

"It was a deer," he said.

It may also have been a hallucination. He wanted deer that badly. You had the feeling he would just punch a deer in the face if he got the chance.

That's when we saw it.

Actually, all we could see were its handlebars.

Bird's three-wheeler had fallen in a deep mud hole cut by a pulpwood truck and was now mostly underwater. This is what he wanted me for. His plan was for me to get in and push, since I had fat rubber boots, while he would help from dry ground, where it would be easier to laugh.

"It's too cold," I said. I was thinking of our hypothermia lesson. They had showed us an instructional video, but the man in the video, he died.

"Just stand in the shallow part," Bird said.

I guess I was tired of seeming like a big fat baby, or maybe the air temperature had briefly frozen my brain. Whatever it was, I stepped in.

What happened next would likely be described by medical professionals as "drowning." The water was five feet deep where I'd gone in, and I went under. I sort of bobbed and floundered there for a second, like a buoy, owing to the many layers of clothing, which proved astonishingly impermeable to water.

I managed to scramble and hurl myself onto the edge of the pool, that carpet of pine needles that served as my own private Normandy. When the mud drained from my ears, I could hear Bird laughing the loudest laugh that had ever been laughed outside of a mental hospital, so loud that any nearby deer would have mistaken it for a distant car accident involving cattle.

"You got a little wet," Bird said.

I wanted to ask him: What does it feel like not to have a human heart? Is it fun?

My gun lay against a tree several yards away. I briefly considered the moral implications of fratricide. Nobody would know. Hunting accidents happen all the time. A gun can slip, fall, accidentally discharge six or seven times in one's brother's face.

I started to shake. Bird attempted to reach his handlebars from dry ground, while I lay there and tried to remember the various stages of hypothermia, which started at anxiety and ended in what I vaguely recalled as "feelings of unreality" and then "death."

"You look a little pale," Bird said.

"What color are my lips?"

"Green," he said.

"I'm going to die."

Thankfully, I was wearing cotton, which was very good at holding water next to the skin, speeding up the dying process. I began to disrobe, first my boots, then my coveralls, then various inner garments. My book fell out.

I had forgotten about my book.

I'd gotten the idea the previous hunting season, as a way to cure the endless boredom. I had been careful not to say anything. Pop would be upset. He'd said to keep reading books, but books had their place, and guns had theirs. Now they'd know why I hadn't killed anything. Literacy was to blame.

"What the crap is that?" Bird said, looking down at the wet paperback.

"A book," I said, teeth chattering. "It's got all these words in it. You should get one."

He was shocked. He might as well have discovered me carrying a gymnastics brochure. It was *Watership Down*, a book about communist rabbits who worship the sun.

"What's it about?"

"Hunting," I said.

"Whatever," he said.

"Don't tell Pop," I said.

Most of my clothes were now in a pile, and my exposed skin burned. The man in the video said you could die in just an hour or two.

I needed to go. Where to, I didn't know.

The best thing about dying from exposure is that it gives you time to reflect. I walked deeper into the woods and thought a lot about my situation and my family and my brother and father and this ridiculous childhood. Why couldn't I have been born to a man who loved circuses, or museums? Where was my mother, at that moment? Strolling down the cereal aisle, I guessed, humming a happy song. In her hands, she would have the coupons I'd helped her clip the previous Sunday afternoon. She was my people. Her father loved movies. He'd run a film projector at the Joy, a movie house in Rolling Fork, Mississippi. Every Saturday, he took Mom. She stayed there all day, watching westerns and monster movies and *Gone with the Wind* about a million times, which I guess is a kind of torture, but it sounded dreamy, sitting alone in the balcony while one's father sat a few feet away threading reels and smoking cigarettes and reading the funny papers. The Joy was her Jitney Jungle. Her father was to her what she had become to me.

Right about then, my book was beginning to chafe.

The feelings of unreality came quickly.

What I thought was, I should get back to my stand and just wait like nothing happened and maybe Pop won't notice that I've lost all my clothes. I walked, and walked: Up trails, around bends, through forks, taking rights, taking lefts: I saw visions of darting brown things. I found myself stopping for no reason, turning to look into the woods. Had I seen something move?

What in the hell was I doing?

What I was doing, I guessed, was hunting.

I looked for the sun, but the sun had wrapped itself in a warm envelopment of clouds. My face felt like the surface of a refrigerated ham. I came to understand how rabbits might worship it.

I could always start a fire, which the video had explained was a way to save my life and also burn down the forest. Since then, I'd taken to carrying matches, which I transported in a small black watertight film canister.

I found a small clearing by the trail and gathered twigs and leaves. I crouched, lit the pile. The fire caught and spread, a very successful fire, and I wondered: When does a fire in the forest become a forest fire? It was an interesting question. And if forest fires are wrong, why does this one feel so right? Is this what they meant by feelings of unreality?

He did what, they would say.

Started a fire, they would say. Because he thought he was going to die.

And they would laugh and laugh.

I put the fire out and kept moving.

I knew what I had to do.

I had to find my father.

I came to a fork, and went toward where I thought he might be.

I put a round in the chamber. Yes. I was hunting now.

Pop had said he was going to the Cutover, a desolation in the very center of these woods, a clearing approximately the size of Central Park and created, not by thoughtful urban designers, but by paper companies who took all the trees and left a bare gray landscape that looked like somewhere you'd find a mass grave or an art project about mass graves.

I walked along the edge of it for a hundred yards or so, and I saw him in a tree. And despite that I had lost my hunter's orange vest somewhere up the trail, he saw me. He waved. I waved back. But no, he wasn't waving. He was gesturing. Pointing at something out in the Cutover, something he wanted me to see.

I saw it. A deer. No. Two.

About two hundred yards away, grazing, heads down. Big one, small one. No antlers.

Seeing *anything* in the wild got the heart pounding. Spit fills the mouth. Blood heats. Intestines tumble. There was no question of my not shooting.

It would be an easy shot, as they were not moving.

So, my first deer would be a woman. Okay, I guess. That was fine. This is what he wanted. I put the bead of my iron sights where the heart was.

Bang.

I pulled up and looked with both eyes. The deer had not moved.

Two hundred yards was far.

Bang.

More nothing.

Bang.

Additional nothing. Three murderous shots and they hadn't moved. It was like they hadn't even heard the gun. Were they deaf? Was I shooting a family of disabled animals? Was that even legal? I looked at Pop, who gave me a thumbs-up.

I put the gun to my shoulder again. I was fine with missing, really. They were so far away. Pop would understand.

But no. They just stood there. Daring me to do the thing that everybody said would make me a man. But I didn't want to be a man. I could settle for being a child forever, or maybe a woman, or a librarian, or anything that didn't have to kill things.

Five rounds left, one bullet for each stage of grief.

Bang. Denial. My gun was broken.

Bang. Anger. I hate my family, and I hate these deer, even if they are deaf.

Bang. Bargaining. Okay, Jesus. Remember how I said I would become a preacher if you let me kill a deer today? I'll do you one better. Not only will I stop touching my penis, except to wash it and dry it, which I think you are probably okay with, but I will become a missionary to some dangerous and alien land, like Java, or Atlanta. Yes. I will serve you. Just please let me explode this deer's head off its body. Also, I will be nicer to old people. Amen.

The deer had moved a little, but continued to graze, unperturbed. Two shots left.

Bang, another miss. Depression. I should do us all a favor and turn this gun on myself, although I would probably just miss.

One shot left. What would this come to? Would I have to charge at them with a stick? Would Pop come down and hand me his gun? In that moment, if I thought it'd have made him proud, I would have thrown a grenade at a whole damned family of deer.

Now Bird had found us. He had heard the shooting. He watched.

One more. Make it count.

A short, naked tree stood nearby. It looked dead. I walked to it, and placed my rifle in the crotch of a low branch. I aimed. Help me, Jesus.

Bang.

I stood ten yards away from the larger deer. It was still breathing. I'd hit her in the gut, but she was not dead. Bird and Pop stood behind me, watching. This was my kill. Becoming a man was complicated, filled with decisions. Such as: Do I just stand here and let it suffer?

"Shoot it again," Bird said.

Pop said nothing. He merely surveyed the fact of what was happening.

But I couldn't do it. How close do you stand to it? Do you put the barrel against its head? I had to work up the courage. This was supposed to be the easy part. It was lying right there. I usually kept one or two rounds in a pocket, just in case. I found one. It was wet. Could I use it? Should I? Would it misfire? Explode? Blind me?

While I was vocalizing some of these questions, my brother shot the deer in the head.

And that's when we saw the other deer, the baby one.

A yearling. The saddest part is how it just stood there, watching, almost leaning into the clearing where we all stood, as though it wanted to run to its mother, but didn't know if it had permission.

For some reason that I'm not sure I know even now, this only embarrassed me further. I had killed this animal's mother. I tried to tell myself that the fawn was not thinking about its dead mother, that when it went to bed that night, deep down in some secret thicket, it would not feel alone for the first time in its life. And that is what made me sad, and I was embarrassed that I was sad, which made the moment even sadder.

Was I reading too much into the animal? Had I read too much into every animal? What was it with me and animals? Why was I reading a book about talking rabbits? Why did my mother give me books that made me feel feelings, and why did my father give me guns that made me hurt the feelings of animals, by wounding them, and their mothers? Even then, I felt there was great portent in this particular moment, that something important had or was happening in real time, and that it had something to do with me and this deer and its mother and my mother and my father. The air around us all was burdened with meaning.

The small deer turned its head, and that's when I saw that the right side of its face was mostly gone. Its muzzle was split in two, bleeding, its teeth and jawbone exposed, the flesh of its jaw a haze of gore. I had done this. But how? Was this the ghoulish result of the final bullet, ricocheting off some dead tree? It would take a long time for this animal to die. It would starve. Get an infection. Die of shock. Never grow up.

It turned and walked away, slowly, into the Cutover, and was gone.

That was the last time I went hunting, or rather, the last time I tried to shoot anything. For five more years, I would get up on so many mornings in November and December and January in the coldest part of night, only this time I made sure to bring books. I read without ceasing, Tolkien and Verne and Dickens and Twain and Poe and Hemingway and Steinbeck, and then moved on to the weird stuff, the Asimov and Koontz and King and *Dune* and *Clan of the Cave Bear*, yet another book given to me by Mom, about a Cro-Magnon girl who wanders the wilderness and is adopted by a violent clan of Neanderthals with a limited vocal apparatus, which reminded me of so many of my brother's friends.

These stories were hearty distractions from the horror.

Pop knew. It was our agreement. I would not resist the hunting, and he would not resist the reading, and every deer season, as if by miracle, my standardized test scores would improve, bringing me closer to such time as I might get my paper, as he occasionally reminded me was how not to be a slave to lesser men.

It was that day, I think, when I finally stopped trying to be like my father and my brother and be a different kind of man, the kind who was more like a woman, which is to say my mother. Yes, the kind of man who only climbed trees if being chased by a lion.

Besides, I'd killed a deer. I'd done my part. Really, I'd killed two. There had been no fanfare. Pop had taken no pictures, sent them to no magazines, put them up on no general store walls. They didn't even make me drink the blood. I hardly remember the gutting.

I just kept reading and didn't think about it.

When I finally did go to college, Pop kept asking me to come home and hunt, and I had all sorts of new excuses: that I needed to study, or work, or was planning to have blood in my stool this weekend and couldn't make it. Eventually, he stopped asking.

It was good for me. I am grateful for the obvious lessons, of patience, and quietude, and reverence for a wild and unruly creation, and how to locate your own genitalia whenever they are hiding under thirty layers of flannel, and how to be a writer, which also involves getting up very early, and sitting, and staring, and going slowly insane.

I sometimes wonder, Will I be able to give my children adventures like those? On Saturday mornings these days, the darkest and scariest place we go is the public library, which, if you've been to some of the public libraries in my town, is a lot less safe than it sounds.

And if they complain, I will tell them: "At least I didn't make you cut out deer anuses."

Sometimes, the old urge rises within. I will step outside on a gloriously cold morning before sunrise, briefcase and book in hand, the stars laughably bright, Orion standing at the ready, a song in my blood. Today the deer will be moving, I think to myself, and I think about those two wonderful men off in the woods—Bird chewing peyote buttons and taking deer scalps, Pop sitting and staring out into the Cutover. I almost wish I was there with them. But these stories aren't going to write themselves.

On the way home from that Thanksgiving, when Pop and I had told and retold all our great hunting stories, we were speeding along the highway, green and brown falling away on both sides, and I found myself scanning the fields for ghosts. And I saw them.

"Deer!" I said, pointing.

"Deers!" my children said.

"Where?" said my wife.

But it was too late: We had passed them. My wife and children are too slow. They don't understand. You must look quickly, or they are gone.

—≈ ✦ ✦ ≈—

·

CHAPTER 8

Every Creeping Thing

—≈ ✦ ✦ ≈—

I had always thought the world was made up of two kinds of people: the Hunter People, who liked to kill and eat things, and the Animal People, who whispered to horses and brought their dogs to cancer wards and let goats live in their houses. But what I'd learned is that I was neither. I didn't have the stomach to kill, but I also probably didn't have the stomach to let a goat live in my house, even if it had cancer. I was a new kind of person, a third kind: not Hunter People, not Animal People. I was Scared People.

Nevertheless, I was blessed to grow up in a place where animals were everywhere, eager to be your friend. I frolicked with many species. *Frolic* might not be the right word. What I did was more like *running away screaming*. Sometimes it was just running, other times it was just screaming, and sometimes it was just standing there and letting my bowels do the running for me.

It wasn't just movies about werewolves and yetis that made me this way. It was also my mother, who played Prokofiev's *Peter and the Wolf* on the hi-fi, which I believe taught me to associate classical music with predators. But there was an artist far more sinister than the Russian composer: Marlin Perkins, of

Mutual of Omaha's Wild Kingdom, a man whose TV show taught me that the Lord's manifold creation was best appreciated by those armed with tranquilizer rifles. The show and others like it, say, *Marty Stouffer's Wild America*, pulled no punches in the animal attack department, with its cascading sequences of violence: snake-on-rat, gator-on-bear, ram-on-ram, raccoon-on-toad, lynx-on-pheasant, cougar-on-elk, cougar-on-bunny, eagle-on-bunny, wolf-on-bunny, basically everything murdering bunnies in the most hateful ways possible.

In Mississippi, it was easy to feel like a bunny.

It's not that I was overly afraid, or even phobic, at least no more than the average human might be. The problem was, Mississippi is not filled with average humans.

Death was all around, and not just at the deer camp: Vast roadside morgues and mounds of torn flesh on the highway, black and brown and red and dead. Hitting them was not fun, although one had the feeling it was fun for some, those rural drivers who learned to operate their motor vehicles by watching *Smokey and the Bandit* and footage of early NASCAR tragedies.

One spring night, on a slow country road, we came upon a bunny.

"Stop!" Mom said.

"Don't hit it!" I said.

And Pop, usually the type to hit a thing on purpose, slammed on the brakes.

It sounded like someone had thrown a golf ball at the bumper. Had we hit it? Also, did you know that rabbits can scream? They do. So do mothers and children.

"Oh, no," Mom said.

Pop drove on.

I looked out the back window to see if I could see it, but all I saw was a big fat dairy moon covering the black woods in milk. Out there, the beauty and the violence were all mixed up.

Like the time I saw the many-pointed buck swimming across the Coldwater River one January day, perhaps the most sublime scene I have ever witnessed, and how my cousin steered his boat that way so he could stab it in the neck with a knife. It would not have been my first inclination to engage the creature in such brutal gang warfare, but then, I assumed that this was what you did in Mississippi, perhaps because there were so few actual gangs.

Or the time, in the middle of a varsity football game one night, when a squirrel ran across the end zone, and a barred owl the size of a harrier jet materialized out of the autumnal ether, its whiteness blazing like an angel under the lights of the field, and all of us gasped at the beauty and the horror that such a thing could descend from blackness unbidden. It gutted the squirrel right there in front of us, and the crowd cheered.

Or the time we found a nest of newborn field mice inside an old tractor seat, still blind and hairless, and how my father dumped them into a garbage fire in the yard. This sort of thing never happened in the city, where small animals, when found by children, were generally given names and a dish of water. Sometimes, I thought, having a small pet might make me less skittish, something small and soft, maybe a whole family of small soft things, and there they were, on fire.

I felt like I needed some way to connect to these animals that didn't involve death, something that might redeem the killing, or help draw me into a deeper spiritual understanding of it, to see it the way Bird saw it, as a natural process, a communion with wildness.

The place really was a zoo: the blue herons, gray bats, green-heads, copperheads, red foxes, white appaloosas, and the cows, the very many cows, an ocean of beef. Much of it was lovely to behold from the safety of a school bus, but these things could hurt you, the alligators who lurked at the margins of our swimming holes, the only lifeguard an indifferent kingfish with no certifications to speak of, the snakes that fell out of trees into the boats that we'd hoped would keep us safe, the panthers and rumors of panthers and bears and odors of bears.

"There aren't really bears here," Mom would say. "Are there?"

And then there'd be some story in *Mississippi Game & Fish* about a bear seen on a highway, and it'd be, like, great. It was chilling to know there were things that could kill you walking the woods or slinking through the water we played in, but also a little sublime. It added voltage to a walk in the woods.

Boys rode bulls, girls showed sheep, and everyone had a little fur and blood on their hands. If someone invited you to spend the night, by breakfast they'd be expecting you to do something to a hog.

My fears were not irrational. I'd heard stories.

"A razorback just about got my uncle this weekend," a friend would say.

What was a razorback, I wondered? Some kind of bird?

But no, I learned that it was a wild hog, and that wild hogs did not usually fly, unless they were dropped from airplanes. I also learned that they had tusks, and that it was not uncommon for them to attack humans, usually during the rut, and that this usually happened in the woods, where we spent most of our playtime, which was upsetting, because I did not generally like to play in places that were full of angry sex monsters.

Up the road, there was a nice boy who'd been made retarded by a horse. They said it had kicked him in the head, and one thing was clear: He could no longer talk right.

"My hurts," he would say.

"Where did you get hurt?"

"Ouch," he would say, pointing to a cloud.

"No," we'd say. "Where on your body."

"Ice cream," he'd say.

"You got hurt in your ice cream?"

"Mmm," he'd say.

The animals could hurt you in all sorts of ways, hurt your body, hurt your mind, make your soul pucker, as mine did the day I saw the dead bull.

He'd bent down to drink from a waterhole and his forelegs had sunk too deep in the mud. We found him bloated, dead many days. The boys whose farm it was lit into action, one fetching a heavy chain, another a tractor, another a gun. A gun seemed odd. I watched them wrap the chain around its hind legs, while the oldest boy stood on the levee and took aim at the bull's head.

"Snakes," somebody said.

The tractor did its work, and the ghoulish head rose from the water, its eyes missing, its wide nostrils wider, dripping, and filled with the heads of many white snakes.

When you see a thing so horrid, you have to cuss, even if you don't cuss.

"Oh, shit," someone said.

"Goddang."

"Motherfucker."

Snakes poured from the mouth and eyes and nose, white snakes, a color we'd never seen a snake be. The boy with the rifle started shooting at them, and more guns were fetched, and I watched more things die and be dead.

Later, we doused the bull in diesel and set it on fire.

There were stories of coyotes who had to be fought out of chicken houses with aluminum bats, of deer who'd turned hunters blind with their antlers, of turkey buzzards that would throw up digested carrion on you if you got too close. Why did nobody seem upset by any of this, by a world where the birds would just up and vomit on you?

My father, of course, was raised on a dairy and courted several young ladies who resembled mules, and he obviously wanted me to have similar experiences. He made arrangements for Bird and me, seizing the moment if an elderly farmer had fallen ill. "Wake up, boys," he would say before dawn. "You got to go feed Mr. May's cows. He's got the walking pneumonia again."

He was always on the phone, searching for some sick farmer who'd had a blood clot or lost his balance and been mangled by a baler. Dutifully, we'd go and do whatever needed to be done, praying that God would stop afflicting the farmers of our community with arterial plaque and vertigo.

Then one day, Pop hit the jackpot. He'd found a permanent job for me on a real farm with real animals. Perhaps, I thought, they would allow me to work with the gentler livestock, piglets or baby lambs or maybe a small and affectionate cabbage.

When I arrived, I met my only coworker, Tom, a boy I knew from school. Tom had always been a large boy, perhaps enjoyed a ham hock or two, and was now likely visible from space. I made a mental note that if any animals attacked, I might seek protection by climbing to the top of him and awaiting rescue by helicopter.

"You any good with animals?" he asked me that first day.

"Like how?" I said.

"Like can you ride a horse?"

"No."

"Ever worked with hogs?"

"I wouldn't say I've worked with them," I said. "I know what they look like."

"Can you feed them?"

"Would I have some kind of a stick or a pole?" I asked.

He had a chew in his mouth. He spit. We talked. Occasionally, I spit, too, and for a minute there, we were a couple of genuine spitting machines. He was installing new emergency flashing lights on his truck, he explained, because he had designs on being a member of the Cato Volunteer Fire Department.

"You ever put out a fire?" I asked.

"Not yet," he said, with a look that suggested he might start his own fire if one didn't immediately present itself.

Tom gave me simple tasks, things that could be done by any village idiot, such as mowing the grass. I did find myself quite close to the animals, but always on the safe side of the fence. It was nice to be close to an animal that you hadn't necessarily shot in the face. Animals are so much more pleasant when they're not dying.

"Sweet horsey," I would say, gently, cautiously, pulling up a fat dandelion to feed the beast. It wasn't so bad. They smelled a little, but it wasn't their fault. Mostly, I just watched them. They had favorite spots, favorite foods, best friends. They were complicated things, got in bad moods, and sometimes they got in good moods, and that's when they had a great deal of sex.

There were a couple of horses whose courtship had its own delightful choreography, which involved the mare staring at the stallion for about an hour, which I thought must have something to do with the stallion's giant penis.

Tom didn't talk much, but animal sex always got him going. He'd come over to the fence and point out some act of lovemaking to see what I thought about it.

"You ever seen a hog pecker?" he said one day.

There's just no good answer to a question like that, so I said, "Sure."

"Then you know it looks just like yours," he said.

I looked down at where mine usually was and tried not to think about it.

"But a boar, see, theirs is like a corkscrew." He made a screwy motion with his finger, as though his digit had temporarily transformed into a real boar pecker and he was some sort of wizard. And in a way, he was.

Hey, dude!" Tom said.

He called out from the dangerous side of the fence, in the midst of about ten thousand cows. Fat or not, he was clearly more man than I. He would do anything to an animal. He would grab a cow teat and spray you. He would pick up a snake and kiss it. I once saw him masturbate a dog, like he was showing me a new magic trick.

"You want to see something cool?" he said.

"Something cool" could have meant anything: porn, a two-headed snake, porn involving a two-headed snake. Suddenly, a sonic horror filled the countryside, like a distant bagpiper being slowly fed into the world's largest garbage disposal. Was that an animal? That couldn't be an animal. It was the kind of sound one normally ran away from, while shouting that we were all going to die.

"I need your help," he said.

Before I knew it, I was over the fence and rounding the barn with him, and there she was, the thing that made the noise, a brown cow. From across the fence, from the road, these cows, they looked small. But this cow was not small. It was the size of a starter home. It was really two cows, I suppose, if you counted the one inside her, trying to get out.

"You got to keep the cow from busting out of the gate," Tom told me.

Whatever was inside her was large and angular and possibly a dining room table. I got a little dizzy. Tom stuck his hand inside the cow, which made her scream some more.

"Hold that gate," he said. "And don't let her get out!"

A gate, that was easy. I could hold a gate. I could hold all kinds of things. My hands, for example, over my face, to keep out whatever demonic odors were currently trying to melt my nose bones. The smell was regal in its unpleasantness, a rich goulash that stabbed at the underbelly of the brain, the odor of an animal that had never bathed and left uncovered stool samples in its bedroom every day. And now, people were in its bedroom, attempting to pull things out of its anus, which made it angry, and so it did what any reasonable animal would do: It urinated on us.

Tom did not acknowledge the Niagara of nitrogenous fluid now covering our shoes and legs, nor any of the other viscous liquids pouring out of her. Instead, he considered how best to tie the cow to the wall, explaining that she might become high-spirited and want to run away, which could kill her and the calf, which, he explained, was not ideal.

"All I got's this twine," he said. "You think it'll hold her?"

My first thought was, I think this cow needs some privacy. My second thought was, What's that in my shoes? My third thought was, Oh, that's just cow urine! It was around this time that I decided to stop thinking.

Thirty minutes later, after I'd achieved a pleasant cataleptic trance and had rededicated my life to serving widows and the fatherless, it occurred to me that if holding the gate was necessary, then Tom was clearly expecting the cow to burst through it. I stood there holding the broken gate shut and wondered what my father and brother would do if a cow charged at them. They would probably punch it in the face and try to put some mustard on it. I wanted to ask Tom how we could quiet the beast, but he was too busy prying around inside its birth canal, a procedure proven to upset almost any species.

The cow looked at me. It was a hurtful look.

What was it thinking? It struck me that I'd never thought to ask.

I tried to let it know things would be okay, that we were trying to help, that it wasn't our fault, that I was sorry, to it and every other animal I'd ever met, sorry for running, for screaming, for shooting it in the face, for letting it get burned alive, for letting it get hit by a truck and eaten by a buzzard and thrown up on a stranger.

What I wanted to say was, I like you, I do, I'm just scared of you.

"I can feel something!" Tom said.

At this point, he seemed to be trying to fit his whole body inside the animal's vagina. He went deeper, and began to pull, and then asked me to pull him, and both of us began to cry out in what I guessed were sympathetic labor pains, while the cow cried loudest of all, and we all seemed to be praying and pulling until the cow threw Tom into a wall, broke its meager twine noose, and got ready to run.

"The gate!" Tom said.

Our eyes met one last time.

This was my moment to make a stand, to let the animal kingdom know I was not afraid.

She lowered her head, and blood poured out of the back of her, and I could not let her run, and so I threw myself between her and the gate, and she charged, and I closed my eyes and did what needed to be done, which was, to climb the wall like a kitten.

"Noooo!" said Tom.

The cow plowed over the earth where I'd stood and was gone, and Tom got up, went running after it. The stall was empty now, save for blood and shit and a dead calf, its legs bent back over it, a monstrosity.

It's a strange feeling, seeing a newborn thing dead. I climbed down from my high place, saw Tom in the pasture chasing the big cow. He caught up with her, pulled out the afterbirth with his bare hands, and I made a mental note to gouge out my own eyes when I had the chance. I turned to look at the dead calf, but it was gone, replaced by a thing that stood up on four legs.

And I heard angels.

I fell more in love with Mississippi on that day, seeing what it could do, what could happen there, all the beauty and life that could come from nothing, so violently, suddenly. And I think it was on that day that I began to love its people, too, the Toms of this wild place, who could reach deep into God's animals and pull forth wonders unbidden, such as other animals. I miss that. I miss those people.

I live in a city now, with completely different kinds of people, the kind who set up playdates for their dogs and allow seeing-eye goats to live in their houses. Which is fine. It feels safer, in many ways, raising our children in the city, where the birds have enough courtesy not to go throwing up on everybody and almost nobody sets their animals on fire.

Just last week, we were watching one of those nature shows descended from *Mutual of Omaha's Wild Kingdom*, but scrubbed of all the animal death. It was a story about a dog who made friends with an orangutan. The dog and the ape cuddled, played, rolled around like old pals. It gave me hope. It was also pretty weird.

"Back in my day," I explained to my children, "animals attacked one another on television."

"Cool," they said.

"And your grandfather made me work on a farm."

Young men today, they have no direction, nobody telling them what to do, and so what do they do? They go to college and ruin their lives. But every American boy deserves the opportunity to be trampled by a large animal, although I hear that this is now possible in many of our nation's most progressive fraternities.

I told my children these stories, about the snakes that came out of a cow and all the other things I saw and did and wished I had not done with animals.

"Did that really happen?" they said.

Maybe they're right. Maybe it was all a dream. But I know this: I came out of it a new man, a man who appreciated creation a little more, and life, and health, and showers. The animals were kinder to me after that. It's like they knew, and were grateful, or maybe it was the stick I carried.

A few minutes after the calf was born and came back to life, Tom wanted to let the world know, so he cranked up the siren on his truck and let it sing. I guess he was just happy. And so was I. It was nice, seeing something not die. I can still hear that siren now, ringing the glad joys of creation in my ear, so many years later, which is about how long it took to get the smell of cattle urine off my shins.

—❧ ✦ ✦ ☙—

CHAPTER 9

·

The Wishbone

—❧ ✦ ✦ ☙—

I was no child anymore, it seemed. I had seen things die and be dead and also undead, come back to life to flourish and fret others, once the beasts had grown large enough. I was getting larger, too. Too large in places, it seemed, not quite large enough in others. Junior high had come and gone, leaving in its wake nothing but questions, generally regarding my genitals, and how large I could expect them to be, or not be, at some point in the future.

And yet, the years dragged their feet like tired children. When would I be grown, liberated of this man who made us work for free for people who hadn't even asked us to, who made us pluck hot organs out of pendulous creatures, and who went into debt just to buy guns so that we could obtain meats that could easily have been purchased at the store, if we'd had any money in the bank, which we didn't, owing to the many guns?

He yelled, whipped, drove us like beasts, was out of his mind. Wanted us to have a life that might no longer be possible, and bent himself and his conscience every whichaway to make it happen. Whatever he did, he did it brutally, but for the most part he also did it honestly. Cheating required skills that Pop did not have, such as the ability to whisper and make at least one good friend. Pop didn't have friends, which he believed were things meant for women and children, as were holidays and happiness. A real man didn't need all that. All a man needed was a gun and a woodstove and maybe, if things got bad, a towel for the blood. He did not cheat unless it served some larger moral good, such as the rigging of the company car into a family car. But that had been justified in his moral calculus, which made it the opposite of cheating: It had been a duty.

He was righteous, and crazy, and liable to explode, but he did not cheat.

Except when he had no choice.

It happened one cool November evening, with the hiss of fried pork chops and the pedantry of *Jeopardy*'s Alex Trebek wafting down the hall to my room, where I was staring into the mirror at my changing body. It was a glorious thing, this body, and I admired it, its pubescent blubber melting away and hair arriving in secret places with disturbing speed.

"You're a man now," I said to the thing in the mirror. I flexed. What power.

There was a knock at the door. I jumped onto the bed, covered myself in a pillow, turned my book over, feigned reading. "Come in."

It was Pop.

There had been a great rift between us for months, ever since I'd stabbed the dagger of treason into his back by quitting the football team, and I had begun to worry that I was no longer a son to him, but a turncoat. Pop had been a football hero, then a coach, then my coach. My quitting was a tragedy, a royal abdication. I might as well have expressed an interest in joining the U.S. Men's Knitting Team.

Something had died between us.

Then came this knock at the door.

"What you doing under that pillow, boy?"

"Reading."

"What about?"

It was a slightly lusty Dean Koontz novel about a hermaphrodite whose sons possess the ability to telekinetically transport themselves through space and time, and so I said, "It's about science."

"Neat," he said. I could tell something was wrong, as my father was not generally enthusiastic about science. "I need you to do something," he said. He was also not a big asker of things. "Fetch them old cleats you got and get dressed. We going to Pearl."

There was only one thing in Pearl worth going to on a Thursday night: a complex of dirt football fields as flat and red as a Mars plateau.

"Why?" I said.

"I need you to suit up."

He walked out.

That was odd. Not because I preferred hermaphroditic literature to football, but because I was in high school, and Pop coached a peewee team. Let me say that again: He coached a team full of ten- and eleven-year-old fatlings, whose soft little necks had trouble holding up a helmet. My neck, along with the rest of me, was fully formed. I was fourteen.

Was this a joke? Perhaps the old man was being funny. And then I remembered, my father did not tell jokes.

The horn on the Dodge bellowed. I grabbed my cleats, ran toward the sound.

Pop, they said, had been a beast on the grass, a true wonder in athletic contests, despite being as round and thick as a mastodon. They could say this because it was back when they had mastodons. The man had a head like a medicine ball, legs like Doric columns, shoulders like two Honey-Baked hams on either side of a very wide room. It was generally agreed that he would eventually play ball for Coach Vaught at Ole Miss or, at the very least, wrestle bears for a living. Then, during a fateful high school game versus Hernando, he broke one of the more necessary bones in his leg, and—just like that—the dream died. And so, since he would not be making any game-saving sacks or game-winning scores, he set himself to making something even better: a little man, just like him, who might fill those cleats and carry the mantle, live the unlived dream. No son of his would have a choice in the matter. The gravity and density of Pop's DNA would be too much to ignore.

It took him three marriages, but finally, he got him a boy.

"Hot damn!" Pop said, that long-ago day, in a hospital just up the road from Graceland. He was excited, because he'd seen a pecker. He devoted the next eighteen years of his life to raising up the little thing attached to the pecker. The little thing, of course, was me.

"It'll make a man out of you," he was always saying. Like the time he told me to saw a deer in half. He handed me a rusty bone saw old enough to have been used by Grant's siege engineers at Vicksburg and told me to run it through the dead thing's pelvis.

"It'll make a man out of you, boy!" he said, handing me the saw. "And don't be sawing through his nuts, neither."

This is advice I've taken everywhere with me: Don't be sawing through an animal's nuts. Speaking of nuts, that's what

Pop was about football. It had everything required to make a boy into a man: brutality, blood, a concession stand.

On the way to Pearl, we spoke little. I had so many questions, like "Do you really expect me to hit all those children?" and "Have you lost your mind?" We powered up Highway 18 in the Dodge, not even a radio station to break the tension. He stared ahead, as he always did, with the frozen gaze one typically associates with Arctic musk oxen.

I was worried. I was not a big rulebreaker. I did not like the idea of flouting what was clearly league policy about age limits. Some of the boys who played up in Pearl, they were big. I might not stand out too much. But still. What if I was caught?

"So—" I said.

"I got you at fullback," he said, looking straight ahead into the black.

"Oh."

"We running the wishbone."

"Good."

I had no idea what the wishbone was. Some kind of formation. Also, a salad dressing. I suppose he could sense my wondering, because he soon explained that he was expecting only ten players to show and needed one more or else he'd have to forfeit. I suggested there'd be dozens of teams at the park and that he shouldn't have a problem finding an eleventh from another squad, some boy of some eager father who wanted his boy to get more reps in.

"Yeah, but you know the plays," he said.

"True, true."

I remembered none of the plays. Pop was always doing this, assuming I knew more than I knew about whatever game it was he'd ordered me to play. Overestimating my talent. Believing his DNA had won the battle with my mother's and that I was like him in every athletic way, even though history had shown us both otherwise.

When I was six, he mounted a basketball goal in our driveway, believing the angularity and velocity of the sport would at least teach me to juke, which would be of help in football later on. But juking, as well as dribbling and shooting, were somewhat problematic due to my enormous head, bequeathed to me by Pop through the miracle of genetics. He could manage his own enormous head fine, having the adult body to go with it, but I could not, and I worked hard to keep it from hurling toward the ground at dangerous speeds, which is what gravity desires to do to all enormous children's heads. Invariably, one of our family basketball games would end with my feebly attempting some sort of layup, while Newtonian physics attempted to introduce my skull to the driveway. I would jump, and slip, and come crashing down headfirst onto the concrete.

Mom would shriek and run to my aid, but not Pop.

"My boy's got a powerful head!" Pop would say.

Next, he put me on a baseball team with boys three years older than me, hoping I'd rise to the challenge. Mercifully, they put me in right field, a clear signal to all that I was mentally disabled. On the rare occasion when a ball limped my way, I'd hurl it toward the infield and would be as shocked as everyone else to see it flying in the wrong direction, toward the heads of children on other fields. The parents shrieked, sought medical help, but not Pop.

"The boy's got a powerful arm, don't he!" he would say, sirens in the distance.

As I got older, I filled out a little, foreshadowing my

future girth and power, but still lacked hand-eye coordination, as well as eye-foot, foot-foot, and head-wall coordination. In games of Two-Hand Touch or the regrettably named Smear the Queer, to be sure, I struck people and objects with great frequency. Once, after scoring a touchdown, I broadsided my grandfather's barn and knocked two planks loose. Cousins ran inside for something to soak up the blood, but not Pop.

"Seems like he's got him some powerful legs, too," he said, while relatives pried me from the me-shaped hole.

When I turned ten, Pop announced that I would play football. The time had come. Glory. It was an August afternoon when he took me outside, pulled from his trunk enough football equipment to make a house payment, and told me to put it on so he could hit me: shoulder pads, Puma cleats, a jockstrap large enough for a Viking warlord. I put it on, and he got down opposite me.

"Say, *Hut, hut*," he said.

"Why?"

"Just say it."

Nothing's quite as horrifying as watching your extra-large father—for all practical purposes the Incredible Hulk with a heart condition and comb-over—squat down, look you in the eyes, and ask you to ask him to hit you.

"Hut, hut," I said, and I soon found myself blessed with the gift of backward flight.

"What are you doing to my baby?" Mom said, as I lay there, my nose bleeding, my life-force pooling into the dry, sandy ground.

"That's how a man hits," he said.

Pop had never been my coach before. He was safer in the bleachers, telling himself harmless lies about his boy. But coaching. Someone could get hurt. Me, for example.

Pop poured everything into my teams, building squads that might array themselves around me and help carry me to some future exaltation. He did this by trolling the playgrounds and trailer parks of our community, filling the roster with previously unknown athletes, boys whose time in juvenile detention had precluded their involvement in youth sports. He made the acquaintance of other large men, who might have large offspring, and many did. He signed up poor black children, whose parents could not afford the registration fee, or the equipment, or the gas money to get to games, and he paid for them from his own pocket. Which is to say, we had a roster full of large, fast, hungry, and very grateful athletes. Also, we had no savings.

"You spend too much on football," Mom said.

"It's his future we talking about," Pop said. "He'll play college ball one day."

"I sure would like to take a vacation one day, or maybe get some new Sunday dresses."

"I sure would like you to cook us some dinner."

Was this how a husband was supposed to talk to a wife? I recognized a superior control in my mother, a Hoover Dam harnessing a righteous fury and turning it into a whole other thing. I could see a regal confluence of grace and power in her body and face when Pop spoke to her like this—was it a joke between them, or not a joke at all? When she looked at him, there was a willful weakness in her eyes, mouth, the closed lips, the unclenched jaw: Was it love, or pity, or a prayer?

I was old enough to know she had options: She could have left him, for example, or poisoned him, which she had many opportunities to do, given that she controlled the means of production of the dinners he so deeply loved, but she wasn't going to poison him and she wasn't going to leave, because she'd been left once before—and so had he: twice. I'm sure she was starting to see why. It was a miracle he hadn't been killed by a woman somewhere along the way, and I think Mom must have known it. She was his protector.

"No other woman would put up with this," she'd say.

"Shit," he'd say. "I'm a catch."

"And I ought to throw you back."

She stayed with him out of love and sacrifice: It would have been a cruel act to release my father back into the world, to devour more women. He was safer this way, steamrolling her. She could take it. She didn't mind lying down. It was a comfortable position, convenient for both napping and reading.

And for ducking the volcanic power of the man, and he was a volcano. You just had to get out of his way, and that's what Mom did. She loved the volcano, saw through his magma to something hurting underneath it. She did not run from the gaping maw, but stood there on its rim and cooked it a pan of cornbread, which the volcano liked very much, and helped calm it down.

Nevertheless, the volcano had no money for new Sunday dresses for her, because of all the spending on football, and so she came up with a plan, which was to tutor local children for extra money in the afternoons at our dining room table, which meant the delaying of the making of the daily cornbread, which typically would've meant the volcano would bring desolation, but in fact was fine, because that meant Pop could keep us longer at football practice every evening and make us run more laps around the field. It worked out for everybody. Mom got a new dress or two, and Pop got his football team, and I got to spend more time getting concussions, which taught me a valuable lesson, which I have since forgotten, due to the many concussions.

We won bowl trophies and whipped many teams across the county. Pop soon became a vaunted member of the fraternity of coaches, a real bootstraps kind of hero. And I am grateful for what he did. It was fun, all the healthy camaraderie, the sleepovers after games, the time spent with my mother in the hospital while suffering from mild brain-bleeding.

I toughed it out, fought through phalanxes of giant corn-fed children, tried my hardest to do something right. I could barely understand the cryptic metaphors Pop used in his coaching.

"Eat his lunch!" Pop would shout from the sidelines.

"Eat his *what*?"

"His lunch."

"What are you talking about?"

"Let me hear some leather pop!"

"Leather?" I would say. It sounded like something he'd pried out of a dictionary of nineteenth-century hobo slang.

"You know," he'd say, clapping.

None of us was wearing leather, as far as I could tell. Should we be? Did he want me to carry some kind of a whip?

"Take a two-by-four to him, Junior!"

"To who?" I'd say. "There's eleven of them."

"Yo deddy crazy," my teammates would say, and I didn't disagree.

If pictures are worth a thousand words, the look on my face in team photos of this era says something like, "I am uncomfortable and hot." My face is strained and stiff, the countenance of a fatalist who is suffering from a high-fiber diet. I seem to be making private signals to the camera, suggesting my location and how a well-trained team of SEALs might extract me.

Over the next four years, I tried to quit football approximately eight hundred and forty-two times. There was one rough game where a fullback, who seemed way too old for junior high, had abused me. His age, of course, was an assumption of mine, based entirely on his lush and rather full mustache.

"I think he collapsed one of my lungs," I said.

Pop, as ever, pretended not to hear. "You coulda eat his lunch."

I dreamt of being in a terrible car accident and losing the use of my limbs, which, I believed, would make it easier to quit. During a physical in Jackson, I got the brilliant idea to have a physician sanction my unfitness to play.

"Our other doctor said I have a heart murmur," I said. "I could die."

"You won't die."

"But I might die."

"Not from that."

"But one day."

"One day, yes," he said, putting a credentialed hand around my vitals and making me cough.

Back at home, I kept trying. "It's just . . . there are so many extracurricular activities I could do," I said.

"We got to get you a multivitamin, firm you up."

"Like maybe the quiz bowl team."

"Make a muscle," he said, groping my bicep.

With my other arm, I extended an envelope. "Did you see this invitation I got to join Mensa?" I asked.

"Men's who?"

"It's for geniuses," Mom said from the kitchen. "My baby is a genius."

Pop looked toward the sound of dishwater, confused. "Your momma's gone crazy," he said.

"It just seems like maybe I should focus on things besides football," I said.

"You mean, like baseball?"

"Like maybe the chess team."

Something inside him turned to ash. You could see it. He stared into the middle distance, as though reaching back through memory for some tenuous relationship between chess and balls.

Soon, I spiraled into a whorl of decadence with the chess and science clubs, learning very different kinds of offensive moves and establishing control groups and reveling in the empirically verifiable company of other disappointing children. Pop and I didn't speak for weeks, until that night when he came knocking and told me to find my cleats.

We arrived at the Center City Complex of Pearl, Mississippi, and I remembered that I did not very much like Pearl—a community best known for its excellent marching bands, violent dogs, and high rates of venereal disease. Their peewee teams were notoriously nasty, unmannered, and good. We didn't know why they had always been so much better and stronger and faster than us, but we suspected it had something to do with having stepfathers who abused them. The only consolation, for those of us from outlying rural communities, was that they would all soon be in prison.

Pop opened his door, got out. It was night. The halogen glow formed a dome around the park, over which moved low gunmetal clouds. A gust of wind blew off Pop's baseball cap, and his hairflap came unmoored, rose to attention.

"I got your pads in back," he said and walked toward the lights.

I found all my old gear, the ancient jockstrap that smelled of spring meadows. I undressed right there in the grassy glen, preparing to don equipment that I had first worn four years earlier, when I was not yet the size of a Viking warlord as I was now, owing to a strict regimen of Cool Ranch Doritos. I had grown as big as Pop, but not in the right way. Not with the muscles.

A quart of sweat later, I made a jarring lurch onto the field, like Dr. Frankenstein's hopeful monster duct-taped inside a protective barrier of sofa cushions. My knees refused to flex, and my shoulders had grown too large for the shoulder pads, which now perched atop my clavicles rather than astride them, giving the effect of small and functionless wings sprouting from my neck.

I joined my teammates, most of whom seemed too small, stunted even.

"Who are you?" a small uniformed boy asked, looking up.

"I'm Coach Key's son," I said.

"You're big," he said, poking a finger deep into the fatty tissues around my exposed gut. More of the younglings gathered around me, as children are wont to do with Jesus and clowns.

"How old are you?" they said.

"He's tall as my uncle."

"What grade is he in? Hey, what grade are you in?"

"He ain't got no grade," Pop said, strutting over. "He's homeschooled."

It was strange to hear my father lie so imaginatively.

"I'm in high school, and I have a driver's permit," I wanted to say. But I knew it would blow Pop's cover. Then, during warm-ups, the taunts began.

"Ain't he a big one?" I heard, off to my right, from the Pearl side.

"The big ones is always stupid," another said.

"Hey, boy!" they said. "I bet you too big even to fit in the short bus!"

They howled. The Pearl parents appeared to believe I was slow of speech and had something of a gland problem.

"Good luck tonight, hon!" a tattooed mother said. "He's about to bust outta that uniform, ain't he!"

I said nothing, just stared dumbly, which only strengthened their belief in my retardation. I ignored them, tried to be the bigger man. I *was* the bigger man. Bigger than some of the parents, even.

"Grab a knee," Pop said.

It was almost time. My teammates looked up to me, and I looked up to Pop, and Pop looked at a point approximately thirty degrees above the horizon, as though he'd sighted a large formation of ducks he wished to murder. It started to rain.

"Lead us in a prayer," Pop said to me, and I did as I was told.

I was disoriented, at first, by the giant-headed children raging around below me in the rain. Then, four plays in, I got steamrolled by a child I hadn't seen coming and landed sideways in orange mud. My teammates gathered around me, their dripping helmets wreathing the dark sky. One of them kicked me.

"I think Coach Key's son is dead."

I elbowed myself to a sitting position. My small attacker was the size of a ferret but appeared to be feeding on amino acids and gunpowder.

"I tole you he was dumb, Rusty!" his teammates said to him, high-fiving. It was embarrassing, getting whipped by a fifth grader named Rusty.

What happened next would become the stuff of peewee football lore.

In short, I sort of became an enraged gorilla. At fullback, I folded up children like bad origami, including Rusty, who soon took to running in the opposite direction, shrieking. I chased down the largest players, knocked them into a new day of the week. I started calling the plays, took the handoff, ran over as many athletes as possible, which required several awkward turns and parabolic vectors, before entering the end zone. On my second—or was it my third?—touchdown, I dragged at least four defenders across the plane, along with one of my own pocket-size teammates, who had become excited and was riding me like a homecoming float.

"It feels so good!" he said.

"It does," I said.

I ran around children, over them, under them, and, at one point, fulfilled a childhood fantasy by throwing and then catching the very same pass. I made their running backs drop balls merely by barking at them.

"He's got the rabies," they said. "He's an animal."

And I was. I played with abandon, both because I knew it would be my last football game ever and also because, owing to puberty and the shrinking properties of cotton, my jockstrap finally fit.

"Thatta way, boy!" Pop said. "Stack 'em like cordwood!"

Ah, yes! The metaphors—they all made sense now. I started inventing my own.

"I just ate a tree!" I said to a fallen Pearl athlete. Or, "I'm about to grow a new head!"

"That don't even make sense," Rusty said, from across the line.

People were starting to talk. I saw them pointing, whispering. I knew there might be inquiries made about the depth of my voice and the hair on my arms and the date on my birth certificate. From what I could tell and hear, it was believed that I was either in high school or the greatest athlete in the history of Mississippi youth sports.

By the time the game was over, the field was littered with bodies. Children cried in pain or wept in joy, depending, rolling around celebrating and/or lamenting in the soupy carnage.

Parents and coaches were on the field to tend the wounded. Referees shook their heads. The score was 63–0, and—I am not making this up—every point was mine.

Pop put his hand on my shoulder, and we beheld the spectacle of the battlefield together, where an alternate history played itself out, unraveling backward like reversed game tape, a glorious past where I had not quit, where I had inherited the best qualities of this beast on the grass that was my father.

"We whipped 'em good," he said.

I couldn't help thinking that he'd wanted me to play, to feel what it was like to be him, at least for one game. To him, it wasn't cheating. It was fathering.

Pop knew what was coming, and we got out of there quick, while children tried to get my autograph or a lock of my hair, and league officials loitered to get a look at the young Sasquatch. On the way home, we spoke little. My ears rang like they always did after games, but now it was from all the cheering. To my knowledge, nobody ever pressed the matter. Pop was allowed to continue coaching and did so for many years.

There in the truck, in the dark, plowing through fat gems of rain, Pop spoke first. "I sure would like you to play again," he said. "In high school at least."

"Pop," I said, "I hate football."

"A man likes to see his boy play."

I had terrorized many young children on that field, had eaten many lunches, had perhaps ruptured important organs and caused internal hemorrhaging. It felt great. Somehow, even then, I knew that this sort of triumphant feeling could never be achieved at our nation's many science fairs.

"It's fun to whip a little ass, ain't it?" he said.

"Yes, sir," I said. "It kind of is."

And for once, it was no lie.

—❦ ✦ ✦ ❦—

CHAPTER 10

·

The Curious People of the Piney Woods

—❦ ✦ ✦ ❦—

Sports taught us a lot as young southern men, mostly how to hurt each other in exchange for the praise of our fathers. I would eventually possess the skill to play one or two sports at the college level, or at least the barber college level, but I had a condition that kept me from excelling as much as I would have liked, what psychologists call "large buttocks," which led to "chafing," which led to "depression."

I was better at baseball than any of the other sports we tried, due to the great deal of standing around doing nothing. My greatest skill was insulting players from the other teams, which, in Mississippi, was considered a necessary baseball strategy. I might not be able to run faster or hit harder than you, but I could say things about your mother that would make you want to shove your bat up my rectum, which was one way to distract you from hitting the ball.

Some players, their insults were just silly:

"Hey, batter, batter!"

"We need a pitcher, not a glass of water!"

"Nice swing!"

I felt my contributions should be more original, so I tried a fresher invective, focusing on how their moms smelled like Doritos and how their girlfriends probably looked like walruses, and my teammates thought it was hilarious because it often distracted the batters and runners and such, but then I would look in the bleachers and see their girlfriends and would feel a little sadness because sometimes they actually did look like walruses.

That was the price of winning, I guess. We needed to win. We did what it took. Sport has always been an important part of southern life, along with other beloved traditions, such as quilting and racism. Racism, we were especially great at that, too.

Satan created the niggers," I heard a man say on TV one day, during some sort of parade. He wore what appeared to be a heavy white caftan and a large conical hat, also of white. "And the Lord Jesus Christ created the whites!" the confused man said.

"Is that true?" I said, looking to both my parents for an answer.

"Absolutely not," Mom said. "Nobody in this family's racist."

We heard the word *nigger* a lot, but not as much as the flags in our house might have suggested. Pop was not all *nigger* this and *nigger* that. We knew: This word was dangerous. If you said it up in Jackson, it might get you shot. If you said it out here in the country, it might make somebody think you'd had sex with your sister. Mostly, the word was used by old people suffering from dementia and young men suffering from mullets, the sort of men who believed in protecting their heritage and defending a noble agrarian ethos so that one day their children's children could wear a Confederate flag bikini down at the lake while listening to Iron Maiden and smoking a joint the size of a grain silo.

I almost never heard Pop use the word, but that didn't mean he was in love with African Americans as a people.

"The blacks are ruining this country," he and other family members might say.

Or, "The blacks are ruining this town."

Or, "The blacks are ruining this movie."

All this ruining of things, I thought, must take a lot of work. I started to imagine all sorts of things the blacks could be ruining: railroads, salads, tariff legislation.

"Fucking and killing, fucking and killing," a man had said at the deer camp one day. "It's they goddamn way of life."

I knew God had made black people, the same way he'd made clouds and hammerhead sharks, and there didn't seem to be anything in scripture about not liking them, so I was confused.

"Why do we hate black people?" I asked Mom.

"We don't hate them."

"Do we like them?"

"Yes, we love everyone," Mom said. "It's just complicated down here."

At school, it was difficult to see exactly what the black people were ruining. I looked closely. They were so much like white children, having most of their arms and legs and the correct number of eyes and eyebrows and so forth. There were subtle differences. Words, for example. What I called an *aunt*, they called an *auntie*, and what I called *fat* they called *stout*, but then so did some of the whites. The boys were Willie and Bobby and Marcus, easy enough, but the girls had names like Toshica and Lachunda, which sounded like the names of Japanese motorcycles or distant rivers in tribal lands.

When our school cafeteria served chicken, many of my black classmates expressed a clear preference for dark meat and also dark milk, which they called *chocolate*, as did we, which seemed fine. Occasionally, this one black kid would take his carton of chocolate milk and just pry the whole thing open, making a little square bowl of it, and then take the dry cornbread muffin we'd all been given and drop it into the milk and pulverize it with a fork and then eat it, which did not make me want to hate him or his people, but did make me want to stop eating for a couple of weeks, so I guess the only thing I ever actually saw a black person ruin was my appetite.

In my daily life, it appeared that black people and white people got along fine. At school, we ate at the same tables, refreshed ourselves at the same fountains, relieved our bladders in the same troughs, where we enjoyed a special brotherhood experienced only by those whose jets of urine had commingled. We knew instinctively that all of us were alike on the inside, that the only true test of a man's character was the muscular strength of his urethra.

Then I learned what people outside our state thought of us.

"They're making a movie about Mississippi!" somebody would say.

And the movie stars would visit and they'd eat and it'd be great fun until the movie came out and we saw that they believed things about us that couldn't be true, like how all of us talked like Foghorn Leghorn and the state lacked even a single building with effective air-conditioning. We'd watch *NBC Nightly News* and get very excited when we heard Tom Brokaw say something about us. Sometimes it'd be a story about how poor we all were, or how dumb we all were, but it usually had something to do with how racist we all were. The message was clear: If anyone was ruining anything, it was the white people.

This one time, on the bus, a black girl gave me a love note.

"You got a nice butt," the note said. "Big and round."

It had never occurred to me that my buttocks could be an object of beauty. Did people from Up North know such things could happen in our state? Why couldn't they make movies about these sorts of things, and not church bombings? Could my buttocks truly be the catalyst for racial healing?

I approached her, sat down. Her name was Shalanda, a name that had long fascinated me, so I decided to start with that.

"I like your name," I said. "It sounds like the name of a river in a fairy-tale land."

"A fairy-tale *who*?" she said.

"Like with elves."

"Elves? What you talking bout, *elves*?"

"Mythical creatures."

"I ain't no creature. Seem like *you* the creature."

She was very angry to have written such a flattering note. I sat down. And I kept sitting down, this time next to solitary black boys in cafeterias. Mostly they stared at their food. I had so many questions. Had they experienced prejudicial cruelty in my new homeland? Did they shoulder the weight of histories I did not understand? What was their position on the appropriate size of buttocks? Mine, for example?

I was usually a pretty good talker, but these boys, they had no interest. I decided they must have been able to detect the radiating fumes of racism emitting from my clothes and hair, the lingering odors of home. I wanted to build a bridge across this gulf of injustice, but they were sphinxes to a man, closed off: riddles, wrapped in enigmas, stuffed inside a carton of chocolate milk.

And then I met Tom.

We hit it off immediately. We liked the same movies, the same breakfast foods.

"You like Pop-Tarts?" I said.

"I eat them every day," he said.

"That's amazing."

He was the first black boy I'd ever heard say things like "wow" and "indeed," which may sound strange to people from progressive places where white people and black people all sound like they work at American Apparel, but in Mississippi, it was no small miracle, like Dorothy meeting a Munchkin who also sang songs about rainbows.

"Can Tom spend the night?" I asked Pop.

I'd probably had a dozen different friends over at some point or other. Pop almost always said yes. He knew a boy needed friends. But this time, he sort of looked at me funny, then away.

"Absolutely not," he said.

"But he's got braces!" I said.

What was crazy was, Pop didn't walk away. He seemed at least willing to engage. The drawbridge of the fortress of his soul came down. It might not happen again for a thousand years. I accepted the offer and leapt over the moat.

I launched a barrage of moral confusion and outrage, all these feelings about race and class and Christian love. I recited scripture, delivered a homily. He was the one who took me to church. If he didn't like what I was saying, it was his fault.

He said nothing.

He stood there. He thought. It was painful, watching him

think, forcing him to do something so unnatural. He made a face, as though he were passing a kidney stone.

"The thing is, son, blacks is different."

"But Moses was married to an African," I said, proudly, righteously.

I'd read something about this in a Bible tract, about Moses being married to an Ethiopian, or maybe it was an Etruscan, or an Ecuadorian. Point was, this celebrated Jew, who we were led to believe was also an upstanding Christian, had a thing for brown women.

"Moses can marry whoever the hell ever he wants to," he said, "but ain't no black boy spending the night in this house."

I didn't get it: Pop was Tom's coach. Why was it okay to coach a kid, but not let your boy be friends with the same kid? He jabbed a finger at me, hard. The message was clear: Stay away from the black boys, and stay away from his finger, which might be loaded. I stormed off, and that was it. The drawbridge was raised, the fortress forever closed.

I'd like to say I got angry, that I burned my Ole Miss Rebels flags and finery in a righteous bonfire in the pasture, replaced them with posters of N.W.A and Public Enemy, and announced my plans to marry a girl like the girl who married dear old Moses, but none of that happened. All that happened was, I was sad.

Mom was right. It was complicated.

Tom and I grew distant, as friends who aren't allowed to be friends often will, and that baseball season ended in a hot, pitiful denouement.

Mr. Brokaw had been right.

"Your father just comes from a different time," Mom said, as though Pop had recently been thawed from Paleolithic ice and was now wandering the backyard hunting woolly mammoths with a rock. And then suddenly, the next baseball season, he evolved.

L et's take a ride," he said.

It was a Friday, early spring. I climbed into the Caprice Classic next to him.

On the dash he pitched a copy of *Sports Illustrated*, turned to the "Faces in the Crowd" section, a monthly lineup of amateur athletic talent from around the nation, including one Roberto Ventura, a young black man from a strange institution up the road: the Piney Woods Country Life School. We knew it simply as Piney Woods, a historically black boarding school for students from places like the Dominican Republic and the Virgin Islands who'd been sent to the American South for some unknown purpose.

Ventura had thrown five no-hitters in a row for Piney Woods and owned a fastball that made white men construct idols in their hearts.

"There's more where he come from," Pop said.

On the way there, he told me what he knew about the school, that it was mostly orphans and fatherless children, some left on doorsteps, others snatched from the unforgiving maw of juvenile detention centers across the crystalline waters farther south, which may or may not have been true, but that's what he'd heard, and that's what he believed.

"Them boys deserve a baseball team much as anybody," Pop said.

These fatherless children, many of whom weren't actually fatherless, I would later learn, were black, right? Was Pop suddenly overcome by kindness? Was he on some sort of a drug that caused unhealthy inflammation of the conscience? What would practice be like? Would he accidentally go calling one a *nigger*? And if so, would I be forced to beat him to death with one of the good Easton bats, or would the players beat me to it?

Our first practice took place at Burnham Field, a wedge of turf scratched out of a weedy plateau of farmland in what looked like the perfect location to burn a pile of bodies. Pop and I got the field ready, moved the livestock off the outfield, drew baselines with bags of lime, and waited for our new team to arrive. Across the road, high on a hill, a horsehead gas well nodded up and down, blessing our efforts.

The Piney Woods van pulled up, deposited several skinny black boys, and a few very large ones, and drove away. They must have been worried, traveling from their Arcadian grounds to this godforsaken field, full of rat snakes. They looked around casually, but warily, as though they might be marched to a ravine and shot.

"You can call me Coach Key," Pop said.

They just stared.

Pop handed out a few leathery mitts, but the recruits quickly tossed them aside and produced some sort of large orb and began to kick it.

"What are they doing?" Pop asked me.

"Playing some kind of game," I said.

"It's the queerest thing I ever saw."

"I think it's called soccer," I said. "I saw it in a movie."

Their names were Clive and Ricardo and Philip and more, and they came from faraway lands like Trinidad and Chicago. They were of many colors, with blue and brown and bright green eyes and some even with hair the color of spun gold, and they spoke a West Indian vernacular both alluring and alien, stacked with blank verse and rhyming couplets and what seemed like nonsense words. I'd experienced this confusion once before when a Scot had visited our church: I understood nothing she said, but hadn't let that stop me from asking her questions, so I could misunderstand her even more, which I found pleasurable. This was how my teammates from Piney Woods sounded, somewhere between that Scot and Bob Marley.

"The batty booty moody fruity," one might say.

"Ah, it do! If the lickety rickety stick to the trickety dick."

"And the moody fruity don't bippety boppity."

"The lady got some grady."

"Dat's for shady!"

"You know it."

"I do."

"Ha ha!"

I very much longed to join in this fun dialogue about the moody fruity and the shady grady lady, so I acted like I knew what in the hell they were talking about. They'd be warming up, tossing the ball, and I'd work my way into the polygon of throwing.

"Dee elephant say the ball boy."

"The toy in the backside."

"Dem latrine the backside."

"Dis for true!"

Everyone would laugh, and so I would laugh, as though I understood this story about the elephant and the latrine, and they would look at one another and laugh harder, and so I would laugh harder, and would realize they were laughing at me, and that perhaps I was the elephant in this scenario.

On the first day of practice, it was clear who their leader was: Michael, from St. Thomas. Pop called Michael to the mound to get a look at his fastball.

"Gimme dat ball, see," Michael said, taking the smudgy orb

from Pop's hand. I squatted down behind the plate, to catch. Michael laughed in my general direction.

"Looka here," Pop said. "What's so funny?"

"Ya boy's funny," Michael said.

"What's funny about me?" I said.

"He got them lodge flaps on his head, like he would fly away."

My ears. They were laughing at my ears. They *were* big, wide and fleshy and pink, like rare and precious tropical flowers, but Pop said nothing, and I decided not to be offended.

"Ready when you are," I said, squatting behind the plate.

This was why we were here, to see which of them could pitch like Roberto Ventura, who had already been drafted by the Cubs.

Michael wound up, released the ball, and we watched it fly over the visitors' dugout. The second and third pitches flew in the opposite direction, sailing into the parking area, so far off course that Michael seemed to believe the pitcher's job was to win the game by hiding all the balls. Our best hope was that he would be able to injure most of the opposing team's batters and we could win by forfeit, while our opponents were on their way to the hospital.

"Don't worry about it," I said to Michael. "You got a good arm."

"Dontcha think I know dat, Dumbo?" he said.

I wanted to say something about his meaty nose, as wide and ridiculous as my ears, but did not, for one does not build a dream on slander, even I knew that. I wasn't afraid of him, really, even though he seemed to hold some secret rage. If we got in a fight, I figured any punches he threw were more likely to hit someone very far away.

In subsequent practices, Michael called me many things: Dumbo and Ears and Lodge Boy and Squash Head and other names that made me sound like a mentally handicapped cartoon character.

"Hey, Captain Batty," Michael said. "Ya walk funny."

"Batty?" I said. "What does that even mean?"

"Butt. Ya butt. Ya batty. Ya got a big batty like a lady fatty maddy paddy daddy."

"What about my butt looks like a woman's butt?" I said.

He demonstrated, walking funny. Everyone laughed, even the nice ones.

Nigger-lover!" Pop said.

"No," Mom said. "Really?"

I stood in the hallway, listening. The story was this: The coaches had scheduled a meeting to discuss the upcoming season and schedule. Pop had arrived a few minutes late and as he entered, he explained to Mom he had heard another coach refer to him as a "nigger-lover."

"What'd you do?" Mom said.

"I about whipped his ass."

"Well," Mom said, "I've heard you say that word many times."

"Yeah, but it's different," he said. "It's some that is and some that ain't."

"And which is which?" she asked. "Who decides?"

He had no answer.

In the days leading up to that first game, he showed those Piney Woods boys how to swing and throw and catch and steal, how to blouse their uniform pants, how to slide, how to wear their baseball caps like real men, high on the head, placed there gingerly, like a cake-topper. He seemed to take real joy in it, picking up the team from their beautiful campus, speaking to them in coarsely affectionate tones, the way good fathers will. They took to him, and he to them, and it forced me to reconsider this man, who had seemed so simple, and now seemed so complicated.

My father, a lover of Negroes.

At every opportunity, every practice, he scuttled me to the back of the line at the batting cage, at the water spigot.

"But Pop—"

"Don't backtalk me, boy."

This got the others riled up. They liked seeing him scold me.

I tried not to get too angry with Pop, even though he had me carry the equipment to and from the truck while the others showered themselves in Gatorade and chatted in their pidgin with my father, who apparently could understand them just fine.

"You da flew in the merry on the jerry berry."

"It's all in the wrists, son," Pop said.

"Is da weet fleet."

"Ha ha," said Pop.

"And beans in ya head boy."

"If you all win, then yeah, we might do that."

Pop coached us with great fury, his eyes glinting with righteous vengeance, chewing his gum wildly, eager to whip someone's ass in the cause of equality. He even brought the boys home, fed them, let them watch our television.

What had happened? How had we gotten here?

Michael was now able to aim directly at the batter's heads, and we were ready to play. At that first game, the opposing parents didn't try to lynch anybody, mesmerized as they were by the curious language our team used.

"Reckon it's English?" I heard someone say.

"I swear if it don't sound like Spanish."

"Hell, they ain't got blacks in Mexico."

"Shit, they got 'em everywhere."

We won that first game, mostly as a result of the other team's batters refusing to stand closer than ten feet from the plate.

But I still hadn't won their affections, which I needed very badly, like so many white people before and since.

Why did they hate me so? They hung about dugouts in a loose cloud, their jocular chatter forming a protective barrier from those seeking brotherhood. Every now and then, when the game forced them to recognize my existence, they included me in their jeering, reciting poetry about my disgusting white body, but I was not invited to retort.

And then one day, I decided I would. After all, insults were my gift, too.

Specifically, what I decided to do was make fun of one or perhaps even several of them, as a way of showing our shared love of humiliating others. Why hadn't I thought of this before? These Piney Woods boys, I knew, would love it. They weren't making fun of me. They were asking me to be their friend. To make fun of them.

All I needed to do was think of some way to insult one of them. They would love it, and laugh, and teach me their secret language and handshake, just in time for the season's final crowning moment, the team pool party, when we would laugh and attempt to drown one another in racial harmony.

That moment came, though not at the pool party, but at one of our last games, dusk settling on Burnham Field. Michael was inside the dugout, making merry, Don Rickles at the Friars Club.

"Potty feece, potty feece, it no boy in the duty truck tooti fruiti!" he was saying, or something like that. I stood on the other side of the cyclone fence swinging a bat, warming up, ready to play.

"Da way dee chirrens be tinking!" Michael said.

More laughter. This was my moment.

"Hey, man," I said, my old swagger back.

Michael turned. "What you wan, boy?"

I could feel the tide of history heave and hold its mighty breath.

"Your mom—" I said.

"My *who*?" he said.

"Your mom—"

His eyeballs grew, expanding marshmallows in the angry microwave of his face.

"What you say, boy?" Michael said. Suddenly, I could understand him, and the violence in his eyes. My mind evacuated and my bowels alerted me of a very similar plan. And I could not remember the end of the joke.

"Your mom, she's just—fat," I said. "Just very, very, very fat. Ha ha."

I am guessing, by the way Michael attacked the fence between us with an aluminum bat, that he must have loved his mother very much. Someone wrenched the weapon away from him, held his arms. I don't remember exactly what he said, only that it had something to do with pulling off my genitals and putting them somewhere inconvenient.

"What's the ruckus?" Pop said, running over. I held the bat in a defensive position, preparing to bunt my way to safety. Michael threw himself to the ground, wailing.

"His mama dead," one of the others said, while Michael cried.

"Yeah, okay!" I said, still holding my bat, not really believing them. "Ha ha."

I waited for Michael to get up and start laughing and maybe hug me and make me an honorary black person, and I waited, and I am still waiting. Turns out, she really was dead. Drowned, they said, when he was a baby.

There would be no pool party, and no triumphant moment of festive We Are All of the Human Race togetherness. It was just Michael, weeping for his dead mother, and me, the white devil, standing over him with a bat.

The last time I was in Mississippi, I beheld many wondrous things.

Black boys, riding horses, carrying shotguns. A white man, in a real Honest Abe stovepipe hat and a black frock coat, decrying Obamacare, and looking really dapper, and also insane. Trailers featuring great big Confederate flags hanging like kerchiefs in the tired light of an afternoon. Cafés with at least four different colors of people, holding hands and praying aloud for anyone to hear, people the color of chocolate and plantains and yams.

And I saw a black woman driving a nice European sedan with a bumper sticker that read: "Remember Freedom Summer."

And I remembered my own freedom summer.

What is there to say about it? It was little league, not a Disney movie. We won some, lost most. There were no riots. But we did see heads wag. And I heard things I won't forget.

"Nigger-lover," I heard them say of my father.

He did a fine job, as fine as could be done with children who had been taught their whole lives that using your hands was a penalty. He'd done what he set out to do. He'd coached a baseball team.

In the years that followed, Pop continued to evolve. It was

no fairy tale, of course. He did not start sending checks to the Southern Poverty Law Center. But he did join a church with a black deacon and more than one black family, which is about as close to a miracle as I've ever seen, and he and my mother even went to a black church for a black wedding, a fact resulting from their having something resembling black friends, and he even moved to a neighborhood in town where black people were reported to live.

"It's some blacks here," said Pop. "But they all right."

"Good," I said. "I would hate to see you join one of their gangs."

He smiled, but did not laugh.

And he coached more black teams, and helped many of those boys in other unheralded ways. He'd had his issues with black skin, but was drawn inexorably toward boys with no fathers, black and white, a gravitational pull stronger than history.

"Your father has changed a lot," Mom said, when I walked into the living room a few years ago to find Pop sitting in his recliner, holding a small black child in pajamas.

"This here's my friend," Pop said.

"We're babysitting for some neighbors," Mom said.

The South is a strange place, one that can't be fit inside a movie, a place that dares you to simplify it, like a prime number, like a Bible story, like my father.

CHAPTER 11

Fight School

What I learned from that encounter with my teammate was that sometimes you can't get someone to like you, no matter how fat you say their mothers are, especially if those mothers are dead. It was an exhilarating thing to come so close to a real fight, the electricity that lights up the bloodstream, makes you come more alive than you were used to, even if it meant ending up in a wheelchair, which felt likely in my case.

Could I do it, could I be in a real fight?

For most of my life I've subscribed to the teachings of Jesus of Nazareth, a homeless Israeli who, when one looks closely at his memoirs, seems to believe that if someone should smite thee, one might actually respond with the counterintuitive choice. There's much talk of cheek-turning, as though one had an endless supply of cheeks. What's not clear is, what if your attacker just keeps hitting all the new cheeks?

The first fistfight I ever saw took place at a football game between Ole Miss and Arkansas, a contest of two esteemed institutions that serve as Arcadian oases for the citizens of their respective states, where the Best That Has Been Thought and Said is both thought and said and occasionally screamed by a drunken man who is not afraid to urinate into an Igloo cooler.

I was maybe eight, nine. We'd just left the stadium. I was smitten by the energy of the place, this paradisiac colony of learning and sport and art, when someone hit me with a turkey leg. We were in the midst of a tangled frenzy of brawling. Mom grabbed me and ran, while Pop marshaled himself as a sort of human shield between the barbarians and us, a Great Wall of Father. I heard shouting, which included some variation of "Go back to Arkansas, you goddamn hillbillies" and at least one reference, each, to "titties," "retards," and "motherfucking shit-ass motherfuckers."

One man wore a bright red necktie, so I assumed this was our Ole Miss man, while the Arkansan assailant was shirtless, which I felt gave credence to his being an actual hillbilly. The barebacked fellow had assistance, too: a young woman, presumably the owner of the titties in question, who was doing her best to concuss our man with a bottle. I remember ice and blood and the hiss of punctured beers and the terrible sickening sound of human meat throwing itself at other human meat, and then they disappeared over the horizon of memory, presumably to the ground, where all real fights eventually go.

I'd gotten into fisticuffs only once in my young life, roundhousing a portly classmate in kindergarten for stealing a potato chip. There was nothing courageous about it. He was chubby and unlikable, the easiest kind of person to hurt. It wasn't even really a fight. It was more like setting fire to a wounded sloth.

I'd much rather set fire to a sloth than get in a real fight, where the blood flows like wine, and Pop must have known it. When I was ten years old, he called me into his office.

You know how to fight, boy?" he said.

All I really knew of fighting I had learned from *The Karate Kid*, having perfected my Crane Technique, a maneuver central to the movie's plot, where you stand on one leg, spread your arms, and assume the position of someone who is attempting to pass a sobriety test while pretending to be a large bird.

I always knew Pop was a fighter. It was in his body, the sheer mass of him. On television, men who were that big were usually hitting things, usually with their fists, occasionally with folding chairs. The stories I'd heard about him were incomplete, partial, obscured by history and rumor. There were tales of schoolyard fights, beatings by principals, followed by more fights, perhaps with the principal, followed by tales of guns and knives and women and gentlemen callers. I asked Pop if he'd ever killed a man, and he didn't say no.

He also once told me about a man who tried to molest him when he was a boy.

"Really?" I said. "What'd you do?"

"I took his riding crop and whipped him with it."

I had so many questions, such as, What sort of a badass must one be, to beat a grown man with his own crop? And also, what is a crop?

First thing you do," he said now, "is ask them real nice to stop."

"What are they doing?" I said.

"It don't matter."

"Like, hitting me?"

"No, if they hitting you, you just hit back," he said. "I mean if they doing something silly, like talking at you funny."

"Like telling a joke?"

"No, no."

Maybe somebody was getting bullied, he said, or was kicking your dog.

"So I ask them to stop?" I said.

"Yes."

"Stop kicking that dog," I said, as a sort of rehearsal.

"Yeah."

"What if it's not my dog?"

"It don't matter. You said stop, he better stop."

I liked the idea that I could just make people stop doing bad things by asking them to.

"You might even say *please*," he said. "You know, be friendly."

"And what do I do if he keeps kicking the dog?"

"That's when you hit him."

"Where?"

"I'd start with the face," he said.

He balled up his fist. It was a mighty thing to see up close, to imagine a rock like that coming at you.

"And if that don't work," he said, "hit him in the tallywhacker. Get you some ear, pull his hair. You fighting for your life here. Stomp on his nuts if you got to. Shit, bust his nuts wide open. And if he gets up and comes at you, there's one last thing you can do."

I waited. What would it be? Brass knuckles? Throwing stars? Did our family possess some ancient Crane Technique of our own?

"Act crazy," he said.

"Crazy?"

"Like, pick up a piece of furniture, maybe, and throw it at him." He explained that I should search my immediate surroundings for anything that can be used as a weapon: lamp, terrarium, potted plant. "You got to be crazy, man. If you hit him with a rocking chair, he won't ever mess with you no more, believe me."

I thought of all the things I could do to seem crazy. Kicking, biting, homework.

I did have some fighting experience with my brother, although Bird called it "playing," as in, "Hey, I'm just playing with you," while I would be on the floor, looking for my teeth. His preferred method of combat was to put a hand on my forehead and keep me at arm's length while I clawed the air with my short, malformed arms. In pickup football games, he'd tackle me with unnecessary zeal, picking me up and then throwing me to the ground in the manner of a small woodland creature you wanted to stun before clubbing to death.

If you threw a sock at him, he'd throw a rock back. If you threw a Nerf football at the back of his head, he'd throw a wooden bat at the front of yours. If you had the nerve to touch one of his Iron Maiden posters, he would place you in an iron maiden of his own devising, throwing you on the ground and folding you in half, bringing your legs up to your face, and then spitting playfully in your mouth while you cried.

Occasionally, I tried Pop's lesson on others—Bird, for example, when he elbowed me in the nose for touching his Twinkie.

"Please don't do that again," I said, tasting a little blood on the inside of my lip.

And, out of respect for me, he did it again.

According to Pop's lesson, this was when I was supposed to go ape, and so I would hurl myself at him like a crazed monkey, and he'd catch my hand and start to hit me in the face with it.

"Hit him back!" Pop would say, now watching.

I'd swing my free hand, the left one, at Bird's face, and soon find myself being beaten with both my hands. Bird would laugh, Pop would seem a little crestfallen. My last option, I knew, was to hit Bird in the sexual area, but it's hard to know where that is when you're being flogged in the eyes with your very own hands.

Pop taught me lessons, and so did Mom. She was a teacher, after all. She'd been teaching since 1969, all over the Delta and then in Memphis and now in a place called Star. She taught fifth and sixth grades, mostly, and by all accounts the students loved her, a hypothesis based entirely on the gifts she brought home on the last day of school before Christmas, consisting mostly of buckets filled with chocolate. Clearly, these students believed my mother was some kind of god.

What had she taught them, that they supplicated her with such precious offerings? Long division and geography and the different types of clouds and new vocabulary words, I presumed. That was nothing to what she taught me, at home. While Pop was teaching me how to bust someone's nuts wide open, Mom was teaching me to make cornbread and sew a button and frost a cake, how to take notes on a sermon and nap and laugh and dance and play records when you clean the house. She taught me to prefer the Life of the Mind, or at least the Life of Reading in the Bathtub, to the Life of the Busting of Nuts.

On slow summer days, after our morning chores were done, while Bird would wander off down the road in the truck and Pop was out selling asphalt, Mom and I would do something that Pop wouldn't really allow in his presence: arts and crafts. I don't know: I guess he found it disagreeable to watch his boy make sock puppets. Calligraphy, shoe-box terrariums, poems on the electric typewriter, we did it all, and I learned to love being a maker of things, even when those things were papier-mâché birdhouses that confused my father.

Pop was very straightforward in his efforts to teach me to

fight, while Mom educated me in subtler ways, like asking me to help her make brownies when nobody was looking or buying watercolor kits and leaving them in conspicuous places around the house, such as on my face while I slept.

"Can I go to work with you tomorrow?" I'd occasionally ask her in late summer, just as I'd done with Pop. Fall would soon be upon us, and Mom needed to work on her classroom at the little school in Star, called McLaurin Attendance Center, and I wanted to help.

"Of course," she said.

Those days were dreamy, walking the hallways of that empty school, nobody there but other teachers—women, you see—pleasant and refreshed from their summer vacation and not yet bitter and haggard, as they would be when the students arrived. Mom set me to designing her bulletin boards, drawing cartoon animals, cutting borders, retrieving butcher paper, stapling, gluing, taping, laminating: a real crafting fantasia.

"Oh, my goodness!" other teachers would say, visiting her classroom, seeing all the work I'd done. "Your son made all this? It's perfect!"

A career in education was starting to seem like the path for me, even though I was barely in middle school. Teachers, I decided, could teach me something, such as what else about me they found adorable.

Can I change schools?" I asked my parents, a few days before I started the eighth grade. I wanted to go to Mom's school, I explained.

"Why?" Pop said.

A child needs two things from his parents, I think, besides food and water and shelter and love, and one of those is the Freedom to Almost Die in a Street Fight, or in some other violent way, because a boy needs danger, and Pop heaped it upon me at every turn. But the other thing I needed he could not provide, and that was the Freedom to Glue Eyes to a Pinecone and Call It Your Friend, and that is what my mother gave me. She let me do what I was good at, and that's why I wanted to change schools.

Pop didn't protest too much. McLaurin had a decent baseball team, at least.

"I guess," Pop said.

Mom smiled. It was done.

There'd been a good deal of fighting, it seemed, at my old school, and I figured the new school to be more civilized. After all, my mother was there, and she was very civilized. I laughed at Pop's silly lessons about fighting. No need for fighting at the little school in Star.

Ah, but I was wrong.

Gone were the rodeo kings and lovely daughters of farmers, replaced by a large helping of relatively normal children and also a few highly interesting persons called "hoods," which was short for "hoodlums," which was short for "youth who like to play with knives at school and tattoo themselves with hot coat hangers as a way of demonstrating their need for therapy."

At McLaurin, there were fewer Good Country People, more Angry Trailer Park People, which was fun. They had a sparkle about them. And their fighting was intense. Even the girls fought. In most fights, the boys scrapped with other boys to reclaim something that had been taken from them, usually things named Sheila or Tammy, while Sheila and Tammy also fought somewhere nearby.

"Fight! Fight!" was not an uncommon thing to hear in the hallway, guaranteed to send a tidal wave of students toward the sound of bodies colliding with lockers, jumping and grinning to see if they could learn a new way to kill someone with a U.S. history textbook. This was the Wild West. No *Karate Kid* here. This was more like *Bloodsport*. Crane Technique? Try Switchblade Technique.

One day, I watched two boys bow up in study hall. One was short, stout, the other tall, blond, muscular. What were they fighting about? Who knew. Metallica's latest album, I guessed, or whose girlfriend was more likely to be featured on *Cops*. The Viking threw himself at the Falstaff with such fury that I worried someone might die. I tried to stay focused on my book, but it was hard when your eyeballs knew they might get to see what a small intestine looks like. Coaches came running, cheerleaders cheered. It was not unlike football.

It was pretty clear that fights were over dignity and honor and women, and since I had no dignity or honor or women, I felt safe. Nobody had any reason to want to hit me. Then I learned that some people will hit you for no reason at all.

The boy's name is unimportant, mostly because he is probably still alive, and probably in prison for doing something to his loved ones with a machete. Like so many other nice people in this book, I'll call him something like Tommy, and I'll leave his distinguishing features to the imagination. Let's just say, he looked like an animal, and I'm not saying which kind, but it wasn't a beautiful animal. Tommy seemed to hold a deep and shameful anger, which we assumed was because of looking like the animal.

I sat behind him in English. We'd never had bad blood. The teacher was not in the room, and he was focusing intently on a piece of paper, drawing with a pencil.

"What are you drawing?" I said, trying to be friendly.

"A picture of your mom," he said.

He held it up. It looked like a manatee wearing a wig.

It was even more hurtful because Mom had, in fact, been his teacher only a few years before. He knew my mother. He knew that she didn't at all look like an aquatic mammal. And you know, maybe it was my hormones, or a bad reaction to the cafeteria food, but I sincerely believed a polite request to stop drawing pictures of my mother would be just the moment of human decency that Tommy required in what must've been a troubled and turbulent life.

And besides, if you just sit there and let someone draw a picture of your mother like that, while other people see it happening, many of them staring, leaning in, lusting for blood and circuses, including several pretty girls, then what would stop others from doing the same, turning every family member into an illustrated monster?

"That's not very nice, drawing a picture of my mom like that," I said.

"Really?" he said, putting down his pencil.

"Really."

I had never noticed how large Tommy was. Did he have a gland problem?

"You don't like my picture?" he said.

"I just wish you would stop drawing it," I said. "Please."

Pop had said to say *please*, but the way it came out, it sounded more like a taunt, more like, Could you remove my head with your bare hands, *please*?

Tommy grabbed my neck with his left hand, lifted me out of my desk, and drew back his right in a fist. He stood there like a cocked pistol, his fist pulled back, vibrating with desire.

"I'll knock hell from you, boy!" he said.

I tried to look casual, as though I'd woken up that day having planned to be choked in public. I looked like someone waiting to be seated at a restaurant who just happened to have an enraged hand attached to his throat.

"Just try and hit me!" he said.

But I couldn't really talk.

"Just try and hit me and you'll see, boy!"

I tried to communicate with my eyes, making them friendly, but also deeply sad at the brokenness of the world, perhaps how the Lord's eyes looked to Pilate. If my eyes were saying anything to Tommy, it was something like, "puppies" or "flowers" or "Christmas."

He let me go. We sat down. The teacher came in. Nobody said a thing.

Later, I slipped out of study hall and walked to my mother's classroom. I had no plans to tell her what happened—it's just, I thought it'd be nice to go somewhere in the building where nobody wanted to see how far my windpipe could bend. Her door was closed, and I peeked in to watch my sweet mother teaching those children, who now seemed so young, so eager, their eyes wide as spring flowers. Mom's back was to the door, and I saw her doing something I'd never seen before: screaming. Actually, it was more like shrieking. She shrieked at her students.

"Chester! Terrence! Billy! I said sit! You people are animals!"

She went on, about how they should be lashed to a post in the hot sun and then whipped with a rubber hose, and how she would do it if they wouldn't send her to prison, and she really seemed like she would do it, like she had been given some drug that made her crazy. I'd never heard Mom speak this way to anybody. From what I could see, the students were perfectly behaved and perfectly horrified at the bloodthirsty woman in front of them.

Was everybody at this institution deranged, including my

own mother? I'd come to school here in part because she seemed the sanest person in my life and because it felt wise to spend as much time around her as possible, where we could discuss films and literature on the long ride to McLaurin, and here she was, secretly a lunatic. She never screamed at home. She sounded dangerous, as violent as Pop and Bird and everybody else.

I ducked my head out of the window and went back to study hall.

It was a year before anyone tried to knock hell from me again, and this time it was no classmate, but a full-grown adult.

"Hello?" I said, into the phone.

"Is this the little shit's been talking shit?" the voice on the line said.

"Who is this?" I said.

"I'm Tom Bishop, motherfucker."

He said it like *motherfucker* was an actual credential, as if he were identifying himself: Tom Bishop, Licensed Motherfucker.

"I'll make you bleed, son," he said.

My heart quaked in its little tin casing. What had I done to enrage Mr. Bishop?

Tom was in his twenties, I knew. I'd only ever met him once, at a football game. All I remember is that he had a mustache and looked very young and was also a pedophile. He was dating one of my classmates, a girl named Casey.

Everybody liked Casey. Some months before, I'd accidentally touched Casey's nether regions. It was a totally consensual accident, on a school bus, where a boy can become disoriented and find his hands inside someone else's underwear without even knowing what happened. Our relationship was intense, passionate, and lasted about three minutes. These days, Casey was into much older guys, the kind with tattoos and children. Hence, Tom, who'd heard of my brief sojourn to Casey's underworld and needed to ensure I would not be going back. He had nothing to fear. Everybody wanted to be in her panties, and I had long ago decided to find a less crowded pair of underwear.

"I know where to find you," he said.

"You don't understand," I said. "That was a one-time thing."

"Good, then I'll only have to whip your ass one time."

"But—"

"I'll see you up at the school."

That night, I couldn't sleep. Would saying *please* really make this madman stop? "Please stop hitting me with that crowbar," I imagined myself saying. I prayed for anything to keep me from school, a fungus, a meteor. If Jesus really didn't want me to fight, then why couldn't he help out by liquefying my internal organs?

I wanted to fight, I did. But I knew instinctively that I was a Man of Peace, and if necessary, a Man of Climbing Trees to Get Away. I was not afraid to climb a tree. That didn't make me a coward. For example, there could be snakes in the tree.

The next day.

Homeroom, nothing.

First period, nothing.

In the hallway, I worried: Will I see him? Will he really come?

Second, third, fourth period, no sign.

Nothing will make you question your life choices like waiting to die. There were so many things I hadn't done yet. Go to prom. Go to New York. Find a sword.

During break, instead of going outside, I went to the library, my old sanctuary, under the guise of studying for a chemistry exam in the following period. The class was hard, and the teacher, Mrs. Nutt, demanded real effort. If anyone liked me less than Tom Bishop did, it was Mrs. Nutt, a small, sturdy matron with magnificently bulbous hair who made no effort to hide her belief that I was born of Satan.

I sat in the library and tried to think about Mrs. Nutt's chemistry, but found the specter of Tom Bishop's promise too real. I looked out the window, and there he was, skulking through the crowd with murder on his mind.

Ohno ohno ohno ohno.

I noted with surprise that he was very short. I hadn't remembered this. Weren't the short ones more violent? He was clearly capable of disfiguring me, although it might require the use of a footstool.

The bell rang. I gathered my courage and walked to Mrs. Nutt's classroom. I sat down. Other students came in, took their seats. No sign of Tom Bishop.

And then: Tom Bishop.

Heads turned. Whispers. People knew.

My heart murmured: fight-fight, fight-fight, fight-fight.

He smiled, nodded at me to join him in the hallway. I froze. It strikes me now how odd this was, that a grown man with no children in the school, other than the one he was making love to in the back of his truck, could walk in and just start challenging its students to duels. Had we no supervision?

I tried to remember Pop's lessons. Something about being nice, then being insane. I briefly considered going right to the insane part, heading Tom off at the pass, but how would I know the precise time to start throwing furniture at his groin? I looked desperately at Mrs. Nutt, for what, I don't know. Maybe she kept some sort of weapon in her hair?

"Hey, boy," Tom Bishop said from the doorway.

"Hello!" I said, as though attempting to sell him life insurance.

He beckoned with a finger. The class held its breath. They knew.

I was about to stand.

"Young man?" Mrs. Nutt said.

Was she talking to me? No, she was talking to Tom Bishop. He stared, bewildered, at the woman with the golden topiary on her head.

"Unless you plan to recite the periodic table," she said, "you may now leave."

In an instant, he withered into a nothing, a sad little imp. He looked around, unsure how to reclaim his virility. Mrs. Nutt walked over to him, looked him in the eye, and gently, sweetly, closed the door in his small, confused face.

Out the window, we saw him leave.

I was ashamed. I couldn't be a child forever.

The opportunity for redemption came, of course, during English. What was it about the study of literature that made people so angry? We were reading through *Romeo and Juliet*, a play that has been enraging readers for four hundred years. I was a little older, a little larger. I had more anger now, simmering as I was with hormones, like the young men in our play.

A boy in the front row was snickering in my direction.

I did not like the look of him. He was not a bad kid, as far as I knew, but he was strange-looking, with a great deal of body hair in places that seemed wrong. His hairline was so low that it looked like his eyes were on the top of his head. You had the feeling that nomadic peoples could have used his back for evening prayer. I found myself angered by his hair.

He snickered some more.

"What are you laughing at?" I said.

"Him," he said, pointing at the young man next to me, a friend of mine, Thomas, who looked a little rough that morning.

"He's laughing at you," I said to my friend.

Thomas shrugged. He was very good at shrugging, his way of demonstrating a practiced apathy to the world. Yes, my friend Thomas needed defending.

"Hey," I said to the boy. "Please stop laughing at my friend."

He laughed some more.

"I asked you nicely," I said. "Please stop laughing."

He kept laughing, couldn't stop.

"I asked nice," I said.

How could somebody with so much hair just go laughing like that?

I stood up.

"Coldcock him!" someone said.

Encouraged by the bloodlust of my classmates, but worried that the teacher might return at any minute, and remembering that I was supposed to be a model student, with regard for our nation's laws and school policies, and that my mother was employed at this institution and that I might require its administrators to write various recommendation letters on my behalf to entities that might help extract me from the miasma of the life that so many who lived here might never escape, including the Laughing Wolfboy, and Tommy, and most definitely Tom Bishop, who'd shown that he couldn't even leave after he'd already left, I made a decision: We would not fight. Not here.

"After school," I said. "At the field house."

It was on.

My secret worry was that perhaps this boy was a badass, had

been rehearsing his own Wolf Technique or Chewbacca Punch for months in the privacy of his bedroom.

"I'm doing this for you," I said to Thomas, while we waited by the field house. He shrugged. He didn't care. I was starting to want to kick his ass, too. A few audience members gathered, friends from the baseball team.

"I can't wait to see this," one said.

It was a lovely autumn day. Here he came, walking down the hill from the band room.

"Why don't *you* fight him?" I said to Thomas, who was now reading a novel about robots on the back of a nearby truck. I wore khaki pants and moccasins and a pink polo. Could I risk ruining these good clothes? These were not the clothes of a fighter. These were the clothes of someone who longs to windsurf.

We faced off.

"Well," I said.

"Well," my opponent said. "Here I am."

We stared.

"You were being a freaking jerk," I said.

"I wasn't even laughing at *you*," he said.

"I ought to punch you in the face."

"I'll hit you back."

"Yeah, well! I'll hit you again!"

We were just a couple of badass motherfuckers.

Bystanders grew bored, drifted back to their barbells, so I decided to up the ante by making fun of his girlfriend, who was widely known to suffer a disfiguring underbite and a slightly lazy eye, so that you never really knew if she was looking at you, which, in Wolfboy's case, was probably ideal. I said many things about her that I immediately regretted, at one point comparing her face to a piece of construction equipment and her eye to a planet that had been knocked out of orbit. At this, he broke. He was not far from tears, as though he, too, knew that her face resembled a backhoe and he was only now coming to terms with that.

This was my Shame Technique.

Only then could I see: I was his Tommy, his Tom Bishop, a sad little animal threatening to hurt others for no good reason. Wolfboy wasn't the monster. The monster was me.

Is this what Jesus wanted? Punching people in the face seemed more humane than what I was doing. The things I'd said about his girlfriend, his father, his single eyebrow. It did not feel great.

"I'm sorry I laughed at you and your friend," he said.

"I'm sorry I said that about your girlfriend," I said.

We shook hands. Nobody cheered. Nobody was even there.

When you leave high school, you realize the world is not a Thunderdome, that you needn't whip a man to be a man. What you need is intelligence, and hard work, and a scholarship, and a career, so that you can have money, so that you can buy a handgun.

The river of my life changed at that school. I had learned so much about the democratic promises of universal education, for one, including the lesson that public schools are about the last places in our country, aside from the Doritos aisle at Walmart, where a perfectly reasonable and healthy human being can come into close contact with people who are actually insane. And that includes many of the teachers, and also my mother. There's just no other explanation for their sweaters.

I guess it's no surprise that I would go on to become a teacher myself, and that I, too, like my mother, have a love for sweaters and a gift for screaming at children and announcing that I would like to hurt them with a length of rubber hose, were that permissible.

But unlike my father or Tommy or Tom Bishop or all the other angry Toms of the world, I never really had an occasion to fight, at least not until I had a wife and children. I have three daughters, and I often find myself standing between them and some danger, some dog, some fire pit, a Great Wall of Father.

"Will you protect us?" my daughters often ask. "If someone comes into our house?"

"Of course," I say, and I can feel the truth of it in my bones. I come from a long line of men who have whipped other men with riding crops, and I have whaled on many things, mostly drums. My daughters are sure I can hurt people, if the need arises. And I believe I could, if I had a folding chair.

I just hope it doesn't come to that, because I'm better at the turning of the cheeks. I've got an endless supply. Just try and hit me, and you'll see.

—≋ ✦ ✦ ≋—

CHAPTER 12

·

This Hurts You More than It Hurts You

—≋ ✦ ✦ ≋—

There's some dispute about what actually happened that Saturday night in the heady days of my seventeenth year, whether it was assault and battery, or just assault, or just battery, but two things were for certain: My father hit me, and I was in my underwear.

It would be the last time that he hit me.

What I needed that night were pants. I have always needed pants. People have done nothing but ask me to put on pants since I first had legs. I was in my bedroom, preparing to go on a date with a girl I'll call Lucy. Lucy had schooled me in the arts of love, had taught me so much about how to treat a woman, and one lesson she taught me was how important it was to wear pants. But that night all the good pants were in the laundry room, on the far end of the house, and so I sought them out with the use of my pantless legs.

It was just us three in the house, Mom and Pop and me, Bird having long flown the nest for places where there were fewer societal restrictions against smoking marijuana in churches. It was quieter now, simpler. I had taken to bicycling country lanes in solitude, trying to breathe in the rich vapors of this place I knew I would soon be leaving. It was no longer necessary for Pop to coach me to do anything, and we saw much less of each other, even during deer season, my revulsion at the tedium of live-meat acquisition having driven me to seek refuge in SAT test preparations and the writing of poems that were so full of nonsense that many of my early readers would have happily rather watched me saw the heads off animals than be forced to read them.

Pop and I had grown distant. He did not like what I was becoming, had become. I hadn't fired my gun in two years, had barely fished, had forgotten how to tie a clinch knot, had quit the varsity baseball team in the year when I could have ruled the outfield, had I made the effort. There was a bitterness in his tight-lipped grin as I shared with him some dubious new enthusiasm: writing, cycling, the drums.

Every son, I guess, wants his father to know: I am not like you.

Some of our fathers are ministers, so we make sex with whores. Other fathers make sex with whores, so we become gynecologists. Or our fathers are witch doctors, so we become wizard doctors. This is the way of things. Fathers can accept it, or they can deny it, or they can do what mine did: get mad.

He was mad about much: his life, his work, his money, his problems, and now, his boy, who was behaving like a homosexual and threatening to go to college with a bunch of Presbyterians, a word that wasn't even in his Bible, and now his boy had taken to walking around the house in his underwear, and he could not abide it.

Something was going to happen. There was a reckoning due. A great battle.

"What'd I tell you about being in your underwear, son?" he said.

They were watching television, he in his recliner, Mom under the afghan. I strolled past them casually in my briefs, as casually as a young man with no pants and a Kodiak bear for a father can.

"Yessir, oops," I said, still pantless, scampering now.

It is difficult to explain how deeply my father hated his wife having to see his sons naked, or almost naked, but one suspected it was rooted in some anxiety over biblical curses and that old Oedipal tug that moves the ancient places of the heart. I thought nothing of my mother seeing my penis, the selfsame penis she had formed in her uterus and powdered for years afterward like it was some sort of little fancy man, much less seeing the profile of the little fancy man inside my underwear, which she washed and folded with such care.

"I done told you one too many times," Pop said, getting louder.

"Sorry," I said from the laundry room, when I heard his recliner squealing shut.

As I dug around in baskets for the required garments, I heard Mom say, "No, don't." And I turned, and there stood Pop. I was as tall as him now, if not as large. Our eyes met. Then I looked down, and saw that he was holding a belt.

The question every boy asks himself is this: Can I take my father? If push comes to shove, can I whip him? Huck asked it about Pap. Luke asked it about Darth. And now, as I stood there between a pile of whites and the dryer, what I asked was, Could I defend myself with an ironing board?

I don't remember the first time he did it. There was never a time when he wasn't doing it. I suspect it started very young, when I was two or three.

It's called *whipping*, and it's as far away from what's called spanking as Mars from Uranus. Spankings were for little girls and puppies, a tender, halfhearted swat by a parent who didn't really mean it. A man who merely spanked his children was probably a florist. No, Pop whipped us like a Mexican grandmother beats a rug, with stoic resolve, dispassionately, purposefully, constantly, and sometimes like a Mexican grandmother who smokes PCP and rules a cartel. It was his understanding that boys who were not beaten in a spirit of paternal affection ran the risk of growing up to become happy, overconfident handbag designers.

"He that spareth his rod hateth his son," says the Book of Proverbs, "but he that loveth him chasteneth him betimes." We heard this verse a great deal in church, a holy sanction for the beating. I pictured the writer of Proverbs with a quill in one hand and a large rod in the other, perhaps of bamboo, beating back the sons he so deeply loved.

"Your daddies whip you to show you they love you," said the preacher, and I thought, Maybe he could just say it with a card.

The way it would always start was, we'd do something we weren't supposed to. Say, throwing rocks, or throwing bottle rockets, or throwing our smaller friends.

"You boys better behave," Mom would say.

And like all boys, we would not behave. We would throw the thing, and something bad would happen: a rock through a windshield, a bottle rocket through a crowd, a small friend through a window.

"Your father wants to see you," Mom would yell out from the back door, as I crouched behind a large shrub and feigned the look of a boy with a great interest in ground mosses, while Bird descended from whatever tree he'd climbed, and soon we were inside, walking slowly toward Pop in his recliner.

"Come around here where I can see you boys," he said, the unmoved mover.

"Sir?" we'd say, trying to look as darling and precious as two young boys can, doe-eyed and full of God's holy light.

"Get around here," he said, directing us to stand immediately in his line of sight. This was his way of suggesting we were not the center of whatever galaxy this might be, that we were satellites at best, distant and pathetic moons that must be hit with things to get back into proper orbit. His gravity brought us to him, not the other way around.

"What'd you boys do?" he said, and we told him. We couldn't not.

"Come with me to my office," he said, closing his recliner with the tortured squeal of its steely innards, a sound I have forever come to associate with anal discomfort.

We followed Pop down the hallway, and I did my best to leave a visible trail of tears and mucus so that the authorities could retrieve our bodies. Pop had no office, of course. What he had was a bedroom, where he selected his belt.

I bawled ferociously and very much wished to run, but he'd spiritually neutralized our ability to flee, the way a tiny bunny can see but somehow cannot run from the large snake. Several belts hung there on his rack, electric eels in slumber. He took one, folded it in half, and turned to us, while I began to affect the look of a child with polio.

"Who wants to go first?" he always asked.

I couldn't imagine watching Bird get it. Bird was a known wailer, with screams like a schoolgirl being slowly lowered into a kettle of hot oil.

"Me," I said.

I stood up, and Pop took my small left arm in his bearish left paw. As soon as the belt made its initial contact—on the bottom, occasionally on the top of the legs, sometimes the small of the back—I abandoned all reason and attempted to flee through the nearest architectural orifice: a door, a window, a wall mirror. But I only got as far as my arm could straighten, for Pop still held it tight, tight as a blood pressure cuff, while my legs continued to assert their right to flee, which led to my being occasionally horizontal, levitated. There was always a sort of call-and-response during this wicked dance, with Pop repeating a few questions that sounded strangely rhetorical, while in response I screamed like Robert Plant in Zeppelin's "Immigrant Song."

"When are you going to behave?"

"Ahhhhhhhhh!"

"When are you going to do what I say?"

"Ahhhhhhhhhhhhhh!"

"How many times do I have to tell you?"

"Ahhhhhhhhhhhhhhhhhhh!"

From the street, it might have sounded like, like, well, exactly like what Robert Plant had been singing about: young children being slaughtered by a Viking.

These were no tender touches of parental scolding, the way you imagine fathers with expensive sneakers would do it, like they were prying ketchup from a glass bottle and regretting every delicate tap, while the children sort of stood there and cried, because it hurt their daddy's feelings if they didn't cry at least a little. No, these were mighty strikes, searing, launching me high into the air, such that I might seek refuge in the ceiling fan, reaching for it, for anything to pull me out of this chamber, a child attempting to catch an escaping balloon while being attacked by rabid fruit bats.

When Pop finally stopped, the sheer momentum would send me from the room with great speed, and I would run around the house seven or eight times, attempting to outrun my own buttocks and the liquid fire that spread over them and up my back, eventually collapsing into my bedroom, where I would use a telescopic arrangement of mirrors to inspect my hocks and wonder if such things happened to the hocks of other boys.

I never thought to ask myself if it was cruel. It was just one more condition of living with Pop, the way people in the Civil War didn't complain about having their legs sawed off. It's just what happened. You got shot, it got infected, they sawed a part of you off. I threw a rock, I got caught, and now, like so many Confederate veterans, I also couldn't walk.

Why did he do it?

The list of reasons is long and unsurprising, the rocks, the clods, the failed *yessirs*, the petulant *nosirs*, all the petty urges boys will have, such as my trying to put a cat in a toolbox, after being repeatedly told that cats do not belong in toolboxes.

"Why would you do such a thing, boy?" Pop would say.

There was no good answer. I just lowered my head, and waited for the executioner to rise and mete out his electric pain. He was right. You can't treat a cat like a set of metric socket extensions, even if cats are full of darkness and evil.

We got older, and the whippings got worse: harder, longer, louder. I have no illusions about any angelic goodness in children, knowing what I know of the heart of man, but this was starting to feel like child abuse.

"If he keeps that shit up," Bird said, "I'll fucking kill him."

And he kept that shit up, and nobody killed him.

Mom would intervene, I hoped, at some point. If it got bad.

I knew she must have secretly believed it was wrong, or a bit much.

"Some parents put their children in time-out," she said to

Pop one day. "Like, when kids misbehave, you put them on their beds or the bottom stair."

"Stair? We ain't got no stair," Pop said. "TV's turning you crazy."

"It's more humane," she said.

"Humane?"

Pop searched his vocabulary for this term, and found only a picture of a florist.

"When do you whip them?" he said. "Before or after the stair part?"

Something was in the air, you could tell. Times were changing. We heard things on ABC's newsmagazine *20/20*, where Hugh Downs would detail the horrifying ubiquity of child abuse in America, calling it rampant, especially in more rural communities, suggesting that if you had at least one relative carrying a shotgun or food stamps, there was a high probability you were being abused at this very moment, but also that signs were looking up, that America was getting wise to its warlike ways and learning to embrace more humane childrearing habits that involved what seemed like excessive talking and hugging.

Around junior high, I read something in one of Mom's *Reader's Digest*s about child abuse, and they provided a toll-free number and a list of suggestions, including the procurement of a camera to document the abuse.

I happened to have such a camera, a Polaroid.

And I wondered.

And I wished.

I wished it were easier. I wished that Pop read things like *Reader's Digest*, so he might be moved by its persuasive arguments about the power of human love and how hitting your children with such violence could lead to all sorts of pathological behaviors, such as them hitting their children, which were your grandchildren, which you had caused to be hit, and who would hit their children, your great-grandchildren, a whole lineage of big people hitting small people, and the small people attempting to flee, to fly, to run far away, so far, perhaps across oceans, even.

Was it really child abuse? How could we know it was wrong to hit things? We grew up hitting things: at school, on the field, in the woods. It was only normal that somebody would want to hit us, and why should we stop them?

All I knew was, I was ready to do something about it.

If Pop hated our walking around the house in our underwear, then he really hated our standing there, watching our mother urinate. I don't know why I enjoyed conversing with my mother while she sat on the toilet, but I suspect it had something to do with every child's fear that when a mother is out of sight, she might be enjoying herself.

"You shouldn't be in here," she said, that morning.

I guess I was about fifteen when this happened.

Mom and I talked about everything: books, foods, comedians we'd seen on *The Tonight Show*, bits I'd heard on *A Prairie Home Companion*, faults of logic she had perceived in sermons, new ways scientists had discovered for children to die tragically.

It was Sunday, the master bedroom, she in the toilet and me just beyond.

"What's for lunch?" I asked.

"Can't I ever be alone?" she said, the tinkle of her sweet, maternal waste plinking into the toilet. I should've let her be, I knew, but she was the closest thing I've ever had to a slave.

"Which tie should I wear to church?" I said, shoving both through a crack in the door.

Pop came into the bedroom.

"Your momma's in the toilet, boy," he said, and then he started hitting me with a hairbrush. Really hitting me. I ran around the room, evading the brush like a raccoon that had stumbled into the cottage of an angry maker of funny raccoon hats.

"Stop, please, no!" Mom said, from the toilet.

"Come here, boy," Pop said.

He set down the brush and took up his belt.

As he whipped me, hard and ruthlessly and with abandon, he made loud declarations about how wrong it was for a boy to look upon his mother's nakedness, and I reeled through the Bible concordance in my mind for some applicable verse, but it's hard to do research when you're being hit with something that used to be part of a cow.

By the time he was done, I was on the floor, a puddle of son.

"Go dress for church," he said.

The only thing I felt capable of putting on my legs was some sort of healing cream, or holy water.

My plan was to crawl back to my room and pray to Jesus for a wheelchair, so I crawled, passing Mom in the hallway. I wanted her to see me crawling, so she would have more to testify about in the trial.

"I'm crippled," I said.

I pulled up my shorts and showed her the stripy welts that had begun to rise from the back of my knee to my lower back, and on my arms, long red ribbons. It was strange, knowing that the worst physical pain you've ever experienced was caused by the man who'd brought you into the world.

She said nothing, tried not to look at me.

"It's child abuse," I said.

I grabbed carpet toward my bedroom, found my Polaroid and the toll-free number. I locked my door, disrobed in the mirror. Was this normal behavior for a father, a son? How many more times would I have to fly through the air, and then crawl through the house? .

I took pictures of my naked bottom, which required my assuming certain positions that might have gotten me burned at the stake in an earlier century. I picked up the phone. What would they do to Pop, exactly? Would they send an agent to investigate? A sheriff's deputy? Would we be on television? *Cops*? Would the world have to see these pictures?

I put the phone down.

I picked it up again.

Was it wrong, what he was doing? Yes. It was too much. I knew that now.

Did I hate him? Probably. I have never really been into hating people for doing terrible things, not because I am filled with tender mercies, but because I have always preferred to hate people for smaller crimes, such as not having prominent moles removed. And to be frank, I couldn't disentangle my hate from my fear. The man was my father. Whatever was in him was in me. A frightening prospect. If there was something about him I hated, I'd just be hating myself, and I couldn't bring myself to hate me, as much as I tried. I just had too much in common with me. We went everywhere together, even took baths together. But not Pop. I took no baths with Pop. And I had a special power that allowed me to go places he could not, which I'd begun to think might be a good idea, to keep him from hitting me, and to keep me from hating him, to keep me from wanting him to die.

And sometimes, that's what I wanted.

Sometimes, I really did want him to die.

However, I also pitied him. The more I read, the more I learned, the more I looked down on him and the smallness of his philosophy.

I was not a bad kid, not really. I could hear Pop now: And how much worse would you be, boy, if I didn't do it? And honestly, I don't know. I looked at the Polaroid. The image of my buttocks was ghastly. I put the phone down. I would not rat out my father. Other things could be done to get justice. I could major in performing arts, for example.

Something inside me died that day; something else came alive.

All boys have a bridge to their fathers, or sometimes it's grandfathers, uncles, teachers, a gangplank over which stagger the lessons of manhood. At some point in the boy's life, that bridge is savagely burned, as if by a retreating army, and the boy will be alone, and no longer a boy, but something not quite a man, and I was coming to see that my bridge was on fire, would soon be gone, and that when it burned to nothing, I would be alone, and free.

I would run away.

I knew that others did it—because they'd been hit or burned with irons or starved or sexually violated. Occasionally some adolescent from our community would go missing, and we'd be told by adults that these young people were "going away for a while," usually to stay with a cousin in Alabama, usually because they needed to work out some things, usually out of their uteruses. But most did not leave.

Why not? Was it something in the water? The irresistible tug of the land? In all our years at this place, Bird and I had mapped just about every square inch of ground on either side of the highway as deep into the trees as any child might want to venture, had found its secret places, its veins of clay, waterfalls, abandoned cabins, springs of crystal waters, artifacts in banks of mud, bones across the roots of fat old trees. Its mysteries were endless, a labyrinth you didn't want to leave, with its own private Minotaur.

We were aware that other places existed, thanks largely to the news: that Los Angeles was a place of Gang Warfare and

Chicago was a place of Gang Warfare in the Snow, that New York was a place where residents enjoyed a tradition of being stabbed and mugged in close proximity to well-regarded museums. Nobody ever came to us from these places, and we knew that if we went there we would get AIDS.

The only other place that seemed to matter was the one where Jesus lived, and we sang about it at the Church of Christ at least once a week. "Some glad morning when this life is over, I'll fly away," we sang. The message of this song was that you could leave Mississippi, but you had to die first.

"I'm getting the fuck outta here," Bird had always said. "And you better, too."

Pop might've been burning the bridge between us, but he was also holding on for dear life. I made many feints at leaving, applications to distant boarding schools that accepted me, offered scholarships, which he ignored.

"Do they even got a baseball team?" he'd say.

I'd be invited on a family vacation by a friend to some distant state, on a mission trip to South America, but always, he said no. Everything was no. Leaving was no.

"He's afraid," Mom said.

"Of what?"

"That you won't come back."

I applied to distant universities, and he lost the applications, or laughed.

"Notre Dame?" he said. "You ain't a dang Catholic."

I felt that since I'd lived through Pop's own inquisition, I could probably handle whatever the papists had in store. I tried to tell him, but he couldn't hear me, that I'd never felt at home here. Books had given me a thousand vistas onto a thousand worlds, worlds without goats on roofs or chickens in trucks, worlds that I'd heard were in fact real, were realer even than anything on *NBC Nightly News*, and which could be reached by conventional methods of transportation, such as burro, or bus.

There was something desperate in Pop during my last few years in the house. He hit me hard, so hard, hard as I'd ever seen him do, but there was none of our old dance. I did not fly. I couldn't. Something inside me had turned to stone. I was becoming a Stonehenge, just like him, and he held me tighter, gripping my arm, because he knew, when he finally let go, I would not be coming back.

And that's when I came through the living room in my underwear.

He started hitting me almost immediately, striking me in thrilling new places, such as my knees, and shins, and throughout the rest of my Demilitarized Zone. Mom shrieked in horror, pulling at Pop to stop.

It was a small laundry room, and we were all in it, along with a week's worth of laundry and a freezer full of deer sausage, and Pop lashed out, literally and metaphorically, at any piece of me he could get at, while I found myself ascending the dryer that held my missing pants, climbing in reverse, as if by magic, without even the use of my arms, which were protecting my tender exposed regions from the cobra of his belt.

"No, no!" Mom screamed. "Stop, stop!"

I have lived a long time in that moment there on the dryer, held it captive like the memory of a first tornado, a last kiss. I go back to it often, and have to admit to myself, Yes, I hated him. Right then, I did. And I knew he would die one day, and I thought of that day often, and what it might free me of, and felt ashamed.

What did he think he was doing? Trying to raise me right? Did it work? Had he prepared me to venture out into the world's most dangerous latitudes, places that scared him so much, such as coffee shops and bookstores, with their dangerous poets and light jazz?

Later, when I went to these coffee shops, and we got to talking, I told a few close friends about it.

"He did *what* to you?" they'd say.

"That sounds like child abuse," they'd say.

Some of these people, you had the feeling, *were* abused, just based on their clothing choices. Somebody had not loved these freethinkers enough to do the thankless work of imparting the most painful and necessary lessons. But there's always somebody else at the table who laughs. They get it. They had fathers who loved them and hit them, sometimes excessively, and they are usually Southern, or Black, or Not American.

"In home country, much hitting of the sons," they will say. "And also much plague of the death."

And I would smile and light another cigarette and go back again to linger in that moment, as I watched my father whip my ass, struck by the tender incongruity of it all, how caring he really had been all those years, loving us violently, passionately, a man better suited to living in a remote frontier wilderness than contemporary America, with all its complexities and progressive ideas and paved roads and lack of armed duels. Despite all the hitting, I knew, he was a good man, and he taught me many things: how to fight and work and cheat and pray to Jesus about it, how to kill things with guns and knives and, if necessary, with hammers.

I climbed higher, blocking him now with my hands and feet.

"What the hell is wrong with you, old man?" I said as he hit me. "Are you crazy?"

It was the first time I'd ever used that kind of language in front of Pop, but also the first time he'd ever beaten one of his children while they crouched on a major home appliance. A day of firsts, and lasts. I did not fight back, as I am sure many young men would have, and I did not cry, and I did not scream. I just looked at him square in the eye, and looked and looked, looking for the man inside, the one I loved.

He stopped looking at my body and looked at me, went from red to nothing, a man who'd woken up and realized he'd sleepwalked his way onto a high bridge.

Mom had collapsed on a pile of whites, weeping.

It was his last real chance to leave a mark on me, to do what he thought being a father was. He dropped his belt and walked away. The hitting of the sons was finished. The bridge was burned. There was no bridge. Just air, and a story.

CHAPTER 13

.

The Magical Christmas Teat

I have an announcement," I said.

Mom put down her fork. She looked anxious.

She was worried that I might be gay. I had been gone for a decade, and I had done many gay things, such as performing in many plays and wearing tank tops. Plus, I'd lost seventy-five pounds. I looked great.

"You look terrible," Mom said.

Pop just looked out the window. He knew what was coming.

I'd betrayed them in so many ways, committing hateful acts in the broad American hell, studying theology and queer theory, buying a European station wagon.

"I just need to tell you guys something."

"You guys?" Pop said.

I'd picked up this phrase in the Midwest, having imposed term limits on *y'all*, which made many Chicagoans believe I would soon be murdering them with a sling blade.

"Tell us," Mom said, ready for the devastating news.

"I sure would like some cake," Pop said.

"I wanted to wait until I was home."

Mom needed to hear my big announcement, to confirm her secret fears, but she also needed to feed her gorilla. She got up.

"Coconut," he said.

She got him his cake, a creamy white wedge large enough to have been hunted by Queequeg. He harpooned it with a fork.

"Are things—*okay?*"

"Let me just—"

"Are you on something?"

"Get him some cake," Pop said.

"Do you take drugs?" she said.

"Get him some cake."

There was a great, heavy, frightening silence.

"It's a woman," I said.

On Mother's face, a Janus-faced look of relief and horror. Relief, that I would provide her with genetically authentic grandchildren, and horror, that I'd gotten some heathen girl pregnant and was about to leave the mongoloid baby with them.

"I'm going to marry her," I said.

"Long as it ain't no Oriental," Pop said.

"He wouldn't marry a Oriental," Mom said. "Would you?"

"No, I wouldn't marry a carpet."

Who was she, they wanted to know, and who were her people, and how many arms and eyes did their gods have, and did they pray to statues of animals, and did that prevent them from wanting to shoot animals, and how did they feel about the most important things in life, such as shooting animals?

"Where's her family from?" Pop asked.

There were many wrong answers to this question, and only one right answer: places where there was a great deal of interest in cornbread.

"Yazoo City," I said.

"I know people in Yazoo," Pop said.

An old Delta town, not far from where my mother had grown up. Very fertile, very cornbread. She and her people, I felt, would not be the issue. The issue would be mine.

I had forgotten so much about my home. The climate, for example. The day was hot, brutal, so painfully sodden with steam that it almost felt good, like a special treatment for the skin that made you look younger before making your lungs collapse. It did not feel like this in Chicago or New York, where they had things called "seasons." I had been places where I finally understood poems about spring. I had seen wonders. I had seen it snow on the Fourth of July. I had seen bison materialize out of geyser steam on a moon-filled plateau. And now I was going to marry a woman and move back for the same reason my father had twenty years before: a job. Specifically, a teaching job at a university whose administrators had been fooled into believing I had qualifications.

I'd missed Mississippi, this funny place, its land vast and green and wide enough to swallow up North Korea, but with fewer people than Atlanta. It is a good thing, too, because if you put all of Mississippi's people inside Atlanta, bad things would happen. Somebody might go see a play.

It was not going to be easy, coming back, bringing another human into this family. Was I embarrassed by them? I knew it was cruel to be ashamed of the mentally ill. But having people meet my family was a secret fear. It would be like taking someone to a dark room to show them my anal fissures, and you can't just go introducing everybody to your anal fissures. Only special people get to see such as that.

What would Pop say to my fiancée? How would he behave?

He was a decent man, but I also knew that he had a condition, an illness that I did not want any future wife to see. There is no name for this condition, and I am sure our nation's richly endowed research foundations have more pressing infirmities to fund. One day, perhaps there might be a Race for the Cure, or at the very least a well-organized car wash. But I dream.

What sort of condition?

My father said things.

Inappropriate things, to women. All the time. About their bodies.

I guess you could say it was flirting, although it felt more like assault. He meant no harm, I am sure. It's just that he treated women like Russian nesting dolls that must be pried, and opened, and pried, and opened, until there is nothing left but a restraining order. All my life, I'd witnessed this perverse flattery at churches and Christmas pageants and our nation's many lovely Shoney's franchises.

"Can I take your order?" the server would say. Her name was always something like Tina, and she was always missing one of the more important teeth, but Pop didn't seem to mind.

"Tina!" Pop would say. "Tina-Tina-Bo-Beena!"

"That's what they call me," Tina says, smirking into her pad of tickets.

Pop's right eyebrow would lift ever so gently, tugged by some lecherous puppeteer.

"Oh, I bet they call you all kinda things," he would say.

"What would you like to drank?" she says.

"I'll have a sweet tea!" he says. "Sweet, sweet tea! Sweet, sweet chariot!" He then starts to sing the gospel tune in the voice of a drunken revivalist preacher. "Do you swing low, Tina-Tina-Bo-Beena?"

All this time, Mom would be staring over the precipice of her menu at Pop like he'd just ordered an appetizer of edible panties.

"You make me want to throw up," she would say, when Tina left.

"Oh, hush," he says. "I'm just friendly."

"She practically put her bosoms in your face," Mom says.

"I can't help it where a woman wants to put her bosoms," he says. "Can I, boys?"

We found it difficult to answer his question, though, as we were slowly sliding underneath the booth, hoping to crawl to the breakfast buffet and perhaps live there until college.

But we didn't want to leave our poor mother. She was a dutiful and long-suffering wife. It is unclear how Pop had ever convinced her to marry him, although there has been speculation that it involved a number of soul records and a carton of Winston Lights.

"I like you," he must have said. "You got big arms like what can hold a baby good."

Sure, he had many great qualities, was a great father, had taken and loved Bird as his own boy, nobly, honorably, but Godalmighty, the man was touched in the head. It was a surprise that she'd stayed married to him. She must have considered it a special calling, a sort of holy mission, bringing God's light to the savage, while he verbally scalped the women of our nation's service industries.

Who knew that this was a disease, and that it could be passed from father to son, not through the genes, but manually, as when Pop made me the messenger of his good-hearted misogyny? The victim was my first-grade teacher, Mrs. Jones, a wild-eyed woman, like Gertrude Stein during a Brazilian wax.

"Your teacher thinks she's cute, don't she?" Pop asked in the car, on the way to the dentist one morning.

"She's kind of mean," I said.

"You tell her if she's ugly to you, I'll take off my belt and give her a good whipping, hear."

Did he mean for me to tell her that, in exactly that way? Because that's what I did, in exactly that way, in front of everyone, when I got back to class.

"Your father said—*what*?"

Her red eyeballs swelled like a pair of overfilled kickballs from behind her desk.

"He said he wants to spank you," I said.

The sickening feeling of knowing I'd said something uncouth rose up through my shoes and shorts and up over my shoulders like liquid sin. Moments like these, I think, are why God invented diarrhea, or some other reason to run screaming from a classroom, or a family, or a man.

I must've known I had the disease, though it was hard to tell back then, when Pop's symptoms eclipsed my own.

"I am not my father," I told myself, starting around junior high. "I am not him. He is a joke. I am not a joke. I am a Bible verse."

I am a proverb.

"A fool's mouth is his destruction," it says, "and his lips are the snare of his soul."

Was my father ensnaring our souls with his reckless banter? It seemed like it in my adolescence, at fall festivals and football fund-raisers. There we'd be, Styrofoam plates piled high with charity poultry, me sitting with cheerleaders and hoping to learn the difference between bloomers and panties.

Pop would amble up, grinning.

"How you fine ladies feeling?" he'd say. "With your hands?"

He would then make a motion with his hands, as though he were kneading something, perhaps a large mound of girlish dough, and everyone would look around and wait for someone to yell *rape*.

"Oh, Coach Key, you're so funny," they would say, lying. "How are you?"

"Me? Shoot. If I was any better, I'd have to be two people."

The whole "two people" thing sounded vaguely sexual, or at least vaguely biological, as if Pop were about to undergo cellular mitosis right there in the school cafeteria.

"Your daddy's so *funny*," the cheerleaders would say, after he walked away.

"We plan to have him murdered after the rainy season," I would say.

As a result of this jejune rambunctiousness, I spent high school and college finding ways not to bring girls home.

"Who are you seeing now?" Mom would ask. "Why can't you bring her over for dinner?"

"She doesn't eat," I would say.

"Oh, is she on a diet?"

"She has no mouth," I would say.

I knew this evasion wouldn't work forever, as one cannot keep dating imaginary mouthless women without raising certain questions about nuclear waste. But I got out of high school without bringing almost any of them to the house, and now I was back, ten years gone, having met a girl with the prettiest mouth I had ever seen. I'd told her I liked her, and she hadn't called the police, and I decided we should marry. And then I remembered that she would have to meet my people, and for a moment I regretted not choosing a Filipino girl, whom Pop may have refused to meet, which would've been safer for everyone.

Bird had already done it a few years before, marrying a nice girl from Louisiana and settling down to life as a yam farmer in the Delta. They'd eloped, which I'd felt was a strategic decision, both to keep costs down and also to prevent our father from saying something terrible at the rehearsal dinner, such as how pleased he was that so many bosomy women had come to the party. But we'd have to have a wedding, I knew, which meant I'd have to introduce my lady friend to my father.

It would be risky. He'd not been around such a striking young woman for many years, and here she'd be, in his immediate line of sight, with a belly-button ring and everything.

I decided they should meet her at a restaurant less likely to employ any waitresses with names like Tina or with rare skin disorders or cauliflower ear. Nothing against these fine women: I just couldn't risk Pop making remarks about what other vegetables the other parts of their bodies looked like.

"What should I wear?" my fiancée said.

"Nothing too revealing," I said. "The restaurant might be cold. You might consider wearing a sweater, or a cape, or a bib of some kind."

The day came, and I was expecting a scene, the sort of moment that made the body's endocrine system pucker and surge, but I am happy to report that it went surprisingly well. We made introductions, sat, ate. My parents were gracious, kindhearted, impressed by her unexpected beauty. There was no talk of the belly-button ring, hidden away quietly, a fact I thought would best be revealed later, after my parents were dead. At dinner, Mom was charming, curious, and Pop was tame, almost soporific, as though Mom had tranquilized him beforehand with Benadryl and a claw hammer. This was going to be easier than I thought. I had worried for nothing. Pop had grown up. So had we all.

And so, we married.

Then came our first Thanksgiving.

Here we were, a family, settling into the tender holiday moment. My wife returned with a bowl of popcorn and sat down, and I noticed Pop looking at her with that old sly grin.

"You know," he said to my young wife, "I think your thighs may be getting bigger."

When he said it, a kernel of corn lodged itself in the vestibule of my nasal cavity, preparing to rappel from my nostrils and subdue the man with a flash grenade. I fully expected my wife to burst into tears and run from the room. Instead, she looked at her new father-in-law in a way that indicated he might want to insert his head up a mule's ass.

"I think she looks great!" Mom said.

"She does!" Pop said. "It's a compliment. I like big thighs."

"I'm right here," she said.

"Can we please stop saying *thighs*?" I said.

"*Haunches* is the word," Pop said.

"She's not a horse," I said.

My wife left the room. Thanksgiving was over.

My fears had come to pass. My wife was finally seeing my anal fissures, and I worried that she might never want to see them again. It was odd, trying to think of a way to explain my father to another human being, a dark labyrinth of psychological conjecture that mere mortals dare not enter. It would be easier to explain predestination to a bowl of hummus.

"I'm sorry," I said to my wife. "It's just—he played football before the helmets."

"Do you think my thighs are big?" she said.

But I didn't answer, knowing it'd be safer to focus on removing the popcorn from my eustachian tubes.

Over the next few holidays, it got worse, Pop saying all sorts of things to my wife in our general area of holiday mirth. By Christmas, babies were all the rage.

"Just whatever you do," Pop said, "I hope you don't breast-feed it."

Alarms rang at the word *breastfeed*, and I quickly called in a Code Red. "Let's watch a bass fishing program!" I said.

"Nursing is the best thing you can do for a baby," she said. She was a woman of strong will, with many opinions, and did not yet fully understand that one does not discuss mammary glands with my father.

"Please, no," I said.

There followed a minor fracas over the merits of synthetic versus natural fluids for the infant, and it became clear that my mother had read an article sometime in the early 1970s explaining that breastfeeding was a primitive custom and that modern American mothers should instead nourish their young with Tang and Mr. Pibb.

"You people are crazy," my wife said.

"Ain't nothing will ruin a lady's chest like giving a baby too much titty milk," Pop said.

If I'd had a gun, I would've just started shooting everyone, to save the world from us.

"Everyone, stop right now," I said.

I could see the disappointment in my wife's face at having married into a family where the word *titty* could be passed around at Christmas dinner as freely as a basket of warm crescent rolls. She looked at me, and I smiled, weakly.

"He can't help it," I said. "He grew up on a dairy, surrounded by animal teats."

"Teats is titties," Pop said.

"Stop saying *titties*," I said.

"It's all nipples," he said.

"What kind of people talk like this at Christmas dinner?" said my wife.

I could tell by her look that she considered me one of these people.

After all, I was having my own problems—not at home, where my wife could hear, but at work, where that old family disease, that verbal dysentery, had begun to pour forth from a new mouth.

"Morning!" a colleague would say in the hallway.

My brain, desiring both to say *morning* and *hello*, simply combined the two.

"Horny!" I would say, as they ran for the fire escape.

In elevators, I would find myself trying to be congenial.

"Have we met?" I'd say to some attractive new colleague.

"Yes," she'd say. "We met last week. I never forget a face!"

"What I remember best are smells," I would say.

And there would be grave, frightened silence, while the elevator lurched, slowly, giving us all plenty of time to smell one another.

I would enter some new university building, and the female guard, really a very nice woman I did not intend to hurt, would ask to see my ID, which was in my pocket, and my hands would be full, and I'd be sweating.

"Can I see your ID?" she'd say.

"It's in my pants."

"Well, I need it."

"Well, how comfortable are you putting your face inside my pants?"

I would try to apologize, but it was too late.

Worst, though, were office kitchens, where I often stumbled upon nursing mothers heaving out their bosoms like sacks of English peas. There I'd be standing next to the mom, and I'd be so flustered, so anxious to fill the blank canvas of the moment with bright, colorful acrylics that I'd end up staring at her and the baby and saying something like, "I prefer skim," or "He's so cute, the part of his face that I can see!" or "Why do people say *suck* like it's a bad thing?"

I couldn't help it. I wanted to. I did.

A year or two into the marriage, and I'd managed to keep this condition hidden from my wife. But then the truth came out, during Sunday school one morning at a church that was charitable enough not to excommunicate me when I used the word *afterbirth* to make what I believed to be a nuanced theological point.

The look of horror on my wife's face reminded me of something, a look I had seen on my mother's face at a Shoney's many moons ago.

"It's a disease," I explained to my wife, later. "It just came out."

"Words don't just come out."

"My brain picks its own words. I can't control it."

"Try," she said.

"*Afterbirth*," I said. "See? It just happens. *Placenta! Vagina! Virginia! Dead puppy!*"

We had spent that particular Sunday school class discussing the Book of Ephesians, a book that contains almost no references to placental matter.

"Why do you do this?" she said.

It's the guileless, childlike part of my brain that desired to speak, I explained. The other part, the one designed to stop suspect words at the security gate of my mouth and request identification, was easily fooled by words like *afterbirth*.

"Let me see your papers," the security guard says.

"I have them here somewhere," *afterbirth* says, searching his pockets, then finding an old coupon for a Dairy Queen Blizzard. "Here it is!" The security guard inspects it carefully, hands it back, waves *afterbirth* through.

Soon came other words and comments and remarks too delicate to mention, pouring forth from my imprudent lips at staff meetings and dinner parties. Words like *vulva*. Again, nothing you wouldn't find in a high school health class, but still. Because now everybody at the fancy dinner party is thinking *vulva, vulva, vulva.*

You were not like this before we got married," she said.

"I was lusting after you," I said. "I'm way more focused when I'm lusting."

I'd spent so much energy putting distance and education between my father and me, learning words and theories that reordered my brain, forever altered the way I dressed, looked, talked. And yet I sensed a deep and long-forgotten pattern, emerging across my person—that my soul was still tethered to Pop's across time and age, as yet unbroken.

Perhaps we were not so different. What other exciting revelations would adulthood and marriage make known? Might I suddenly be overcome by the unexplained desire to coach a sports team while wearing shorts cut short enough to frighten small children? Might I wake up one morning to find myself soaked in coyote urine and wanting to climb a tree with a weapon of some sort?

I would embrace it. This wasn't a disease. It was a gift. It bound my father and me together. My mouth may be my destruction, but it is also my birthright. Some people inherit land and bullion and horses, but not me. I inherited the ability to say *hemorrhoid* at a baby shower.

"Stop," my wife learned to say, when it's about to happen. She could sense it.

Like all heroes, I learned to control this amazing power.

We were at a family funeral, gathered at the ancestral farm to mourn the passing of our patriarch. The great and august man was buried in the sacred earth of a North Mississippi hill and we were back at the house disabusing ourselves of woolen slacks and hateful neckwear, preparing to baptize our heads in buckets of wine and chicken.

Knock, knock.

It was a family friend, bearing one such bucket. My grieving father met her at the screen door and transformed instantly into a garrulous, chipper troll. Pop remembered this woman and dressed her down with questions of family, engaging her with the intensity of a French furrier scrutinizing a fresh mink pelt.

"I believe you've gained some weight," he said to the nice woman. "Seem like your legs is thicker." The remark, as sudden and surprising as a summer tornado, sucked the air from the house.

I tried not to look at the poor woman, who'd believed she had come here to assuage the bereaved, only to discover that it was a wake for the body she once had. The woman soon left, I assume, to pilot her car into a nearby ravine.

We gathered around the old Coldwater table one last time, ate, drank.

"Why would you say such a thing?" Mom said. "That poor girl."

"What?" Pop said. "I like big legs."

My wife looked at me.

I said nothing.

"She had some hocks on her," Pop said. "Didn't she, boy?"

"I'm more of a breast man, myself," I said, reaching into the bucket.

CHAPTER 14

A Gamboling Problem

My new wife was very progressive. For example, when I was about to say things about bosoms or afterbirths, she had a very progressive method of dealing with it, which is, she would hit me. Or when I asked her to bring me something—a beer, for example—she had this fun thing she would do where she would not do it. She'd spent many years waiting tables and continued to do so a year or two into our marriage, so I guess she'd reached her quota on bringing beers to people who really wanted beers.

"Um, are you crippled?" she would say.

If I was in distress, she might bring me the beer, but in general, she made it a habit not to bring me things, which made me stop asking her to bring me things, which made her happy, and her happiness was important to me, in addition to beer, which I often had to locate myself, using a special device reserved only for emergencies, known as my brain.

This was fine, but also unexpected, because I had come from a family where women brought things to men. If you told a roomful of my male relatives that dinner was ready, they'd walk to the unset table and sit like dutiful children, waiting for the meal to be chauffeured to them by the nearest woman. If

these men were in the living room watching football and desired a glass of tea, they'd announce this need into the air, as if
calling an audible at the line of scrimmage.

"Tea!" Pop would say. "Woman, brang me some tea!" And
Mom, no matter where she was, would brang him that tea. Or
cake, or pie, or whatever.

I grew up believing this was the way of the world, that
women did things for men, and that men let them. And perhaps this really is true in places like Iran.

I can remember one especially tender moment during graduate school at the home of a girlfriend, as we shared a sofa and
watched a movie. She was a fibers artist, a muse to many, sensitive, fractious, heavily medicated. She sat up, for what reason
I know not, maybe to fashion a handbag from an afghan or to
construct a bottle tree from her prescription vials.

"Hey, could you bring me a glass of water?" I said.

It should be noted that I had not yelled my demand from
another room and hadn't addressed her as "woman," but she
still looked at me like I'd asked to wear her grandmother's
panties on my head.

"Get it your goddamn self," she said.

Things didn't work out. And despite the fact that I was sure
this woman would have inspired me to write many fascinating
tales of psychological terror shortly before murdering me with
a darning needle, she did teach me an important lesson, which
is to wait thirty minutes after your lover takes her meds before
asking her to bring you a glass of water.

In the early years of my marriage, I told myself to be more
sensitive to the balance of power in our little two-person fam-

ily. I'd never lived with a woman besides my mother, and I had no other template for how to behave around one who hadn't birthed you. It's a shame. Men with older sisters know things the rest of us don't, such as how to read their moods like the weather across a pasture and how to sense if they're about to burn you with a curling iron.

I did work hard to ask less of my wife than my father asked of my mother, but I would learn, in time, that it wasn't enough. I'd need to do more, ask less.

The childless season of our marriage was tender, sweet. We owned a television, but it picked up no stations, and we rented only the occasional movie, spending most of our time playing cards and board games and Pictionary, which, with two people, required more than love. It required imagination. It was in this season that we learned to make each other laugh: her, by playing games of memory with such frightening speed as to make me worry that she might have a brain disorder, and me, with my unsurpassed enthusiasm for deforming my body in the service of charades. It was a good marriage, I thought.

At the time, all I really asked of my wife was that she manage our checkbook and prepare the occasional taco. I did not ask for the bed to be made, although she did it anyway, as if to prove a point. I did not ask her to wear pearls to dinner, or even to cook every night. I *liked* leftovers, begged her not to throw them out. And I didn't ask her to stop texting her sister about their diarrhea, because I knew diarrhea was important to her.

I didn't even ask my wife to make sex with me every night, as would've been my preference. Or really even every week. Sometimes, I forgot what she looked like naked.

"Stop it," she would say. "We had a meeting just two days ago."

That's what we called it: a meeting.

"I think we need to schedule a meeting," I'd say.

"But we just had that other meeting."

"That was two months ago," I'd say.

"Days," she'd say. "Two *days* ago."

After she got home from the restaurant, she did the bills, and when I got home from the university, I did the lawn, and so on and so forth, but there was something I had begun to ask of her, a simple request that she refused to honor. Each time, she denied me.

I wanted her to dance with me.

"Um, no," she would say, whenever we found ourselves at a bar or a party or a festival where tribal rhythms had lured my buttocks into sinuous articulation.

"Come on," I'd say, my pelvis having begun to undulate against my will.

"What is wrong with you?"

"I can't help it. My body does things."

And her body would do other things, such as slink away in horror.

One thing's for sure: Dancing isn't what it used to be.

"Oh, we had all kinda dances," Pop would say, when I was younger. "We used to dance all the time."

"Like, in pairs?" I asked.

"Oh, yeah, man. That was how you did it back then."

He told stories about dancing at Hernando's Hideaway and barns and honky-tonks and lakeside pavilions between Oxford and Memphis. What I wondered was, How did you know how to dance? My grandparents didn't dance, I knew that much. Our family's particular brand of Christianity believed such behavior would lead to sex, which, of course, it does, if you do it right.

I attended my first real dance in the seventh or eighth grade, where it was explained that it might be permissible to dance with a girl.

"How?" I asked Mom.

She went over to the console, turned the radio on. It was George Strait singing about his many ex-lovers in the Republic of Texas. She showed me where to put my hands, and when the rhythm swung around, she started to move. We swayed and pitched gently, two boats in a safe harbor, and it was nice.

"How do you know how to do this?" I asked.

"Your father," she said.

I found it hard to imagine this man, a teetotaler who no longer owned any records, doing anything with his legs that did not include battering the walls of a medieval fortress. But every June, according to Mom, when he took all of us to the Mississippi Road Builders' Association Convention at the Broadwater Beach Hotel in Biloxi, they'd slip off for a little strutting in the ballroom.

"He can cut a rug," she said.

He never struck me as the rug-cutting type. Tree-cutting, yes. But Mom spoke with great awe of his ability to turn, twist, swing.

"And he'd whisper in my ear," she said.

"What'd he say?"

"Oh, nothing," she said, with more love in her eyes than I was used to seeing when she talked about my father. It felt good, knowing they danced. I'd heard them fight. I'd seen him demand glasses of tea. I'd seen her send him to hell with a look. But as long as they danced, I felt, things were pretty good.

That night, I went to the dance at McLaurin. It was pretty amazing. The girls put their hands on our shoulders, and we put our hands on their hips, and we rocked slowly to Phil Collins's "A Groovy Kind of Love," each couple like a pair of metronomes with giant baby heads. From a distance, we might've looked both beautiful and sad, a gymnasium full of elderly midgets trying to pass wind.

It would be many years before I'd learn to dance with anything like style. Some of the girls in my high school could do things with the lower halves of their bodies that made you believe their buttocks were powered by some sort of generator, and some of the boys broke it off fierce, too, as we used to say. They did the Worm. They did the Moonwalk. They did This Thing with Their Heads Like They Were a Malfunctioning Robot. I tried to do that last one in front of a mirror and looked like I'd hit an underground electrical wire.

The same year of my first dance, we took a field trip to New Orleans, where we were to be inspired with the biology of the Audubon Zoo. Instead, it was the anatomy of the French Quarter that consumed our psychic energies, hypnotized as we were by the pair of mechanical legs that snaked out of a hole in the wall of a Bourbon Street teat facility. Our teachers marched us from Café du Monde to the Ripley's Believe or Not! Museum to see a shrunken head, but our eyes were detained en route by the Polaroids outside a strip club, depicting the very unshrunken breasts of naked dancers in various attitudes of sexual degradation.

"What are they doing?" we asked our teachers.

"Gymnastics!" the teachers said.

Walking through the city, my skin absorbed a strange music—funny, old, cartoonish, a sort of Americanized theme for *The Benny Hill Show*. They called it "Dixieland," but at the time, I had no name for it and was forced to define it simply as "not Phil Collins." Something in the music made me want to move.

On subsequent visits to the city over the next decade, I was further exposed to the alluring contagion of this sound, until such time that I rounded a corner in the Faubourg Marigny and was confronted by a jazz that sounded less like Pete Fountain and more like the Isley Brothers played at very high speeds. Where Dixieland musicians looked like porters at the Hotel Monteleone, this band, standing in the middle of the street in wading pools of their own perspiration, looked more like Public Enemy playing battered instruments that had been run over by a school bus. Rising above it all was the colossal floret of a tuba whose sound throttled my intestine, the call of a drunken elephant seal in rut.

Immediately, I started to dance. Right there in the street, with Holy Ghost Power. It was a new kind of dancing, not really like dancing at all, more like fighting off an invisible swarm of bees while simultaneously trying to complete a walkathon and a bowel movement.

"What is this glorious sound?" I said.

"A funeral," they said.

After that, I was a dancer. I danced everywhere, at college formals, at bars, in buffet lines. At least, some called it dancing. Others called it assault. Furniture became a tool, a prop, a weapon. I made love to the music. Occasionally, the music made love to me. Sometimes, the music and me got in a fight, and then we would make up, and then we would make babies. Most of that's a metaphor.

Sometimes, I had friends who would dance with me. Old black women liked to dance with me, at Field's Café in downtown Jackson, where they taught me how to Walk the Dog, which is more like Riding a Burro. Also, crazy drunk white girls would sometimes dance with me, although the sober ones almost never did. I never understood why. Mostly, it was other sober white guys who danced with me. There was one guy in college who danced with me a lot. We did a pas de deux to "Total Eclipse of the Heart" that made a lot of people pray for us.

Dancing with your hyperdramatic man friends is one thing. But I knew a day would come when I'd get to dance with my wife, a woman I'd seen dance on many occasions. Granted, it was ballet, which some consider dancing. And which others consider boring. But not me. When she danced, it was magic.

I'd also seen her dance in a less magical way at a venue known as the Catwalk. In college, long before we dated, when she was a mere acquaintance, a young girl too interested in men who wore tattoos and cologne to be taken seriously, I remember seeing her and her roommates do things at the Catwalk that would've qualified them, I am fairly certain, for psychiatric evaluation. They tried doing the motorized-buttock thing, which proved difficult given their general lack of buttocks, so they concentrated on their upper bodies, doing what looked to be a combination of cheerleading and enthusiastic aircraft carrier flight crew training. They danced mostly with one another. No guys allowed. Occasionally, I would have a total eclipse of the heart right down through the middle of their girl party, but they'd just ignore me and shuffle off to the bathroom.

Early in our courtship, nearly a full decade later, I decided to find out just what sort of music she liked. On our second date, feeling roguish enough to pry open her case of compact discs, I discovered names like Creed and Edwin McCain and the Backstreet Boys, which made me wonder: Is this woman emotionally stable? Only moments before, she had seemed so healthy, so beguiling, so richly manifold in her proclivities, and yet her musical tastes suggested an undiagnosed mental illness.

On one of our first dates, she pushed one of these discs into its felted playing slit.

"Backstreet's back, all right!" she sang.

"Where have they been?" I yelled, over the music.

"What?" she said, turning it down.

"I was just wondering where they went."

"Where who went?"

"The Backstreet Boys," I said. "They said they were back. Where'd they go?"

"I don't know."

"Maybe they went to hell."

"Maybe that's where you can go," she said.

It was hard not to love a woman with timing like that.

Like Scarlett and Rhett, we honeymooned in New Orleans, which I felt afforded an opportunity to redeem her musical failures and show her what real dancing looked like. I would take her to the Maple Leaf.

"Wear comfortable shoes," I said, smoking a cigarette on the balcony.

To say that my wife was attractive would be silly. Her body had been shaped by decades of balletic exertion. In public, heads turned, people wondered what sort of drugs I had given her to hypnotize her into a relationship with me.

"How do I look?" she asked, stepping onto the balcony in a fitted dress and heels that made me feel ashamed at having fooled her into marrying me.

"I said comfortable shoes."

"These are all I have."

"You can't dance in those."

And she did not dance. Instead, she stood on a bench, against the wall, two feet above the boiling heads of the crowd, far and away the best thing to look at in the building, friendly enough to allow young Tulane boys to present her with offerings of gin and flattery before introducing them to the modest array of gems and precious metals on her ring finger.

"I'm married," she yelled over the music.

"To who?" they yelled up at her.

"The one by the stage, having a seizure," she said.

A year later, we went back to New Orleans, and I took her to see another brass band, but by then the Saturnalian glow of our honeymoon had dimmed, and instead of standing on a bench, she stood in the bathroom and cried. She hated the music, she said. It was too loud. It hurt her ears. She covered them with her hands and asked me to take her home. There would be no dancing.

All the usual metaphors for what it means to dance with someone played through my head. Had I married the wrong woman?

In those first happy childless years of our marriage, we'd be in the truck, and I'd put something entirely pleasant and fun and lively into the stereo—James Brown, Zeppelin—but always, she hated it, turning off the music just as it was getting good.

"Oh my *word*," she would say. "This music is making me crazy."

"Don't ever do that again," I'd say.

But she would, again and again.

"It makes me sad that you hate my music," I said.

"It's just so *loud*."

"It's joyful."

"It's noise."

I didn't know what to say. The woman listened to the radio. *The radio.* She could memorize entire songs by pop starlets and other melodious necromancers in two or three listens, like some kind of savant. I'd long since stopped taking her to bars, saving myself the disappointment of having the most beautiful woman in the room refuse to dance with me yet again.

Occasionally, we found ourselves at galas and other fund-raising events where middle-aged men in wingtips got weird with their thick-necked wives, jowl to jowl, hobbling ever so lightly to "Mustang Sally"—just the sort of place where I suspected my father might have started hurling my mother around the parquet. I knew better than to have a total eclipse of the heart in such a place, or to shake anything larger than a finger or have one of my mechanized buttock seizures, but I did ask my wife to dance.

"No," she said.

"Come on."

She glowed brighter than the other wives, I felt. Heads never failed to turn, the righteousness of her neck and back, the shoulders possessing a firm grace that suggested wings, a posture so courtly you could practically see the underside of her jaw. There was no arrogance in it. It was natural, as natural as the uncontrollable gyrations of my chassis during "Brick House."

"Stop it," she'd say.

"Why won't you dance with me?"

And then I'd wander off by myself, to look for some drunk old coot whose husband was dead or bedridden, and we'd cut rugs together.

"I just don't understand," I'd say, on the way home. "Wives are supposed to dance with their husbands."

"What you do is not dancing."

"Then why don't you show me how to do it right?"

But this she ignored.

I tried to change. Sometimes, if I could get enough gin

down her gullet, I might get her out on the floor, sway with her sweetly for a few bars, but then something would come over me, and before you knew it, I'd find myself spanking her like a pony who wouldn't behave.

"What are you doing?"

"Hush, little pony," I'd say, and she would run off to greener pastures.

She'd be mum all the way home, and the next gala, the next fancy ball, the next good band in town, she'd make excuses, say she had nothing to wear, say she was ill, or wasn't in the mood, and before I knew it, I was going to all the events by myself. I'd dance all night with fading bachelorettes with a taste for conga lines.

Hadn't my wife promised to honor and cherish me, in sickness and in health? And didn't I cherish her? And wasn't my dancing a kind of sickness?

When I die," I said, "I hope you'll at least dance at my funeral."

"What are you talking about?" my wife asked, the first time I brought this up.

"It will be a jazz funeral," I said. "It's in my will."

I lied, of course. I didn't have a will.

"We'll just have a normal funeral," she said.

"You know, drums and horns and whatnot. Maybe a sousaphone."

"A *phone*?"

"No."

"At your funeral?"

"It's a tuba."

"There will be no tubas at your funeral," she said.

"And trumpets," I said. "A whole parade."

"This is a funeral you're talking about, right?"

"Don't you love me?" I said.

She paused. She had to think about it.

She wanted to believe she was the pragmatist, the realist, the *adult* in the marriage. This, from a woman who once spent thirty minutes trying to explain to me how humans breed with vampires.

"Would you at least be sad?" I asked my wife. "If I died first?"

"A little," she said. "Maybe."

"Would you get married again?"

"Um, *yeah*," she said. "A real doctor this time. Also, he will be nice to me. A nice, gentle anesthesiologist, who dances normal."

"You two sound very happy."

"We will be."

She was funny, you had to give her that much. Then one night, she said the funniest thing of all.

"Do you want to go country line dancing?" she said.

"Ha ha," I said.

There we were, in a vast dark room lighted on one end by a television the size of a Flemish tapestry and at the other end, a spotlight projecting onto a mechanical bull, and in the middle, a dance floor, and against one wall a large boot the size of a small Soviet satellite, in which a disc jockey presumably hid himself out of shame. The name of this bar, she explained, was Saddlebags.

People gathered around the dance floor, and the music began. I like country music, I do, but I do not like line dancing, or any sort of dancing where men hold their belts like their jeans might try to run away, as any sensible pair of jeans would want to do in such a situation.

"Are you two going to dance?" one of our friends asked.

"Oh, no," I said.

And yet, to my surprise, there she went. My wife. Dancing. Without me.

This woman, I mean.

A woman with posture and grace like that stands out on any floor, and it was no different that night, as the cowboys and hillbillies and swamp angels gathered around to watch. She was so pretty in the lights, a map of stars playing over her face.

The music started, and she danced, and honestly, it was the dumbest thing I'd ever seen happen on a dance floor. Was this how my dancing seemed to her? I tried to imagine her asking me to have country line dancing at her funeral. I'd have laughed, too.

She was right, maybe dancing with your wife should generally not involve spanking, or treating her like a pony, or a burro, or any sort of farm animal.

I had a lot to learn about dancing, and marriage, and this woman.

She did not know the steps of this particular line dance, but after a lifetime of learning *Swan Lake*, it did not take her long. I found purchase on a step above the dance floor, to see her better, over the heads of the gathering horde, my wife, skinny jeans tucked into a pair of cowboy boots she'd borrowed from the babysitter. She kicked her boots, turned, laughed, still the best thing to look at in the building, and I made a mental note to schedule an important meeting with her later.

"Is she with you?" a cowboy asked.

"I think," I said. "I hope."

—❦ ✦ ✦ ❦—

·

CHAPTER 15

The Great and Holy Siege of Vicksburg

—❦ ✦ ✦ ❦—

Do you want kids?" my wife had said, back when she was barely my girlfriend, and we were on our second date. The honest answer to such a question, I knew, was to open the door and throw myself from the car, in hopes that my extensive background in watching television had prepared me to roll in such a way as to not die.

"Kids?" I said.

I tried to remember if I'd ever actually seen one. At the time, the ideas of "a child" and "children" were but Platonic notions that hovered in the rear parlors of my brain, somewhere near other concepts that had nothing to do with me, like "cholera" and "hair care products."

I can still remember when my first good friend had a baby.

"It's a girl!" he said.

"Wow," I said. "I just bought some new socks."

And yet, when the prettiest woman in the world asks you if you want babies, you should probably say yes, because there's always a chance that she might want to make them with you. This woman, she was pretty, and funny, and she liked me back, which was all I'd ever really wanted in a wife, not to mention all the qualities she had that I'd never even thought of wanting, such as hair and an unhealthy fear of bridges. Did I want to have a baby with this gorgeous, funny woman? She might as well have asked me if I wanted to ride a unicorn across a prairie of starlight.

Besides, what is a baby? A baby is an idea, a theory, really, abstractly good in the way that life insurance and riding lawn mowers are good.

"Sure, I like babies," I said. It was true. I had been a baby my whole life.

"Show them how you can read," my mother would say, and I would read something, and all the women would applaud.

"Show them how you can dance," an aunt would say, and I would do my funny dance, and they would cheer.

"Do your memory verse," an aunt would say, and I would recite a psalm in my best Ronald Reagan voice, and they would laugh and laugh, turning me into the monster I would become.

"My baby's so smart!" my mother would say.

I was the baby of the family, blessed with the gift of ignorance. When I was eleven, I still held out some hope in the reality of Santa Claus, and when I was twelve, after hearing about masturbation for a couple of years, I had come to the conclusion that it must be some sort of advanced first-aid procedure. At thirteen, I still didn't fully understand how babies were born. I had seen enough farm animals to know the basic mechanics, but that didn't stop me from believing that babies came out of the anus.

"No they don't!" a girl on the bus said.

"I know!" I said, lying.

One day, six months into our marriage, when we were having soup, she announced that she was out of birth control pills, and

I suggested she get some more, and she suggested I did not love her, and I suggested that I was confused, and she suggested I was selfish to not want a baby, and I suggested that nobody had been talking about babies, and she suggested that now was the time to have a baby, and I suggested that now was the time to finish our soup, and she suggested that I perhaps look into making travel arrangements to Hades, and then she started crying and throwing dishes into the sink, and I made a mental note to contact an exorcist.

"We hear you don't want children," my wife's aunt said, arms crossed, standing at my front door a few weeks later.

"Eventually," I said.

"We're praying that God will change your heart."

"Yeah, well what if Jesus doesn't want us to have babies?" I said.

"Then he will close her womb," the aunt said, pointing at my wife's abdomen. My wife just stood there, enjoying her womb's moment in the sun. This is what happens when you move back to Mississippi. Your wife's relatives show up and try to make your penis a part of God's plan. I didn't know what to say, so I said nothing, and my wife stopped taking the pill, and I did what I was told.

We made sex for a long time. Years, it seemed. I found this quite enjoyable, but also upsetting that it should take so long to make a baby, given the ease with which others became pregnant in my youth, such as high school cheerleaders, who could get tossed up into the air during a football game and come down to the earth bearing twins.

What I would learn is that the whole process of making a family is quite ugly. There's yelling, biting, the rending of garments, the setting of fires, and that's just the sex part.

Why had nobody told me it would be this hard? The world was full of liars.

The first lie is how long it takes to make the actual baby, which sounds like great fun, having sex over and over again, like eating delicious pizza and never getting full. More pizza, please! Nope, not full yet! This is how it was at first, while my wife cried in the corner.

I wondered, Why is she crying? Everyone likes pizza!

My wife would mark the calendar on the days we were supposed to consume the pizza, and we would shuffle into the bedroom and eat in silence. Occasionally, my wife would say something especially sweet, like "Are you still awake?" or "I can't breathe." We tried just about everything short of having a fertility specialist mate with my wife for me.

We had a very small bed, which compelled us, when sleeping, to fold our bodies into a Celtic knot, and if you do that long enough, eventually you're going to penetrate something besides an eye. I guess that's what happened.

"I'm pregnant," she said, shocked.

It was a relief. We could finally stop having sex.

We now lived in a small village called Port Gibson, a lovely little town with more churches than people, a town known largely for U. S. Grant's uncharacteristically noble decision not to set fire to it, because, as he said, the town was "too beautiful to burn," although he was also overheard saying he was "out of matches."

It was a verdant paradise, the Natchez Trace Parkway running through our backyard, the Mississippi River a few miles off the front porch, the most fecund soil in creation, nothing but horses and trees and barely a quorum for the dying Sons of Confederate Veterans. The perfect little place to have a baby, especially if we wanted our baby delivered by a veterinarian.

My wife prepared largely through books, empowering volumes that spoke of the birth canal as though it were an embattled isthmus of Palestine, holistic books about how to grow a baby while eating nothing but gingerroot and one's own hair, and books about how to "listen to your body," which I assumed was saying something like, "Stop eating your own hair."

There were books by enlightened activists who wanted us to have our baby in a solarium filled with hibiscus, and books by wizened midwives who wanted us to return to the purity of the eighteenth century and give birth to our baby on a kitchen table, preferably while someone nearby died of injuries inflicted by Choctaw.

The strangest books were the oldest ones, from the 1970s, books on natural childbirth that were full of ancient photographs depicting women giving birth in meadows, women who were naked in almost every picture, as were their husbands.

"This is pornography," I said.

"This is how I want to do it," my wife said. "Natural, like Mom did it."

If my wife had a calling, it was being a mother like the one who'd made her, a woman who died too soon, in a heartbreaking story that's better told another time, and who left behind her a cloud of witnesses who would've told you that when it came to mothers, they didn't make them any better than her. A part of me thinks my wife must have wanted to suffer, as a visible sign of the suffering she had already passed through in the unseen corridors of her heart.

"Natural, okay," I said. This was her rodeo, her heart.

It sounded pleasant. Blue skies. Rainbows.

But I worried.

I had seen a natural birth before. In a barn. Blood. Screaming.

My wife soon found herself under the influence of friends who announced that childbirth had been "medicalized" by the gynecological-industrial complex and that hospitals were "death traps" and "full of sickness" and that if you wanted your baby to be healthy, you had better have it in a chicken house.

"You're not sick," one angry mother said. "So why would you go to a hospital to have your baby?"

My thought was, Because that's where they keep the towels?

They told us that hospitals didn't offer the kind of "peace" or "tranquility" or "sitar music" required to give birth in a more happy, natural way, explaining that we needed to find ourselves a "doula," which I assumed was some sort of tropical fruit that would bring good fortune, but was actually a kind of nurse without all the baggage of medical training.

"You surely have a birth plan?" they asked. This, they said, was a memorandum to the physician, a sort of Declaration of the Rights of the Mother. "It's a letter where you tell them what you want and what you don't want, and they have to agree to it," they said. "Whether they like it or not."

"Some of these mothers seem very angry," I said to my wife, later.

"We need a plan," she said.

"God has a plan," I said. "That's what your aunt said."

"What about the episiotomy?" she said. "What about Pitocin and the placenta?"

What I wanted to say was that "Pitocin and the Placenta" sounded like the name of a band I saw in college, and I didn't like them at all.

Up until then, everything I knew about childbirth was learned largely from television, which taught me that when a pregnant woman is in labor, she moans in a humorous way, usually while at a restaurant, perhaps while eating a salad, which is followed by a great deal of funny breathing—there's a special guild for screenwriters who write nothing but funny woman-in-labor-breathing scenes—and then the baby comes out and then there's a commercial. Giving birth, I learned, was fundamentally no different than having diarrhea.

In the sixth grade, they'd taken all the girls into a classroom and showed them a film about their changing bodies, while they corralled us boys into an adjacent classroom and made us do homework. We knew, vaguely, the subject of this secret film. We were envious, because this film would likely contain images of female breasts, as elusive and desirable as a pair of rare African birds. Surely there was a male version of this sex movie, one that might tell us precisely at what age our penises would grow to enormous size?

"Do your homework," the teacher said.

The real homework was in the other room.

Write this down," my wife said. She was my teacher now.

I never really expected to find myself typing a sentence like, "I would prefer to keep the number of vaginal exams to a minimum." It was very upsetting. How many times was too many? "And I definitely want perineal massage," she said. "Put that."

"What's that for?" I said.

"The perineum."

"And what is the perineum, exactly, and why do you need it massaged?"

"It doesn't matter why."

"You know, this thing is at least half my baby."

It wasn't my fault I didn't have a uterus. If I could help

make the baby, I would. I would make the hell out of that baby. But Nature denied me that. Nature said I got to watch, in horror, helpless, while somebody massaged my wife's vagina. Because, as she explained, sometimes the vagina is too small for the baby.

"Sometimes they have to cut it," she said.

"They *cut* it?" I said. "They cut your hole?"

I understood, finally, why they hadn't invited the boys to watch that film.

We finished our Birth Plan. It had many great lines, such as, "I want to be able to squat during labor" and "I want the baby to be put on me immediately after delivery." Where else would our doctor put the baby, a Presto FryDaddy?

And what about this line: "I am aware that many pain medications exist, and I'll ask for them if I need them." What would the nice physician think of this one? It would be like pulling one's attorney aside and explaining, in a whisper, "I am aware of laws."

We drove to the doctor's office in Vicksburg, thirty miles north, a drive that never didn't make me think about General Grant. He, too, had marched from Port Gibson to this town, and here we were, with our own tactical plan, which I handed to the doctor and smiled.

He read it over, courteous, nodding, thanking us for being insane.

"The main thing is, we don't want to know the sex of the baby," I said, trying to sound as uncrazy as possible. His nurse did not like it.

"Come on, Dad!" she said. "Don't you want to know?"

I looked at my wife.

"We are aware of science," I said.

The sun rose and fell, and people kept lying to us, telling my wife how luminescent she was, because she was now the size of a small moon.

"You did this to me," she said.

She resented those mothers who stayed thin by eating nothing but hay. According to my wife, the best way to deal with those mothers was to hate them and assume their fetuses also hated them.

"That baby's hungry," she would say, and then feed our unseen baby a dish of banana pudding.

Soon enough, our doula arrived, a sweet woman with many children and cattle of her own, and they hit it off, speaking of terrible things as calmly as the weather.

"When should I expect my bloody show?" my wife asked her.

What in the hell were these people talking about? It was like my asking a neighbor, "When should I expect to have my heart ripped out by a robot?"

Women suffer, I knew that. They grow. They hurt. They look in the mirror and see a thing that looks like a mother. But men. We look in the mirror and cannot see anything, because our wives are in the way, and they are so big.

I waited for a moment of blinding enlightenment when I would feel like a father who had fathered something. At baby showers, I stared into the eyes of fathers when they were looking away. Were they different from me? Yes, but how? Pop came to a shower, and I looked at him, deep into the dark place behind his eyes, but found no comfort there, no lessons.

It's time," my wife said.

She had begun to make noises, like something you might hear at the Dixie National Livestock Show.

"Are you okay?" I said, and she threw a trivet at me.

We went to bed. It didn't feel right, lying down next to a creature making those sorts of sounds, but I wanted to be there for her, although it felt safer to be outside for her, perhaps behind a blast wall.

Around 11 p.m., she began to thrash.

"It's time," she said again.

"You said that already."

"Get out."

I went to the futon, or as I liked to call it, the Iron Taco. I lay down, said a prayer for my wife, and looked forward to having scoliosis in the morning. At 1 a.m., she woke me.

"I'm in labor."

"Again?"

The plan had been to do all the laboring at home, so as to give my wife the greatest chance at bleeding to death in her own living room. But my wife needed sleep and was getting panicky, parts of baby protruding from her body at upsetting angles. At 2 p.m., twenty hours after my wife had first announced that her labor had begun, and both fifteen and fourteen hours after she'd also said it had begun, she said that, finally, at last it had begun.

She was trembling. I'd seen that look before, the last time she'd been forced to drive over the Lake Pontchartrain Causeway.

"I want to go to the hospital," she said.

I reminded her about the medicines they would try to give her. I didn't really care. I was merely being argumentative, which I felt was my role.

Then she started moaning louder, louder, building, bracing herself on the frame of the door, the whole world contracting, ripe with fleshy bounty.

"What do I do?" I said.

"DON'T LET ME DIE," she said.

My poor wife was about to give birth to our child on the front porch, like some kind of animal and several of my second cousins, and I still didn't feel like a father.

Let's have this baby!" a nurse said, and then abandoned us.

"Where'd everybody go?"

That's another lie they tell you, that when you're ready to have a baby you go to a hospital. You don't. The place where you go is more like an expensive and very cold motel where strange people come in, make vaguely dark pronouncements about your wife's cervix, and then charge you five hundred dollars for a commemorative bedpan.

Natural childbirth, I noted, made my wife appear very unnatural. Like she was—what was the word?—ah, yes: dying. Somewhere in the epic of her suffering, she had taken on the noble aspect of a dying ruler, fading, fading, staring down ghosts, a flash of recognition, a pitiable sadness, a very real loneliness, locked as she was in the private chamber of a pain only she could understand, a pain other mothers knew, closed off forever to a world of men who were not competitive eaters.

Hospital staff came in and stared, whole gangs of nurses.

"Don't see much natural these days, seems like," one said.

I found this hard to believe. This was Mississippi, where just two or three decades ago, everybody had been giving birth in cotton gins.

"I bet she'll cave," another whispered, on her way out.

Late into the evening, I found Pop, sitting alone.

"Hey, boy," he said.

We sat there for a while, quiet. I thought this might be a

good time for him to provide some counsel about how to be a father, or even to feel like one.

"Were you in the room when I was born?"

"Shit no."

Pop came from an older generation of men who believed delivery rooms were dangerous places, full of cats and evil spirits. I felt a little sorry for him, and jealous, for I knew I would have to be in there and would have to see the spirits.

"What do you remember about the day I was born?"

"Lemme think," he said. Here it comes, I thought. He was about to drop some serious wisdom. "I reckon we was about to go see a movie and your momma was frying some pork chops and she come to hollering and there you was."

It was a touching story.

Mom came staggering up from a darkened corridor.

"You done had a cigarette," Pop said. "I can smell it."

"Kiss my butt," she said.

"It'd be a lot to kiss," Pop said.

These were my role models.

"I don't even know how to hold a baby," I offered. I'd held only one or two babies in my life and found the experience upsetting.

"Your father knows how to hold a baby," Mom said, patting him on the arm. He was a known Baby Whisperer.

"Shoot, babies like me," Pop said.

Was it in my bones to do what he did, and to like it?

He stood up. He could only take so much emotion before he became gassy.

"You're not staying for the birth?" Mom said.

"Did you know I was a boy?" I said to him, desperate to learn anything.

You could see the fire in his eyes, this unquenchable desire to place firearms in the hands of small boys and watch them maim things. He needed a grandson. He smiled. He left. We sat there, Mom and me, and my wife lay there, somewhere down the hall, and distant cannonade could be heard in this or that room, and the siege continued, forever, into the dark maw of the Mississippi night.

My wife was hyperventilating. I looked at the clock. It was midnight. She had been awake for forty-six hours. The doula was there, with her pillows and massage oils and a large yellow fitness orb in case my wife wanted to work on her abs. Hours passed. Devices beeped. Nursing shifts changed. Sanity departed.

"WHAT ARE YOU DOING I HATE THE BEEPING WHERE IS MY ICE?" she yelled.

She had turned against the doula, too, who at around 2 a.m. of the second night had attempted to nap behind a potted plant in the corner.

"ALL OF YOU PEOPLE ARE ASLEEP AND I AM DYING!" she said.

"I love you," I said.

"I DON'T CARE I HATE YOU GET ME MY BALL."

I picked up her Golden Orb of Suffering, and the doula and I lowered her onto this object, which, it was explained, would relieve pressure on her cervix. She ripped off whatever wires and tubes they'd put on her, various alarms rang out, and she squatted on the orb. I stood in front of her, holding and rubbing her arms, and she buried her face in my chest, in what I thought was a pathetically loving sort of way, and she seemed to be weeping.

This is love, I thought. This is family.

When she started biting my nipple, I wanted to scream out, but knew that this was my role now, to give my wife something to latch on to like a fruit bat. Perhaps that's what being a father was?

The contraction passed, she unlatched, looked up at me, a suspension bridge of spittle connecting her mouth to my shirt.

"Don't let them give me anything," she said.

There were medicines in every darkened nook of this facility, drugs that could induce hallucinations, deaden whole regions of the body, heal the nipple.

I got her back to the bed.

All through the dimness of the room she wrestled with the demons of her suffering, her past, the memory of her mother, who was never not present, rendered almost material by the wailing, the shelling of the city of her body by nature's best artillery, and just when it was darkest and bleakest, when the hours had grown too many to count, when all sanity and reason had been bled from the room, she sat up in bed, suffused with light.

"She's pushing!" the doula said.

"Put this on!"

Somebody threw me a freeze-dried parcel of blue napkins. What were these? Ah, the scrubs! It was happening! I was so excited to wear the scrubs, so energized by the sudden burst of activity that I removed all of my clothes, and I now wore nothing but the blue napkins, which did not seem to offer sufficient protection from the lights that had dropped from the ceiling, which were burning my skin, or protection from my wife, who clearly was trying to eat me, and I found myself at her right hand, in the Universal Place Where Fathers Stand When Babies Come Out of Their Wives, and there was screaming, and barking, and yelling, and pushing, and more screaming, and I found myself screaming, too, just like I'd done in that barn so long ago, and the lights burned and then.

And then.

And then.

Nothing.

Our doctor was looking down, something was wrong. And so I looked. And what I saw was a shock. The place where the penis was supposed to be was no penis.

Our son had been born without a penis.

They said nothing. They were waiting for me to say it. To declare it.

"It's a girl," I said.

It had been three days. I looked down, expecting my beautiful wife to smile and cry and talk to the baby, but her eyes stayed closed. She had other business, deep inside. She was talking to her mother.

Watch her neck," my wife said from her wheelchair, the day we left the hospital, as I tried to put the baby, who looked more like an undercooked pastry, into her car seat, a seat that had seemed so small before but now seemed designed for an adolescent narwhal. Many people had come to see the baby in the hospital, including Bird and his wife, who lived just over the river, not far at all.

"You got to keep that baby clean," Bird said. "You got to change its diapers."

"We had planned on letting it stay dirty," I said, "but maybe you're right."

It was like a novelty baby, a joke baby. We took her out to the car, and I got the straps around what I guessed were its arms and legs, although it was possible she was upside down.

Why had so many people lied about how hard it would be, making it, growing it, pushing it out into the atmosphere?

"The birth of a child is a beautiful thing," they say, as though it's a rainbow, or a sunset, and I guess that's true, especially if you are looking at a rainbow, during a sunset, while someone sprays you with amniotic fluid.

I wanted other young idiot fathers to know that these things happen, that it's a Greek drama, that the place where the baby comes out might actually tear, as it did on my wife. It tore. *Tore.* We had to pay a man to sew it back. He went to school to learn how to do it. *School.* What did you study in school? I studied paragraphs.

The doula, nurses, doctors, I bow to them, low and full. They work at the gates of hell. They work until the walls of the city fall.

That first night alone, I tried holding the baby, not ceremonially, but actually, the way Pop had done with me, rocking, while my wife slept long and hard. I tried talking to this new person, which felt strange, but became easier, the more wine I drank.

It cried, and I tried to stop it, but could not. I was no Baby Whisperer. Not yet.

Fatherhood had not fallen on me like a Damascus light. It would be long and slow in coming, with furious bursts, like labor, but it would happen.

"Hush, little baby," I said, and she did not hush.

There can be only one baby of the family, and I'd just handed the torch to this one, and she'd pass it to others, too, in time. There was still much I didn't know, such as how many holes were actually on the female body. Too many, it seemed. They're a mystery, these women, and their numbers in my house had just doubled, and so had the mystery, and the light.

CHAPTER 16

·

The Horror, the Horror

—❦ ✦ ✦ ❧—

So, we had a baby.

In many ways, it felt like having malaria. Meaning, you don't think much about either babies or malaria until they happen to you. I knew that having a family was, prima facie, good, like peace treaties between warring tribes on distant continents were good or innovations in trash-bag durability were good.

My spouse was different. She had a gift. Her knowledge of babies and how they work was vast and frightening, even before she made one of her own. She preferred babies to college. Babies were her college, she their professor. Women with broken babies would bring them to her to fix, asking her questions about how to make them sleep or eat or generally behave in a way as to not be filled with devils or vomit locusts, and she answered these questions with alacrity and compassion.

"Are your nipples cracked yet?" she'd say, on the phone. And then she'd say, "Oh, you're just engorged," as if being engorged, which sounded like an adjective that happens to you maybe right before your brain explodes, was no big deal. "It's probably just mastitis in your milk ducts."

"How do you know all this?" I asked, while she rolled

her eyes and walked away. She was an expert, and I could not fathom the abyss of her baby knowledge. For my thoughts were not her thoughts, neither were her ways my ways.

When we got a child of our own, I was excited that my wife could finally experiment on her own baby. I was proud, how she powered through an epic birth like some kind of Icelandic sea monster in the World's Strongest Pregnant Sea Monster competition. She had earned the right to do whatever she wanted with our baby. Which was how I wanted it. In that first year, I mostly just shadowed my wife, following her lead, doing whatever she did after I watched her do it, which was a great way to make sure she did everything.

I had some role in this drama, I knew, though it was unclear what. I would have to learn. And one thing I learned is, when you have babies, people will ask you about them.

"How's the baby?" they would say, during that first year.

"Fine," I would say, lying.

I had become one of the lying liars of the world.

Because sometimes, it's not fine. Sometimes, it's like riding a Greyhound bus across the country with tiny people from the state hospital who have the same last name as you and are very likable but also want to bite you and pee on your suitcase. And you can't get off the bus until it stops, eighteen to twenty years from now. But you can't say that. You have to keep lying. Because you have to keep making babies, so society's adults can have something to take pictures of besides the ocean.

Sometimes, my childless friends would want to know.

"I mean, what's it like, anyway?" they'd ask, with a cadaverous smile, the way you ask somebody what it's like to date a girl with no ears. It was a sick question, designed to make themselves feel better about their life choices. "Do you *like* it?" they asked. "Is it *fun*?"

Ours may be one of the first generations in the history of human breeding to ask such a silly question. I could think of a hundred good reasons to make a baby, but *liking* it was not one. I didn't like having children any more than I liked having cartilage. A blessing? Sure. But so is cartilage. One helps me ride my bicycle, the other one poops on my floor. Is that what they wanted to hear?

We started potty training our first daughter when she was still a year old. I cannot explain why we started so young; my wife led me to believe that our child's learning to use a toilet before age two would be something along the lines of memorizing the periodic table or the Chinese alphabet. It would be a real accomplishment, she said, and she wanted to try. She was an ambitious young mother.

"But she seems so young," I said.

"She's very advanced," my wife said, remarking on the child's other talents, which were largely focused on distinguishing between the sounds of ducks and nonducks.

"What does the duck say?" I'd ask.

"Quack-quack!" she'd say.

"What does the sheep say?" I'd ask.

"Quack-quack!" she'd say.

"She's so smart," people would say, as a courtesy.

Some friends said go for it. Force the toilet issue. Incentivize it. These friends came from the school of parenting who strongly inveigh against the commodification of youth and believe that any capitulation to the needs of the young will end Western civilization and reduce our nation to something resembling an early Charlton Heston film. Others told us to let the child decide when she wants to use the toilet.

"Just let it happen," they said, which seemed the very opposite of what you want to do with feces.

The most normal friends suggested we buy a small, colorful, cartoonish children's potty. "The ones with the pictures of princesses on them," they said.

"Ariel!" our daughter said, when we brought the pink bedpan home.

"Yes!" I said. "Now you can poop on her!"

I laughed about this, but not my wife. No. She would not laugh for many years. Because she knew that potty training was going to be an endless campaign against the inevitability of the rectum and the deep Freudian fears of the young, a war fought with love, and prayer, and sullied brown hands, and Skittles, which my wife poured into a mason jar.

"What are those for?" I said.

"One Skittle for teetee and two for a stinky," she said.

I explained to my wife that I would join PETA before allowing the word *stinky* to occupy my brain's language centers.

"Stinky!" our daughter said, holding her nose. At twenty months, she was roughly the size of garden gnome, with a Magellanic Cloud of curly brown hair spiraling out from her head in every available direction, which made her look not unlike a walking toilet brush.

"Stinky! That's right!" my wife said, handing her a Skittle.

The training started on a Monday and consisted of these ten simple steps:

1.   Remove diaper from child.
2.   Walk child to toilet.
3.   Point to toilet. Smile.
4.   Point to child. Smile.
5.   Point to floor. Frown.

6. Point to the places on child where the urine and the feces come from.
7. Say, "Woo woo."
8. Make the child repeat, "Woo woo."
9. Point to toilet again. Smile. Show teeth. Seem crazy.
10. Wait.

I received calls and updates throughout day one. The first came in at 11 a.m., when my wife reported that the child had urinated in every room of the house and was now hiding underneath one of the beds. She'd been wearing, for the first time ever, what are called "big-girl panties," which is, I believe, the technical term for "underwear soaked in urine."

By the end of day two, most of the house was covered in sheets, towels, and other textiles in various yellows and browns. But it worked. I came home and—wonder of wonders!—heard the sound of tinkling. It was the child, on the adult toilet, in the act of voluntary micturition. Day two! It was such a glorious moment, everybody had a Skittle.

That night, I dreamt that every poop that had ever been pooped in the world was represented by its very own Skittle, and the jar reached up to heaven. It was big and wide and pretty, a jar of joy. My wife had done it. No wonder all those moms had called her, and still did. She was some kind of baby wizard.

"What about number two?" I asked the next morning.

"Oh, that'll happen soon," she said.

And she said it with such confidence, such hope.

Over the next few months, what happened was, the child pooped in all the closets. She pooped in her room, our room, the guest room, the living room, but not the bathroom. She did all her urinating during the day, in the toilet, Curious George panties pushed carelessly around her dangling ankles; but her poo, like the nine-banded armadillo and certain species of wombat, was nocturnal. Only when her rectum was cocooned in the palliative barrier of absorbent garments would her gastrointestinal tract release its malodorous bounty.

She would find a dark place somewhere in the house. We would hear her talking through walls and could often smell her pooping through them.

"Who's she talking to?" my wife said.

"The dark lord she serves," I said.

She would poo and then just keep talking, possibly to the poo, because she loved it and was not ready to say goodbye. Sometimes, she loved it so much that she wanted to keep it inside her, compelling my wife to feed the child various accelerants designed to loosen the bowels. Every morning and night, the woman stood in the kitchen and mixed liquids and powders like a medieval apothecary, shaking and stirring and going mad. She poured these tonics into our child, whose bottom opened like the Grand Coulee Dam. Around suppertime, the baby would begin to hold herself in unusual ways, grasping the front of her crotch with one hand and the back of it with the other, apparently trying to lift her entire body off the ground and throw herself out the window.

"LET'S GO POTTY!" my harried wife would say a bit too loudly, smiling a bit too brightly, the way crazy people do.

"No," the child would say. "No! No! No! NOOO!"

It was not an angry kind of NO. It was the kind of NO you hear when you ask someone if they want to throw themselves from the top of El Capitan. My wife fetched her tools, most notably an enema the size of a large handgun, while I chased the child, picked her up, carried her to the toilet.

"NOOO!" the baby said.

"Listen, we don't want to *throw* you in the toilet," I said. "Unless it will help you poop."

"Stop scaring her!" my wife said.

Please note that I was not the one holding a turkey baster full of nitroglycerin.

My parents had taught me so many things. My mother taught me to read and write and paint, and to love the act of learning, and my father taught me to skin a buck deer and even nonbuck deer and even nondeer deer, and also how to run a trotline, as well as how to run dogs and bases and people off your property with axes and mauls. Those had been relatively complicated things to learn, involving much nuance and tenacity, and yet I had learned them. How could we not teach our child this most basic task?

I wanted to help, or at least sufficiently get in my wife's way in a way that angered her. But she wouldn't let me, her logic being that the woman who'd pushed the baby out could teach the baby to push other things out, and so she held the child over the toilet and the child wailed and looked down into the hole for baby alligators.

"Go away," my wife would say, through the closed door.

Then the door would fly open and the incontinent child would escape and run around the house frantically, looking under things, as though she had lost a precious jewel or her mind. It seems so natural: you eat, you form waste, your body and gravity have a meeting, come up with a simple plan: a location, perhaps some light reading material, and a candle for illumination and mood. Nature runs the meeting. You are merely attending, participating. After all, your attendance is required. You could call in sick, and the meeting would be rescheduled. You cannot get out of the meeting.

"We really need to have this meeting," Nature says.

"I'll be here all day," Gravity says.

"She can't keep putting this off," Nature says.

And that was the problem. The child became so distressed at the sight of the toilet bowl that she lost the ability to go *anywhere*: the toilet, her Pull-Up, the closet. She kept rescheduling the meeting, until it was no longer going to just be a meeting. Human resources would have to be there. Security would be called.

To prepare for this explosive day, my wife became an ethnographer of the body's lower functions, studying the child, making field notes.

"She's got to go," she would say, marking the calendar.

"How can you tell?"

The child would be walking very slowly and sort of leaning back, the way some people approach limbo poles or hurricanes.

"It's been five days since she went."

"The toilet will not eat you," my wife said to the child.

"But if you don't give it your stinky," I said, "it will come into your room at night and take it from your bottom with a fork."

The child cried, ran away.

I didn't understand. She was three now, could read chapter books and run effectively from cats and recite creeds dating to the late Roman era.

Sometimes, if we were lucky, nature blindsided the child with a surprise emergency meeting that she could not postpone. We'd be in the front yard playing, and she would grow quiet and sidle under one of the tall camellias by the front porch and squat down and do it right there like a war vet.

"What are you doing?" I asked.

"A stinky," she said. "In the garden."

The neighbors stared from their porch, concerned.

"She's very advanced!" I yelled, a bit too loudly.

How did you potty train me?" I asked my parents on the speakerphone, while my wife and child wrestled just beyond earshot.

"Actually, I never did," Mom said.

"You done it yourself," Pop said. "You was smart like that."

"THAT'S NOT TRUE," my wife said from the toilet. "THEY'RE LYING."

Were they? I followed the odor of memory, and it sent me back to 1978, a time for *Grease* and inflation and a new trend known as airplane hijacking. There was a party at our house, I remember. We had guests. The Bee Gees were there, on the stereo, wafting through the air, wanting to know how deep our love was. Also wafting through the air: an odor. The Brothers Gibb sang about feeling something and not wanting that feeling to go. I was only three and didn't understand who the Bee Gees were singing this to, but found that it was a fine expression of the love I felt for my feces, because I did not want them to go, either.

"And it's me you need to show," they sang. "How deep is your love?"

To whom were they singing this song? Even at the age of three, I felt confident that they were not singing to their feces, as one should probably not address one's own excrement in any form, except to flush it, which was a problem, because while the song had distracted me, my feces had decided to make an illegal border crossing.

Something bad had happened. I locked the door. I was not sure what I could do, there in my room, with a locked door. My only real option was to bury myself in the toy box and hope that my family moved to a new house. Mom knocked.

"What are you doing in there?" she said, rattling the knob.

"I'm in here, pooping on myself," was not an option. So

I did what anybody does when a frantic person is trying to knock down a locked door while you're emptying your bowels: I climbed out the window.

Throughout the house and pouring out the windows, I could hear the Bee Gees asking again, how deep was our love? They really wanted to know, they said. They were living in a world of fools, they said. Breaking them down, they said.

I hit the hot grass and looked both ways. Should I run away? Should I dig a hole to China, as I'd heard was possible? Should I dig a hole for my stool, which jangled in my shorts like a smuggled gem?

I knew what to do. I would check the mail.

"What have you done?" they'd say.

"Look!" I could say. "The new Sears catalog!"

After walking in the midsummer heat, I knew it was going to take more than toilet paper to clean me. It might take a garden hose, perhaps some sort of heated cauldron, perhaps all three of the Brothers Gibb working in harmony. I walked back into the house, past our guests, down the hall. I wrapped my brown underwear in the mail and knew to place them somewhere innocuous, such as behind the television. Nobody would suspect a thing. They would just think Mom was making her goulash.

It was all coming back to me now, how hard it had been to know what to do with my own bowels. My parents were clearly approaching senility. You have to, I guess. You have to forget about how hard everything was, such as the pooping, which I was already wanting to forget. Otherwise, you hate your children forever, and I did not want to hate my children forever, and I am sure my wife didn't, either.

What we needed were not Skittles and enemas. What we needed was patience.

"Patience," I said to my wife.

"Patience?" she said. "Patience?"

"Yes."

"Do you know where she pooped this morning?"

"No."

"The floor."

"The floor?"

"The mothereffing floor."

How deep, I wanted to know, was our love?

The child was sending us a message. The message was: "Cleanup on aisle two."

Let me tell you something. Poop smells bad wherever it is, but when it's just lying there on the floor like a dead squirrel it does a whole other thing to your nose. It gets into your brain, makes you want to hurt people. It infected my wife's brain, made her crazy. She'd get this wild look in her eye, surrounded by various anal creams and ointments, suppositories and laxatives, fibrous hardeners and softeners, rubber gloves and trash bags and spray bottles of antibacterial cleansers and bleach and gasoline, towels, buckets, mops, masks, anger.

"Are you okay?" I would ask.

"Do you smell something?" she would say. " I smell something."

"I think it's you," I would say. "You haven't showered in three days."

"I'm waiting for her stinky. I know it's coming."

She would be looking out the window, up into the sky, as though it were coming by air. When it finally did drop, I would offer to clean it up, but the wife refused, entering the bedroom with her gear and closing the door and alternately retching, gagging, cursing her offspring, gagging, cursing her own gag reflex, and then retching some more.

"Breathe through your mouth," I said, from the safety of the hallway. "Let me know if you need some help." I explained that I would be at the airport, leaving the country.

If the floor was unavailable, the child would poop in the bathtub. The wife would scream. The child would scream. I would run into the kitchen and return with a weapon.

"What's that?" she said.

"A slotted spoon," I said. "It's perfect."

"But what about English peas?" she said.

"I hate English peas."

And so I would use the slotted serving spoon to fish out the intruder, while my wife disinfected the tub with the diligence of a serial murderer, scrubbing and boiling bath toys with a dangerous fire in her eyes. She wanted to boil everything: the toys, the house, our daughter.

"You would make a great murderer," I said.

Sometimes, my wife was not a murderer, but a midwife.

I would get calls at work.

"It's been a week. A *week*," my wife said.

In the background, I could hear the child, alternately laughing at Bugs Bunny and then screaming in horror at her impacted bowels.

"Ha ha, Mommy! Look at Daffy Duck!" she said. And then: "Ahhhh! Help! Ahhhh!"

"Is someone sawing her legs off?" I asked.

"It's been like this all day," she said.

The kid's dung had hardened into the density of an adobe brick, and she would lie on the floor, in my wife's arms, as though in labor, pushing, pushing, screaming, sweating, the baby turd beginning to crown, and then pouring forth into the world, a little Baby Turd Jesus.

Sometimes, it would be big. Very big.

"How does that even fit inside her?" I said.

"That's at least a foot long," my wife said.

I had seen adult ferrets smaller than that.

"We should name it," I said.

"We should take a picture of it."

She got out her camera. We put a dollar bill beside it, for scale. So future generations would know. So we would never forget what happened here.

Seasons passed, more babies were born. There were now two little girls. And then three. It was crazy how they just kept on coming, but I guess there was just so much screaming and crying and disinfecting going on, it's quite possible my wife and I had sex without even knowing it. Soon all three were giving birth to adult ferrets in and around our house and their clothing. We stopped caring. We had to. In time, my wife voluntarily disarmed, reducing her arsenal to one product: the Fleet Pedia-Lax Liquid Glycerin Suppository with Child Rectal Applicator. If it sounds like a machine designed to destroy families, it is.

My wife called it Special Cream, while I simply called it what it was: the Ass Grenade. If ever you have been walking by our house and heard what sounds like the interrogation of terrorist detainees by rogue federal agents, fear not. There were no terrorists here. It was only my wife, sitting on top of one of my naked children on the floor of the bathroom, injecting a medicinal payload into its tailpipe and lying about how it won't hurt a bit.

"You should work for the government," I said. "Any government."

The Fleet box featured a happy penguin, with great big distended penguin eyeballs, as though he had just sat upon his own rectal applicator. In the right light, the penguin looked upset, possibly wrathful. My children knew and learned to fear this penguin, and very likely all other flightless birds.

And then one day, it just happened. Just like that.

The oldest one, she did it. No screaming. No crying.

I had stolen a quiet moment away from my family in the bathtub, which was the only place in our small house where one could read a book without being molested with questions about tornadoes or sharks, and the child, now five years old, really more of a kid, entered.

"Hi, Dad," she said.

"Hello," I said.

She closed the shower curtain between us. I continued to read. I was in the middle of *Heart of Darkness*, reading of the savage horror of it all. I heard the kid mount the toilet, and then a gentle grunt, then something more painful, a horse passing a kidney stone.

"Wow," I said, trying not to breathe from behind the veil. "You did it."

"Don't talk to me," she said.

"Thank you for doing it so closely to my face."

"Mom!" she said, sounding far too old. "Come wipe me."

My wife entered, wiped. I lay down quietly behind the screen, Conrad's young Marlow on the strange waters of a new land. The kid left. I pulled back the curtain.

I loved that woman. She was a beast of a mother, fearless. Our family's own Kurtz.

"Hi," I said to my wife.

"I'd love to have just one day," my wife said. "Just one day where I didn't get someone else's shit on my hands."

"I like it when you cuss."

"Shit," she said.

"Let it out," I said.

"Shit," she said.

"Actually," I said, "in this house, we call it *stinky*."

Nobody tells you this about marriage. That you will love your wife, and she will love you back, and you will journey together on the Greyhound of your shared life to the ends of dark continents only you can know, and your love will bring life into the world, a new person, buses full of people who share your name and imperfections and who will love you, and hug you, and shit on your floor, and in your garden, and in the same bathtub where you choose to read the works of Joseph Conrad, because it's the only bathroom in the house, and you're all in it together, the bathroom, the bus, the cruising yawl of Nellie up the Congo or whatever this thing is supposed to be, this life, and all you have at the end of it is a question:

How deep is your love? I really need to learn, because we're living in a world of fools, breaking us down, when they all should let us be.

CHAPTER 17

"Somebody Stole My Baby! A Reader's Digest True-Life Story"

—≼ ✦ ✦ ≽—

Throughout my life, I've always known that if either of my parents was mentally ill, it was my father, although, to be fair, my mother had her own psychiatric health concerns. She was nervy, fretful about spectral dangers others could not see, dwelling alone inside a magical realm where children's clothing was designed to burst into flames and gangs of electrified toasters roved the countryside, seeking to jump into bathtubs full of her loved ones.

People like to think that we live in anxious times, what with all the concern over apocalyptic peanut jihads and whatnot, but the 1970s and '80s had their own unique fears, such as nuclear meltdowns and the teeth of Jimmy Carter. One of the big fads back then was child abduction. Everybody was doing it. This was before you could dial 911, when if something bad happened, your only options were dialing the operator or going outside to scream while being murdered with a lawn dart.

We humored her, allowed her to search our Halloween candy.

"I have to check your chocolate," she would say.

"For why?"

"For straight pins and razors."

The world wanted to hurt her children. She knew it, could smell it, could taste it in our candy, which she ate.

When Bird was five or six, back when we were still living in Memphis, he was kidnapped.

"He went to the bus stop one morning, like he always did, to wait for the school bus," Mom says when she tells this story. "It was right down the street. I remember looking out the window and seeing him there, the sweet little towheaded thing, so small, all by himself."

A few minutes later, she looked out again and he was gone.

She ran outside, panicked. Others came out of their homes.

"Have you seen my baby?" she said. "My baby!"

Soon, she'd marshaled the whole neighborhood, mothers in house shoes carrying confused infants, milk bottles dropped, family pets running wildly through the streets to locate her firstborn. She called the police, lost it, fell to the earth, an exposed nerve on the lawn, wailing. Her child could not be found. He would never be seen again.

"We found your boy," an officer said, later that day, grave. They told her the bad news. He had been found. At school.

How did he get to school, you might be wondering.

The bus.

Which is what happens when you take your son to the bus stop to go to school.

Mom tells this story so we will understand why she worries, but to us it was just a story about how she was no saner than our father.

In the eighties, when the prevailing wisdom was that American cities were full of gangs, drugs, homeless people who raped joggers, joggers who raped the homeless, and Satanists who sat around sacrificing children and playing Dungeons & Dragons, the narrative of many a film was "moving out to the country" to get away from all the danger. But we knew what the movies did not: that the country was much worse. We had no Satanists, but we did have tractors and hay balers, which I am pretty sure killed more children during that same period than Satan ever could.

Drownings, snakebites, sharpened hatchets, antler impalings, alligators, hunting accidents, runaway pulpwood trucks barreling down gravel roads: Every week, we had a new disfiguring injury to report. A friend whose face had been melted off by an exploding backhoe battery; a boy whose hand had been blown away while cleaning his gun; another one who'd been accidentally shot in the stomach by his brother; a family duck dog killed by a nest of moccasins, the slick wet chocolate scales coming up from the holes in creation to feast on us all.

We got bored, we did things. We climbed on top of our houses and jumped into trees. We built boats from buckets and tried to cross uncrossable rivers.

Shouldn't they wear helmets?" Mom asked Pop, when he bought us our three-wheelers with money he didn't have, so that we'd have a new way to die.

"Helmets?" he said. As we all knew, the only self-respecting men who wore helmets while operating motor vehicles were in outer space.

"They could be concussed," Mom said.

"Hell, they done been concussed."

This was back when all-terrain vehicles could only have three wheels, because of the Wheel Embargo. These were basically giant, high-powered tricycles designed for hunters, so that you could go deep into the woods, far away from medical assistance. That's why we loved three-wheelers so much, because they could take you really far from hospitals, and far from the phones that would be necessary to call the hospitals to come get you, in case you were dying, because of the three-wheelers.

"Slow down!" the poor woman would yell from the back porch, while we motored off toward the veil of woods beyond.

"We can't hear you!" we would yell back.

It felt great, knowing that we were enriching Mom's prayer life so deeply.

I can remember riding in the back of a pickup truck down I-20 during the middle of December, something Mom made Pop promise he wouldn't do, and which he let us do anyway, the winter wind as brutal as clutching the wing of an airplane at forty thousand feet. I tucked myself between the wheel well and the cab and watched the sharp cold sky while my eyes followed the fractals of flocking blackbirds all the way down the highway.

It was dangerous, sure, and for that reason, special.

I will remember this, I remember thinking, and look: I did.

And what I also remember is that a thing was only worth doing if it frightened a woman who loved you—that, if it didn't, you weren't doing it right. It's how we knew we were becoming men.

"Watch out for falling icicles," she'd say.

"Shit, woman," was Pop's stock rebuttal. He'd laugh, we'd laugh, and she'd clutch her Bible. Didn't she know what joy we got out of running off to places where we might get killed? Did she know nothing of men?

It wasn't just our fault. Mom put herself through much of the agony she endured, mostly by reading a provocative magazine banned in many countries for its subversive messages.

It was called *Reader's Digest*, a title that never didn't make me think of the intestines.

What a great magazine, perfectly suited for mothers and grandmothers, with its light humor, word games, medical news, and stories about schoolchildren being mauled by bears.

"Watch out for live wires!" she said to us one morning, before we went fishing on the Pearl, a river not usually known for electrification.

I recalled a similar story in one of her recent issues of the *Digest*, a tale about a swimming pool that had somehow been filled with murderous levels of voltage or piranhas or lava, it was unclear. She bookmarked these stories, so that later, before bedtime, she could make her prayers as specific as possible. Only the Lord could keep her sons from ending up in one of that magazine's true-life stories, eaten by giant catfish at the bottom of a spillway or carried off by muscular fruit bats.

And then one day it actually happened.

It was a cold February day when Bird and I walked into those woods with our fishing poles. It was too cold to fish, but we went anyway, exploring new thickets and copses, hopping fences we hadn't permission to hop. We had asked if we could go, and Pop had said no, since that particular farmer who owned that particular land where a particular pond was to be found was a very particular kind of jackass and didn't want happy children on his property, and I don't know what came over us, but we went anyway, and we stayed gone for hours, tramping over hill and dale, giddy with discovery, not like Lewis and Clark, but more like a pair of dogs that had broken the leash and could not handle their freedom.

We wore ourselves out in our muddy peregrinations, became red-cheeked and filled with that electric joy that one finds from great physical exertions in cold weather, and marched home across the pasture proud and tired but in high spirits like Don Pedro and Benedick arriving at Messina, home from war, while Mom ran through the pasture toward us.

"Hey, Mom!" we said, smiling.

She had already mustered search parties, called the authorities. Every man and boy in our community with boots had formed a dragnet across the countryside, searching for our bodies, our abductors. It didn't matter that both of us had knives big enough to have gotten us out of Cambodia alive. She wasn't having it.

She ordered Pop to beat us severely, and because he was as good a husband as he was a father, he did. He beat the living Hades out of us, he beat us because he saw how scared his wife had gotten, but his heart wasn't in it. He knew what she did not: We were just being like we'd always been taught to be. Reckless, wild, perfectly wild.

If there was anything I learned out in the country, it was that the things that can kill you can make you alive, and that you are never more alive than when you are getting beaten by your father because your mother thought you were dead.

And while to the casual observer I may not have turned out much like my father, I came to see in the first years of my marriage that I have proudly carried on this tradition of scoffing at women who are concerned for my safety, as I did with the woman I would marry.

Sometime during our courtship, before we married, I set off on a hundred-mile canoe trip with a friend, deep into a gorge, very much in the spirit of the movie you are probably already thinking of, maintaining important verisimilitude by bringing along a stringed instrument and a complete lack of knowledge of the terrain or the ways of its people.

"You'll die," my fiancée said. "I'll never see you again."

"Shit, woman," is not what I said, but I did tell her all about the bottomless caves into which we would swim and the cliffs off which we would dive, watching her turn pale. She did not want me to hurt myself, she said, and I felt again the powerful tonic of hearing such entreaties from a woman you love.

Once we were married, she became even more like my mother, which I made sure not to tell her.

"Don't throw the children at the ceiling fan," she said one night, while I was throwing one of our children at the ceiling fan.

"But why?" I said.

Honestly, all I was doing was throwing our daughter up, higher and higher, and then catching her. We were nowhere near the fan, mostly because I'd already accidentally thrown her into it, without telling my wife, and the kid had been fine, mostly. "The fan is scary, which makes it more fun," I said.

"She could die."

"I've been thrown into many a fan, and look at me."

What I didn't say was, I had very important reasons for throwing my child into the ceiling fan, and those reasons were that I wanted to see what would happen. This was my responsibility, as a man, to endanger the people I love in the service of knowledge that seems important at the time.

She asked me to stop it and all sorts of other silly things, such as to not let the baby stand on the counter and to keep the fireworks away from their faces and to lock the doors.

Lock the doors! Ridiculous!

She was complaining because, at the time, I left our house very early in the morning, so early that it was actually still night. I left early for many reasons, but mostly because I found it so pleasant to leave my children in one building while I went to another building, usually to write stories like this one. It could be almost any building, preferably one that was far away, where the children could not find me.

When I would leave our house in the gloaming, tiptoeing quiet as Tom Tittlemouse with my briefcase, I just didn't think locking the door was important. It would make too much noise, all the keys. We had two babies in the house then, light sleepers. If I jangled a key, my wife might lose an hour of sleep, and in those days of everlasting infants, she coveted sleep even more than wine.

"Somebody could come in," she said, about the locking.

"Silly woman!" I wanted to say.

It's not like this was Mogadishu. Nothing was trying to get into our house between five and seven in the morning. Home invaders, I explained to my wife, were generally not morning people. Lock my door? What was I afraid of?

Later, I told Pop about my wife's unreasonable suggestion that I lock our front door, and we laughed. These women! We are men! The world is full of danger, and we fear it not!

Those were heady days, before something came through the unlocked door.

The unlocked door was not in Mississippi, nor was the rest of the house, nor the people who lived there, given that we'd moved to the wild and reckless city of Savannah, Georgia, where anything was liable to happen, such as naps, picnics, and garden parties where people did things that were literally insane, like wear straw boater hats. A college offered me a job, paying me money to do things I had been doing for free for so long that it seemed silly to say no, so we went.

Our cul-de-sac emptied out onto a quiet, lazy boulevard

and a glennish copse of approximately five acres. This park was usually empty, surrounded by homes with one bathroom and driveways paved mostly with dirt. It was a park for children, but also the occasional armed robbery and what looked to be, in my headlights one evening, a prom date–slash–youth breeding experiment.

"Be careful," Mom said, on the phone, warning us about all the things in the city that might kill her grandchildren, such as farmers' markets. It was hard for her, our being so far away. Without her guidance, we might do something careless, like put one of the babies in the microwave or allow one of them to be asphyxiated in the night by plastic grocery sacks that had become sentient and homicidal.

On their first visit, she saw something troubling in a neighbor's garage.

"Oh no," she said, sounding upset. "Look!"

I fully expected to see a Burmese python swallowing a small baby.

"What?"

"*That.*" She pointed to a small refrigerator. "One of the babies could get in there and die."

I explained that the youngest could not yet walk and that the other was so scared of clouds and gravity that she would not leave the house without a Secret Service detail and a diaper over her head. She could barely look out the mail slot without hyperventilating.

Mom seemed as crazy as ever for suggesting it, but she had an uneasy feeling. You could see it in her face.

Not long after, I had my own uneasy feeling.

It was August of our second year in Savannah, about eight in the morning, the world's color strangely muted, the picture dimmed. Our end of the street is adumbrated in live oak and sweet gum trees, but there was something more, some ecliptic phenomena, that arrested everything in gray-blue half-light, like somebody put in the wrong bulb. It was supposed to be a day like every other. I'd left in the dark, had stared at a cup of coffee and tried to get it to tell me secrets about what to write about that day, and I stared and stared, and maybe wrote a line and loved it, then erased it and planned a botched suicide attempt about which I would tell nobody, but which would hopefully inform my work in new and meaningful ways, and now my work was done and I was driving home, to dress for my day job and pretend to be normal for the rest of the day.

The world should've been waking up, but on that late summer morning, everything looked asleep, even the police car idling at the mouth of the cul-de-sac, and I saw that the neighborhood was not asleep, but heaving with held breath.

I passed the policeman, turned onto my short, stubby street. I worried about hitting one of the pets who lived there, lazing across the cracks of the old pavement like lions at the zoo. It would be easy to hit one of the cats. They are petulant and troubled. They don't move.

I pulled in, parked, tramped across my sandy driveway, through the unlatched gate. When I opened the door, I expected my daughter to be standing there, as she always was in those days.

"You came back!" she would say, running to me.

It was hard not to wonder at how much joy the world can bear. One minute, you entertain thoughts of Ending It All. The next, a small human buries her little baby Medusa head in your lap because your arrival has brought her new and everlasting joy. You spend your whole life walking into rooms and the world couldn't care less, people barely look up from their salads, and then suddenly there's this person, these people, tiny though they be, who find you more interesting than almost any food product. They grapple you, tug your pants, want you to come with them to see things, pictures, clothes, toys, forts, bowel movements, anything. They have made them for you, and want you to see.

But when I opened the door that morning, none of that happened. Nobody came running. My wife was standing there in the middle of the floor, not looking good.

"They found her in the park," she said.

"Found who?"

Everything got loud and superheated and accelerated backward and forward. What had happened? I stared at my pale wife staring back at me, telling me that our two-year-old daughter was gone, and the past unfurled like an old carpet with hateful baby snakes in it and the future like an unread, black-edged scroll.

I heard the newborn in the other room crying and saw the toddler in between my wife's legs, hiding, bright-eyed and not scared at all, but the look on my wife's face hadn't changed.

What had happened?

"The police came," my wife said. "There was a man in the house."

"Who?"

"The police."

"Who was in the house?"

"The police."

She had been up much of the night before, nursing the new little baby, barely a month old, and so she had been sleeping extra-hard, extra-deep when she had been pulled up from the dark by the sound.

"A burglar," she thought. "A home invader."

I still didn't understand, and then I understood.

"The man was yelling into the house. It was the police," she said. She did not even stop to put on clothes, stumbling into the living room toward the sound of the man through the fog of a tired mother's sleep. A tall, uniformed officer stood on the porch, looking through the wide-open front door, holding our toddler.

"I don't understand," I said. "She got out? How long was she gone? Did someone take her?"

"We don't know."

"She never gets out. She's too scared."

"I know."

I sat down, not on the furniture, because that seemed too casual to fully contain the white-hot fear that heaved my bones, so I sat on the floor, where I thought I could catch my breath, as I remember seeing my mother do when news hit her too hard and we would laugh.

"Did you leave the door unlocked?" my wife said.

Yes, of course, of course.

Of course.

My daughter ran to me, and I held her.

When you've always laughed at people for worrying that a family member might die, you don't know what to do when, of a midsummer's morning, it's you who can see nothing but a dark hole inside you with death at the bottom.

What did the policeman say, I wanted to know.

He got a call, she said. A baby in the park.

"Where?"

"The tennis courts."

"Who called?"

"We don't know," she said, still dazed, looking off. She was already in the first-person plural, the mode of the newspaper, the authorities, reports, notices, obits.

"He said something about a school bus driver," my wife said. Maybe the bus driver saw her, called it in? I am spiritually assaulted at the thought of her walking, or being carried by some unknown entity, across that wide street where school buses lurch and race and have crushed more cats and squirrels and birds than I want to imagine.

The idea of this child, alone in a fallen world, in a park with dogs and owls and used condoms and discarded brassieres, alone with no shoulders to climb—it was a sickening thought. I would not eat for two days.

Kids die all the time.

"Did you go to the park?" I asked my daughter.

"Yeah," she said, almost embarrassed. Her eyes were dreamy and make-believe.

"What happened at the park?" I said.

"I got on a school bus, and the man was there and the blanket."

"What did you do on the school bus?"

"I cried and cried," she said.

"How did the policeman know where we lived?" I asked my wife.

"The lady who lived across from the tennis courts," she said.

She was a short little lady, round and squat as an egg, the kind who comes outside when she sees police cars.

Sitting there holding my child, and rocking a little bit and trying not to scare her and going ahead and deciding that maybe I would have to lose my shit later at work, in the bathroom so nobody could see, and feeling the great deep chasm inside me that had been revealed through this terrible story that wasn't terrible in fact but only in potential—this was the moment when I finally felt like a father.

It was a long time before I could tell anyone that story. I still haven't told Mom.

Something very large had happened in my heart, and I did not understand it, something too big to be removed through the mouth, in a story. Sometimes, it came out of my eyes. Everywhere I looked, I saw things that wanted to kill my daughters: cars, heat waves, large birds of prey. I tried to remind myself that God didn't make the world to kill us, but he did seem to make it easy for somebody else to do it, and I didn't get it.

Is this what it felt like to be my mother? In the days and weeks after it happened, when it all settled down into something low in the valley of the shadow of memory, I couldn't help but think of her.

She'd lost so much in her life: a father who'd left when she was five; a brother who died too young; then her own mother, who died in a bed in Greenwood, Mississippi, with nobody there to help but her. My mother had no family but us, and every time we left the house for some river, some woods, she didn't know if she'd lose us, too, and frankly, she almost did, many times. She was the brave one. Not us.

I'd always thought it was the things that could kill you that made you a man, that made you alive. What really makes you alive is love.

Nowadays, I still throw my kids up into the general area of the ceiling fan, and I put them in a boat and take them into the Atlantic Ocean, and I let them sit on the counter while I do the most dangerous thing known to humankind, preparing uncooked chicken.

But I do lock my door now, because one day, all of us will look up and see the door open and know that we might never see our children again.

We'll never really know why she went, how she got out there, whether something took her, a home invader with a heart of gold, or whether she went alone, tried to climb up into the baby swing on the playground or padded across the park toward the place where the city turns on the sprinkler in the summer or cried and called for us or wondered at the wide gray world and just stood there, smiling, with her little bunny rabbit.

I'd always thought it was *Reader's Digest* that made Mom crazy. Then I remembered: Those stories had happy endings. People almost never died. They were tales of survivors. What they were, were stories about her.

CHAPTER 18

·

The Ballad of Jimmy Crack Corn

—✦ ✦ ✦ ✦—

There's just something about knowing your daughter could have been killed in a neighborhood that makes you fall in love with a place. After all, she hadn't died. Could the neighborhood somehow be responsible for her not dying, and if so, how do you thank a neighborhood? By continuing to live there and love one's neighbors? And what if, as soon as you'd moved there, you had begun making plans to move away, mostly because of the neighbors, whom you did not love?

It was easy to love our closest neighbors, the two or three families from whom we borrowed eggs and ladders, but just beyond the mouth of the cul-de-sac were graver dangers we hadn't noticed until it was too late: Renters. Not the good kind who grow their own flowers and poison their weeds, but the kind who poison their flowers and grow their own weed. The housing market was a goner, and the renters poured in two by two, and it was not long before their homes started to look as though pornographic films and ritual murders were being filmed inside: the venetian blinds tattered, a front door that appeared to have been clawed at by a large mammal, strange garbage by the road-side: empty boxes of Milwaukee's Best, cartons of latex gloves, discarded tubs of what appeared to be monitor lizard food. These lizard people were up to no good, one feared.

"Where do you live?" people asked me. That's a popular question anywhere, but especially in an old city like Savannah, the answer sure to give the asker clues as to how comfortable you are with your children having friends who have witnessed a murder or know what a bail bondsman is.

On their first visit to the city, my father grimaced at every home in our neighborhood: The tall grass, the weedy flower beds, the sunken roofs, the disturbing shortage of American trucks. This was an unfit place for his boy. His boy, after all, was a doctor.

"This is my son, Dr. Key," Pop had begun saying to his cousins at family funerals.

"How impressive!" they'd say, preparing to invite me to study their growths. "And what kind of doctor are you?"

"I'm an English teacher."

"What kind, you say?"

"I treat people who are having trouble with their colons."

"Oh."

"And semicolons."

"Oh! I see!" they'd say, more confused, looking around for assistance.

My wife would intervene.

"He's not the kind of doctor who helps people," she would say.

"I thought you said he was a doctor," they'd say to Pop.

"A professor!" he'd declare with visible pride.

Professors were supposed to live in big old houses in places where American flags and wisteria whipped in the tastefully scented wind, and it would have been too difficult to explain to Pop that those days were over, that universities were indeed lovely places to work but the salaries for people who scanned sonnets for fun was somewhat less than for those who scanned tumors.

Had he really worked that hard to give his boy a life in a place where everything was smaller: the bathrooms, the dogs, the guns? The house was so tiny that I'd had to put my drums on the back porch, which pleased my wife, because she believed they'd be easier for someone to steal, but I didn't like it, and neither did Pop. Playing drums was strange enough; keeping them on your back porch was just trashy. Born in 1942, right there in between the Depression babies and the boomers, Pop came from a generation where everything got bigger and better every day in every way, and that included your income and your square footage and your prospects and your BMI. I wanted to show him that a smaller house didn't necessarily mean a smaller life, that I thought it would be good for my offspring to grow up in a place where the children didn't all look alike and they could learn the virtue of humility and what sorts of trees to climb when chased by marginalized dogs.

"It's a starter home," I explained.

"Yeah, good," he said.

Humble people come from places like this, I thought, in addition to felons. Things were looking up. Houses had been flipped, flower boxes mounted, picket fences installed. For every discarded Magnum Lubricated Condom, there was the sudden appearance of a jogging stroller.

On the corner lot of our street lived a sweet man, a blind veteran we called Old Man Winter because he was old and grizzled and when he spoke you could sort of feel the shiver of death, and also because we could not remember his name. He usually wandered in the street, gathering tennis balls knocked over the fence from the small public courts the city had installed to attract the sort of people who might not keep lizards. Old Man Winter gathered these balls, which were the last remaining objects he could see besides the sun, and handed them out to the squirrels, who he believed were our children.

"What's your name, again?" I asked him, often.

"What's that?" he said.

"Your name."

"Tennis balls," he said, handing me one.

"Your name."

"Tennis balls!" he said, pointing.

He would sit in the shade of his trees on a lawn chair and tell me about the trees, bigger than any dogwoods I'd ever seen, which he explained had been purchased by his dead wife in the mists of prehistory from a mail-order catalog, which he spoke about with great awe.

"It was a book full of trees," he'd say.

"Amazing," I'd say.

In spring, these dogwoods bloomed bright white like an earthbound cloud bank that made it almost seem like heaven, so pretty you thought you wanted to find a way to live there forever, because you'd always wanted to live in a place where people planted things that would outlive them, because real beauty took a lifetime.

He was a good man, and the neighborhood had others like him, GI Bill homesteaders who had made it a pretty place, but they were dying.

Then came the day that every homeowner knows too well, the day when you see a naked man fighting with the shrubbery.

We pulled into the cul-de-sac, and we saw him in Old Man Winter's yard.

"Is that man naked?" my wife said.

We parked, tried not to stare, but before I could get inside the house, the naked man was standing behind me.

"I got a flare," he said.

I turned around and was pleased to note that he was not naked after all, just wearing flesh-colored shorts designed for a toddler.

"A flare!" he said again.

"A *flour!*" the large woman behind him said, holding sheets of paper.

They had come right up into my yard, opening the gate of my little picket fence as if it were their very own, a small but telling detail.

"A *flyer?*" I said.

"You bet," he said. "I can do it all: trim, chop, lop, rake, cut."

"He can do it all," the large woman said.

The man was what my father would describe as "squirrelly." Like a squirrel, he jerked, stiffened, shuddered in fleshy paroxysms the way most people do when filled with Holy Ghost Power. Unlike a squirrel, he seemed overly concerned with rubbing himself in general and his nipples in particular. He was muscular, his abs defined, what my brother would've described as "ripped." He also appeared high on the drugs, perhaps of the Moon Rock variety, or whatever the youth call it these days. Kibbles 'n Bits? I had seen this sort of human before, but could not remember where. Maybe a TV show: *Divorce Court? People's Court? Cops?*

The woman behind the naked man explained that she was Old Man Winter's granddaughter. She was a big gal, and the eye was drawn to her hair, which could best be described as

Thunderdome-era Tina Turner. It was red, and it swelled up and out from her skull, a rare and deadly tropical flower.

They spoke to me, handed me a flare, and were gone.

"I'm just glad we don't live next to people like that," my wife said.

"We're very lucky," I said.

A few months later, I noticed an ambulance in Old Man Winter's driveway. Father Time had caught up with the man. They would have to saw him in half and count his rings. For a week, his family sat Shiva in the carport, which they transformed into a saloon. He had begot a tribe of excellent drinkers and smokers who seemed to find great pleasure in yelling at one another on a variety of topics, from the temperature of their beer to the proper usage of panties and tongue rings.

On the day after the funeral, I saw Captain Squirrel and Lady Thunderdome carrying what appeared to be laundry baskets full of garbage into Old Man Winter's house.

"What are they carrying?" my wife said.

"Their stuff," I said.

"Oh no."

In the weeks that followed, cars packed the dirt driveway, clogged the street, parked in front of our house. Cats came, too, so many cats, urinating in my yard, sleeping on my car. There was something vaguely menacing about it, this excessive parking, this cat business. They were blocking my view. And I knew it was wrong, to want to firebomb these cars.

Apparently, Old Man Winter's children could not decide what to do with the house, so they let one of the grandchildren squat there until plans could be made to burn it for the insurance.

"I don't like this," my wife said, looking through a slit in the blinds.

"Relax," I said. "Show some Christian hospitality."

But really, I didn't like it, either, and I didn't like that I was aware of not liking it, which meant I was probably too weak to go through with any sort of firebombing plan. What would Pop do? He would do the reasonable thing and start by shooting all the cats. He was a stronger man than me, not so prone to questioning his own motives. He kept a stick in the car just for hitting people.

Later, while cutting my grass like a responsible citizen, I noticed on my property what appeared to be the feces of a large mammal. And then I noticed something far worse: a small boy, on my back porch, sitting at my drums.

"Hello," I said. "Who are you?"

"I'm a drummer," he said.

"What's your name?"

"Cody."

The little towheaded boy with the earring seemed nice enough, even though he touched my drums, which in an ideal world would result in his public execution. But I remembered Christian charity and explained that I would give him lessons, after he answered some questions.

"How big is your family?" I asked.

"I got, like, four brothers and two sisters," he said.

"And a mom and a dad?"

"It's like three daddies."

"That's not possible."

He shrugged. Anything was possible.

"What does your momma do?" I asked.

"She's in the beauty school," he said. "She can do hair pretty good."

I asked him who pooped in my yard.

"It wasn't me," he said.

I woke at midnight. In the distance, the cannons boomed.

"What is that sound?" the wife said.

I went to the window, eager to espy these people launching field mortars into the park. But nothing, not even a flare. Dark. It happened every night for the next many nights, boom, boom, boom. At midnight, and two, and four.

"I want to murder them," my wife said.

"Go to sleep," I said.

"You have to stop them," she said.

"I'll go talk to Jimmy," I said.

"Jimmy" is what we had been calling him, which was short for "Jimmy Crack Corn," which was long for "crack," which we were very confident he smoked.

I slinked into the backyard and surveiled across property lines with a headlamp and a new stick procured expressly for hitting people. I saw what was happening. This was no mortar fire. These were doors. Doors that slammed with great force. Sliding van doors, car doors, tailgates, shed doors, screen doors. The back door, in particular, slammed with such booming fury that it sounded like someone was hurling manatee carcasses into the bed of a pickup.

What was this? A meth lab? A manatee death camp?

I needed to do something before my wife poured a bottle of Benadryl into her soul. In a burst of courage, I dropped the stick and removed the headlamp and stepped around the bamboo curtain. And there they were: Jimmy and his woman, him sweating like a can of beer, searching through boxes.

"Evening," I said.

What happened?" my wife said.

What happened was, I apologized for my family's vulgar

habit of sleeping at night, while Lady Thunderdome belched out what sounded like a whole onion and Jimmy C.C. made some barking noises. I explained all this to my wife, who slammed her head into the pillow in an effort to induce an aneurysm, which she believed would help her sleep.

It kept happening, every night, the Battle of Verdun.

"What are they doing, you think?" I said.

"Drugs," she said.

They acted just as unhinged during daylight, when Lady Thunderdome piloted her van like a banking jet, her regal mane attempting to escape its life of hair-sprayed servitude through an open window. She rocketed past her driveway and slingshotted herself from the rounded end of the sac and came to a neck-breaking stop in front of our house. Then she would pull up. Then back. Then up. Then back. Then into her driveway. Then out. Then in.

"What is wrong with these people?" my wife said.

Lady Thunderdome would then remove from the van a pale, thin baby made of gray plastic. It did not cry, despite its recent jaunt in the G-force simulator. The baby just stared at you. It was a *Deliverance* baby. It knew things.

I felt bad about thinking the baby should be in a remake of a Burt Reynolds movie and resolved to be kinder, more compassionate. And then one Saturday, there Jimmy was, on the legal side of our picket fence, drinking a Miller Lite and staring like he had a secret.

"Howdy," I said, walking over to say hello.

In a frightening burst, a barking animal rushed from the piles of refuse in his carport, a wiener dog, a long turd of a pet the color of a bratwurst, and it barked with fury: deep, amplified, angry barks. I had always believed small dogs were sent by

God as a judgment to his people and greatly desired to see this one fall into a deep hole or be swept out to sea. The dog stuck its head through a gap in the pickets and barked again. It came through the fence. It coughed. It yakked. It vomited.

The dog was now eating its own vomit six inches from my shoes, on my land.

"I fed him a sirloin," Jimmy said, proudly.

"He appears to be eating it again," I said.

Part of me kept wanting to hate them, maybe because it was in my bones to be in a blood feud with such people, but then I would beat back the dogs of my Scotch-Irish bellicosity and try to be a better man.

Sure, Jimmy didn't appear to own any shirts. Sure, he'd transformed the corner lot of our cul-de-sac into a sort of Hurricane Katrina–themed terrarium, rolls of sodden carpet leaning against trees, velour recliners exposed to the elements, dead sticks of furniture lazing in the sun like poisoned cows. Sure, he was a liar, lying about all sorts of things, like how he was an entrepreneur or how he could get me a backhoe.

"Why would I need a backhoe?" I asked.

"To dig shit up," he said. "It's always shit needs to be dug up."

He pointed around my yard at various shit that was in the ground.

I did like the way Jimmy talked. It reminded me of home. It was hard to describe, something like the sound of a distant chainsaw pinched in a knot of pine. Was it possible to construct something like mutual respect, if not outright friendship, with this man?

He explained what he was going to do to Old Man Winter's cottage.

"We gonna make it a beauty parlor," he said.

Stunned, I nodded and drifted off into a nightmarish reverie where the cul-de-sac overflowed with large, loud women and their skyward hair, pouring out the front door of Old Man Winter's home underneath a sign that read "Tina's Kut n' Kurl" or perhaps "The Mane Event." Like *Steel Magnolias*, except where all the women carried knives. Jimmy said his construction plans involved destroying most of the sixty-year-old azaleas and dogwoods that remained the property's last redeeming features.

"Can you believe it?" I said to my wife later. "A beauty parlor."

She had no time for beauty parlors. "That dog attacked our children," she said.

"When?"

"Just now."

I found the middle child, then three years old, in the bedroom, lying motionless like a wounded soldier and covered excessively in *Dora the Explorer* bandages.

"It tried to eat me," she said.

Love thy neighbor as thyself. What does it even mean? Does it mean you're supposed to make friends with a man who has been seen on top of his roof waving borrowed lawn-care tools angrily at low-flying aircraft? Does it mean you smile when he informs you proudly of the roll of chicken wire he found by the highway, and how he intends to use this chicken wire to build a play area for his youngest son, because "kids like to climb shit," but instead chooses to build what appears to be a large sculptural installation, in which various birds and wildlife become trapped? How many children is his dog allowed to eat before you're allowed to stop loving him? How many times is he allowed to ask if you like the Steve Miller Band before you're allowed to beat him to death with his own dog?

"I should shoot that animal," I said to my wife.

"Don't be ridiculous," the wife said. "You should shoot *him*."

I had already started trying to get my parents to move to Savannah. Maybe even to this neighborhood, if we stayed. How fun it would be, where my mother could be near her grandchildren and Pop could say fun things to my wife's friends about their thighs. But I could not move them here, not to this.

"We have to move," I said to my wife.

There were a few more Jimmy Crack Corns in the neighborhood already, and more coming. The writing was on the wall. It was a shame. Such a nice little house. Maybe Old Man Winter's family would wise up and sell and stem this tide. Maybe somebody would buy it. Nice yard. Great trees. The best trees in the whole neighborhood.

Give it time, I told myself. This guy's just trying to scratch out a life here, just like you. We at least still had those gorgeous trees. A few mornings later, we woke to the sound of a chainsaw.

Dear Lord," I said.

"Is that *legal*?" someone said.

We were standing in the street, trying not to stare at the rape of the natural world currently taking place in Old Man Winter's yard, where Jimmy Crack Corn was clear-cutting and burning the dogwoods.

The trees were on fire.

"What's he *doing*?" someone said.

"Destroying property values," another neighbor said.

Events had taken a bad turn. Jimmy Crack Corn and Tina

Turner had started asking people for money. The story was, they'd lost their debit card and just needed a little cash.

"For what, do you think?"

"For crack," my wife said.

"For chainsaws," a neighbor said.

They lost their debit card a lot.

It was Tina who did the asking, their thinking, perhaps, that it would be easier to give money to the future valedictorian of the region's most prestigious college of beauty than to a man who operated his nipples like a pair of important toggle switches. The other neighbors were angry about this, but I tried to withhold judgment. They had asked just about everyone on the sac, and we knew they were coming for us.

"Look at him," a neighbor said.

He had felled two or three dogwoods already and had started pulling azaleas out of the earth with his truck, leaving nothing but a row of divots like shallow baby graves. The corpses were heaped on hazardous bonfires in the yard, around the stumps of the fallen trees, on which Jimmy had also dumped clothes and other garbage.

"Somebody should say something," they said.

Everybody looked at me.

"You live next to him," they said. "You're the one who talks to him."

What would my father do, I wondered? After Bird and I had left home for good, he and Mom had moved from the country into the paved environs of Brandon, Mississippi, where Pop quickly installed himself as president of his homeowners' association. He had rules about where you could put a boat, putting up fences, how tall the grass could be. For example, it was not the kind of place you could just spray down an old bookcase with lighter fluid and set it on fire in your yard, as I'd seen Jimmy do.

"The power's gone to his head," Mom had said.

Pop had been a suzerain king of the Pecan Ridge subdivision, ensuring clean, tasteful homes by patrolling the streets with his four-wheeler, menacing his constituents, waving documents in the air, threatening legal action if they did not roll up their garden hoses properly. He hired neighborhood youth to work on defunct properties and launched a beautification program with proceeds from the association, sometimes paying out of his own pocket. Every time I visited, he had poor young men, shirtless and overheated, doing his bidding.

"Those are his slaves," Mom said.

"They get paid," Pop said, although he didn't seem happy about it.

Is that how you loved your neighbor, by enforcing a sort of fascist purity on the land and its people, keeping property values and blood pressure high? There didn't seem to be any radical Nazarene love in Pop. He was all Pilate, or Mussolini, or some other Roman. Which would I be? Should I speak harshly with J.C.C., or would I try to love him, and was there a difference?

The next day, Jimmy was back at it with the chainsaw.

"Beer?" I said.

"It's hot as a motherfucker," he said.

We chatted: about life, and weather, and why he decided to destroy the trees.

"They were all so pretty," I said.

"Yeah, they pretty *dead*, now. Ha ha!" he said.

He looked happy, destroying nature.

I finished my beer and departed, but not without hope. Those beers, I decided, were the right approach. Pitchforks and angry mobs and legal documents weren't the way to get Jimmy C.C. to change.

"It's him," my wife said late one night, seeing his shadow through the window on the door. "Do not give him drug money."

"What if they need food?" I said.

He needed fifty dollars, he said. For supplies.

I wanted to say yes, to give freely. I also wanted to say no, because I had a mortgage, while Jimmy Crack Corn was a shiftless, freeloading job-lot whose only vocation appeared to be arson.

"What kinds of supplies?" I asked.

He told me a heart-wrenching tale with many incongruous references to banks, checks, paydays, President Obama, University of Georgia football, and the murder of his father during a home invasion not too far from here sometime during the Johnson administration.

"Wow," I said, explaining that I carried no cash, in this modern age. "You know, it's all debit this, debit that."

He left.

I was torn. Here was a man living in a free house who had farmed out most of his children to various scorned lovers and distant kin and who spent his jobless days setting the cul-de-sac on fire and his nights preparing for the South American tour of *Stomp* while my wife contemplated murder under a threadbare comforter. It was time for a confrontation, not a friendly one.

I planned it out.

I would say, Hey, man. Are you okay?

Why do you keep lying about money!

Stop burning your garbage. This is not a Cormac McCarthy novel!

If you build a beauty parlor here, I will beat you to death with a shovel!

But it would be fine if you burned the dog!

My wife took to locking the screen door on the porch, to prevent them from knocking at midnight, but they found a way around that, too.

"They are knocking on the window, the window!" my wife said.

I steeled myself.

It was time.

"Tell him," my wife said. "No more."

I opened the door, and there was no him to tell, but a her: Lady Thunderdome. She stepped into the bright rhombus of porch light and related a sad tale about—actually, this is quite amazing—a lost debit card.

"For what?" I said.

"For diapers," she said.

Thirty seconds later, I was shoving into her hands the legal tender of Huggies, which I offered in lieu of U.S. currency. She seemed disappointed, inspecting the diapers a bit too closely, assessing their potential as barter goods.

She marched back into the night, vacating the porch-light rhombus, which cut across the yard, and showed me a shadow that looked a lot like my father's, and I wasn't sure if I liked it.

In the story of the Good Samaritan, a lawyer asks how to inherit eternal life, and Jesus gets the man to recite what he knows about loving God and one's neighbor, and then the law-yer says, Yeah, but who's my neighbor? So J.C. tells the story of the man from Jerusalem who got his ass whipped on the highway, and the people who should've helped him—the

people who came from his part of town, say—did not help
him. The one who helped him was a man from a whole other
town, practically a hotbed of terrorism or a Canadian, and the
Canadian terrorist did first aid and put the hurt Jew on his
burro and took him to a safe place and found people to take
care of the man.

The Bleeding Ass-Whipped Jew, that's your neighbor, said
J.C. Now go be a Canadian Terrorist First Responder.

Were Jimmy Crack Corn and Tina Turner by the proverbial
roadside, their asses whipped? Was I really capable of behaving
like a Canadian? In the story, the guy's hurt and about to die.
Jimmy C.C. was not about to die. If anybody was going to die,
it would be one of my people, from the falling timber and the
furniture fires and the vomiting sausage beast.

"Hey," Jimmy C.C. said one night, at my door again. He
had that hangdog look, the money-asking sag about the shoulders. He needed maybe twenty dollars, he said.

"I'll give you two hundred," I said.

"Shit," he said.

"To paint my fence," I said.

He paused, pondering this strange idea of exchanging labor
for money.

You paint your fence?" Pop said, on a visit.

"Paid the neighbor to."

"Good," he said. "Yeah, that's real good."

And then, they disappeared, sort of. Somebody had gotten word that J.C.C. was working construction on a con-
tract for the U.S. Army, while others said he'd come by
asking for money and mentioned something about going
away for a while, to do electrical work at a hospital or in-
stall Sheetrock at a university or burn all the trees on the

Yucatán Peninsula. The story changed a lot, but one thing was certain: Things were quieter.

Their injured cars remained, four in all, furred in thickening coats of pollen and ash, but it was a haunted house. Cody and the Fake Gray Baby were scarcer, too. Rumors spread. They would be evicted, kicked out, a splinter in the Old Man Winter family tree. Strange cars had been seen. A crime scene van, on a Sunday morning. Crimes against humanity or specific people, it was unclear.

Weeds choked up through the baby graves. Remnants of azalea root stems shot up springlike, green as new money. The concrete column of a birdbath jutted into the sky, bathless. The black sooty heaps of garbage remained cancerous, threatening to darken everything. The few surviving dogwoods did bloom. We would have to postpone selling. The sac was a mess.

But my wife calmed down. She had been lately moved by an encounter with a Filipino missionary who visited our church and who spoke of maggots in her cupboards and children in need of shoes.

"It gives you perspective," my wife said. "I could do that. Be a missionary."

I told her I believed we were missionaries already, that we were just really bad at it.

Jimmy Crack Corn remained elusive. Occasionally, he would return from whatever districts of the world he'd been terrorizing and would wave from behind a shrub, where he could be seen urinating in beer bottles. On these furloughs, we could still hear him at night, throwing manatees in trucks or whatever it was he was doing. My wife slept through it now, because she had a new migraine pill that induced a coma. It was better this way, my wife on drugs. Safer, happier. "Jimmy Crack Corn, and I don't even care," she would sing, floating off to a happier place.

Since he was around less, there were fewer incidents. In a way, I missed seeing him rape the natural world, but I guess there's only so much nature to slash and burn.

Last December, we saw him, presumably returned for the holiday, and he was at it again. There'd been talk, relayed by neighbors and screamed by Tina Turner through windows and over fences, that Jimmy C.C. was back for good now, whatever that meant. And then I saw him one night, through distant and growing flame, lording over another fire in the front yard, high and proud and bright as a column of midnight sun. It was a big fire. Too big.

"What's he burning this time?" my wife asked.

She no longer sounded upset, just curious. The firelight capered around the tops of the trees in a festive manner, and then, driving closer, I saw.

"A couch," I said. "And what looks like most of their furniture."

"Oh, good."

"Maybe they're getting new furniture for Christmas," I said.

We pulled into our street and watched him, this shirtless beast of a man in the cold black of this season of Advent, holding what appeared to be a piece of the sofa high over his bespectacled head, his eyes blazing with two lesser fires. He threw the wide, fat cushion through the curtain of flame, and the flames rose higher.

We parked, and went inside, and sat down to dinner.

"Who wants to pray?" I said, the firelight dancing wildly now through the windows.

"Me," one of the kids said.

"What do you want to pray for?"

"That our neighborhood won't burn down."

"Great," I said, and she prayed, and it was a fine prayer, and I prayed in my heart, too, that we might be like the seed that falls on good ground, that we might grow tall like trees from a book.

"Amen," my daughter said.

"Amen," I said.

In the distance, we could already hear the fire engines.

CHAPTER 19

Space Invaders

Hey, man, we got robbed!"

It was Jimmy Crack Corn.

"Robbed?"

"They stole my boy's bike!"

He showed me where the criminals had come into his garage, where the bike had been. We soon found ourselves discussing rising crime rates, hooliganism in today's youth, and what Tina was going to do to the wayward youth who had stolen one of their bicycles.

"You own a gun?" he said.

"Pardon?"

"It's a lot a burglaries around here," he said. "Man, you got to protect your babies."

He pointed at various homes where he'd heard of burglaries. Up yonder, he said, and over down yonder, and right over yonder.

Tina Turner came raging up into the driveway in her minivan, screaming.

"I fucking got that motherfucker!"

"Did you get him?" Jimmy asked, and it sounded a lot like

maybe she'd run over the kids who'd stolen the bike. She'd found some boy riding the bike, she said, had run him off the road and taken the bicycle back.

"Them bikes ain't cheap," Jimmy said. "It's all kinds of criminals around here. And you know what criminals got."

I didn't.

"Guns," he said. "Almost seem like you got to have one these days."

I had known J.C.C. was a nut, but not a gun nut.

Was it wrong to be nuts about guns? And could I tell if he had a gun in his pants right then? Because maybe he did, maybe he didn't. This was his right, as an American, to put or not put things in his pants.

Growing up, my family were not so much Gun Nuts as Nuts with Guns. It wasn't the guns we were nuts about, but rather the things they helped us acquire, such as food and decorative hat racks. For my tenth birthday, Pop presented me with a Remington 12-gauge pump. "This gun right here can kill a grown man," he said, which made it sound like we'd been trying to kill grown men for many years without success.

I sometimes wondered if I could kill a man. It's something I'd thought a lot about, given my childhood fear of a home invasion. Church didn't help matters, where we were reminded that Jesus would return to earth like a thief in the night. Son of God or not, I just didn't like the idea of a man coming inside while we slept.

When I grew up, I didn't so much renounce firearms as leave behind the life that required them. In graduate school, I found myself in all sorts of places where guns had no quarter: research libraries, cast parties, pagan meditation labyrinths, underground contemplation orbs. I felt it was wrong to bring a gun to an open-mic poetry night, even when people were reading Pablo Neruda.

And then I married a woman who had not grown up with guns and could not understand how people who lived with guns close to hand were not just lying around dead all the time.

"Guns in the house, it just doesn't make sense," said my wife. "It's weird."

"That's how we always felt about cats," I said.

They were dangerous, sure, but back then our world was full of danger—drifters, snakes, meat. Now that I was grown up, my life had grown civil. And so when I took up housekeeping with my city wife, there was no talk of firearms. Instead, there was talk of spatulas, of obtaining as many bamboo-handled silicone spatulas as possible. Only once did I bring up guns. There had been a murder near our home. Was it possible that someone might want to come into our home and take our spatulas?

"Maybe we should get a gun," I said to my wife.

She reminded me that she would not feel safe with a gun in the house, and I didn't argue with her. We were not Gun People. But then, we had children. How would I protect them from thieves in the night? With prayer? With kitchenware?

When we moved to Savannah, it did not take long for us to see that we had moved to a whole city of Gun People. Our first week in town, we noted with regret that the sound of gunfire followed us everywhere, even at the Walmart.

"Oh, that's the gun club!" our new neighbor said, when we recounted the horror of our shopping trip. "Right there in back of the store."

"That seems safe," I said.

"It is!" he said. "They got a wall."

"Like in Berlin."

"And they got a bar, too."

Our new friends were not so much Gun People as Let Me Show You My Gun People and What Kind of Gun Do You Got People, and My Wife Doesn't Feel Safe at the Piggly Wiggly Unless She Can Stop a Charging Bull Elk in Rut People. At dinner parties, the subject often came up.

"Want to go in the back and see my guns?" a new friend would ask.

Twenty-five years ago, it would have seemed a perfectly normal thing to ask, but now it sounded queer, as though they'd asked me to step into their dungeon and see their collection of gilded maces and monkey skulls.

"Sure?" I'd say, before following him into the back.

Entering the master bedrooms of married people always made me uneasy. I was afraid I'd see things that cannot be unseen, such as tubs of Vaseline or some sort of agricultural harness. These nice people would invariably lead me to their private bedroom nook, where they'd reveal between one and eighteen pistols and tactical rifles.

"Look at this puppy," they'd say. "It's called the Basilisk."

I'd take the weapon and wave it around good-heartedly, so as not to suggest that I think it's odd to own a $1,500 handgun named after a mythical lizard.

One night, I drank a beer with a compassionate and learned man who held many academic degrees, and he invited me out for a moonlit promenade on a beloved Lowcountry marsh near his home. Before leaving, he stuffed a .38 into his pants. We were in the country, with nothing to see on our walk but barred owls and fiddler crabs. Had there been much gang violence on this here marsh? I was confused.

"Are you expecting an attack?" I asked.

"You never know," he said.

It all seemed very silly. What were these people afraid of? Being attacked by owls?

There are many things I do not wish to see in my living room at 5:30 a.m., and they generally fall into the categories of Bears, Lava, and Open Windows. It was the last of these that I saw on a morning I shall not soon forget.

"Why is that window open?" I said to my wife.

She hates open windows more than I do, mostly because our neighborhood is home to many creatures my wife believes would like to lay eggs in her face.

"What window?" she said, sitting with the baby.

"That window," I said, pointing.

She looked, inhaled that sort of terrified gasp that mothers make.

We had been invaded.

It is difficult to describe the primeval dread of seeing that open window, the material evidence of malice in our little sanctuary. Who had come into my house in the night? Were they still there? Were they crouching just beyond the window, looking in?

The only weapons in my immediate reach were candles, a large baby, and several throw pillows. Could these pillows truly be thrown? And why did I suddenly feel naked? Was it because I was wearing no clothes? Or was there something else, too?

"The girls," I said.

Despite the dreadful closeness of their door to the open window, I found them in their room, asleep. It was a small house, with few hiding places. I checked the laundry room, the kitchen. I checked the oven. Was that silly? It didn't seem silly. I've got nothing against tiny people who might like hanging out in my oven, but that doesn't mean they don't have something against me.

I put on some clothes.

"I'm going outside," I said. It was still dark.

What I needed was a weapon, but all I had was a serrated bread knife, which might come in handy if I came across an angry Bundt cake. I extended my kitchen utensil into the dark and crept forward, around the house. The scooter, unmolested. The truck windows, unbroken. The shed, locked. The thieves had taken nothing. Back inside, there were no drawers open, no overturned chairs or muddy boot prints. It was quite possible that one of the children had opened the window, but then none of our children had ever voluntarily lifted anything that was not filled with ice cream. Why hadn't our throats been slit, our children taken? What if one of them had gotten up in the night to use the toilet and seen the monster? Would one of them be dead now?

And then I knew.

"My briefcase," I said.

Every day when I came home, I dropped the fat green thing into the chair next to the window. That chair was now empty.

What was in that briefcase?

Nothing. Everything. My wallet, for one. But more than that: my computer. Twenty thousand hours of work. Fifteen thousand documents. A play about a goose. A poem about a duck. My first book, my second book, my third and fourth and part of a fifth, all unpublished, all not worth the paper I had not thought to print them on.

"Oh, no," my wife said. "Your stories."

Listen, I got it. I had not lost a leg or a loved one. What I lost was a great deal of literature about waterfowl. I would tell you why it was not backed up, but it is a long, dull tale about institutional policy and sloth. Also in the briefcase: my wallet.

I called 911 while my wife called the bank and wept with a volume she typically reserved for childbirth, and I felt sorry for the nice lady who had to listen to her cry.

I waited for the police.

A small part of me believed that when the officer arrived, he would hand me a tactical shotgun. "Let's ride," he would say, and we would confront a gang of card-playing criminals in their smoky den of vice. "We've come for the poem about the duck," the cop would say, as I pumped a shell into the chamber like the vigilante poets of old.

But the officer was a short woman who did not appear capable of administering street justice. She was sweet, understanding, a ponytailed little gnome, like an aging Olympic gymnast who'd been attacked by a law enforcement accessories catalog. She took my statement, supplied a case number, and left. For compassion, I gave her the bronze. The sun rose.

"I'm going out," I said.

After all, hadn't Tina Turner recovered her child's bike in this manner? Could I run a man down, by the roadside? My plan was to drive around and look for my briefcase in a gutter, perhaps soothe my rage by running over a few dogs. But as soon as I stepped off the porch, I saw it. There, in the yard, my empty briefcase. My wife came running, fell to her knees, cried out. I held my bag like a hurt child. Then we saw her blue handbag in a neighbor's azalea, and she lost it.

"Our things!" she said.

You know how when people in developing nations experience one of those tragedies that are always tragically happening to them, like a hole in the earth opens up and swallows a school of leprous toddlers, and their mothers are on the news wailing in this kind of sickening, bowel-loosening way, and it's so sad that you kind of want to watch *Wheel of Fortune* instead? That was what it was like watching my wife cry in the dewy grass.

Then the children woke up, came out, and cried with her, un-sure of why they were crying. I stood in the middle of the road and watched the flesh of my flesh and fruit of my loins lying in a heap on the sod. A hole in the earth had opened, sort of.

I had failed to protect my things, my people.

"Don't tell the girls," I said to my wife.

I come from a long line of hunters and trappers and home-steaders, virile men who would horsewhip other men for no reason at all. When attacked, they did not just sit there. They got on their mules and rode to town and hit people in the head with hammers. It was justice, and that's what I wanted. To open a good, old-fashioned can of Cold-Filtered Whoopass Ultra. But all I had in my pocket was a Leatherman Multi-Tool, which was really more appropriate for opening a can of Campbell's Chunky Soup. Why were all my weapons designed for the kitchen? It was embarrassing. Maybe I was Gun People after all.

I need some ammo," I said to a neighbor, the kind of man who I knew might have some extra munitions lying around because he spit a lot and watched television inside a shed in his backyard.

"You got a *gun?*" he said, surprised.

"Hell yes," I said, trying to sound like somebody who be-longed to the gun club.

My father had brought my old shotgun to me a few years back, in case a lost herd of mule deer ever wandered onto my property, and I'd shoved it under the bed. The gun sort of embarrassed me; receiving it was like being presented with the tiny bra of the first girl I'd ever groped. I promised my wife I'd keep it locked, out of sight.

But things were different now. The morning of the inva-sion, I pulled out the weapon, pumped it nice and loud. The sound alone would be enough to strike fear into an intruder, alerting him that he was in imminent danger of seeing his own small intestine without the aid of medical imaging equipment.

"Cool!" my six-year-old said.

"What is it?" my four-year-old said.

It was embarrassing that my children did not know what an actual gun looked like. Or was this a good thing? I no longer knew. They reached up, pet its stock like a new puppy. I thought of how close they'd come to being hurt, all of them, my sweet little Hobbit children—it was enough to send the mind into a real Mirkwood of the soul. Did having the gun make us safer? And why did I suddenly desire to own many of them, perhaps one named after a mythical lizard?

"Do you know how to use it?" my wife said.

"There's more redneck in me than meets the eye," I said, and pumped it again so loudly that my children ran screaming from the room. My plan was to stay up all night on the couch with the gun. I didn't have the heart to tell my wife that our neighbor had given me a box of slugs designed for the killing of bears. If I shot anything with it, I would also likely destroy furniture and load-bearing walls. The newspapers would tell the story.

"Suspected Burglar Dead, Head Missing."

"Man Gunned Down by Area Nut Who Feared Bear Invasion."

My wife kissed me on the forehead, went to bed. On the coffee table lay my tools: a headlamp, more ammo, car keys in case I needed to give chase to wounded enemies, and a copy of *Absalom, Absalom!* in case I had any lingering questions about human frailty.

Nobody came that night. Instead, other people came.

"What can we do?" a friend asked.

This was a family who wanted to help, and they had money, and they were too kind, and if I didn't come up with something, I knew they'd take it upon themselves to invent their own solutions, sending over a team to surround my home with trained baboons and moats of boiling sulfur.

"I guess we could use some motion lights," I said.

Before I knew it, a barrel-chested electrician was standing in my driveway, asking where I wanted the lights. "I can put them anywhere," he said. "The corners, the trees, the roof." He was wearing a serious man's tool belt and appeared to be considering the installation of motion-sensor lighting on my forehead.

"Just put them all over, I guess."

This is exactly what he did.

When I drove home from work that night, it appeared from the end of the street that our house was on fire, and I was reminded of scripture: "And the light shineth in the darkness, and the wicked shall flee, for the 240-degree swiveling security lights doth illuminate the cul-de-sac in heavenly brightness." Pulling into my driveway, I felt very blessed, like one of those people who get to meet Jesus, mostly because I was now blind.

"I love the lights," I said to a bird in the flower bed, mistaking it for a family member.

Other friends tried to help, bringing food and hugs. It was unnerving. Late one night, everyone asleep but me, I heard the crunch of gravel and prepared to shoot the maker of this sound, gun in hand, until I saw out the window that it was merely a friend who was attempting to place a bottle of Shiraz on our porch, something to make us feel better.

"Oh, hi," she said, when I came outside, without the gun.

Savannahians were Gun Nuts but also Wine Nuts, and I was glad. I thanked her. Later, having drunk the wine, I slept.

The next morning, my wife announced another new change.

"We're getting a dog," she said.

In my father's house, having indoor pets was always a sign of moral decay, assumed to be clear evidence of mental illness and possibly drug addiction. If you wanted to get an animal into his house, you had to tell my father that you intended to eat it. But less than forty-eight hours later, my family and I were at a large concrete building full of dogs.

"We're getting a dog!" our children said.

They were looking for a cuddly one, while I looked for a pet that had been trained by Germans to remove human hands.

"Which one do you think will protect us more?" my wife whispered.

"An alligator," I said.

We narrowed it down to a black Lab and a docile German shepherd with a strange growth on its anus. I liked the idea of the German shepherd. These dogs have one look, and the look says, "Can I chew upon your genital region?"

"But everybody loves Labs," my wife said.

Which is how, a week after the burglary, I had a hundred-pound black Lab named Gus sleeping on my couch, sitting in my chair, and watching me urinate.

"If someone tries to break in, are you sure he'll bark?" I asked my wife.

So far, the only security he provided was filling the yard with heaps of his malodorous dung, which could've been used to build a wall around our house. He didn't stay in the living room, where the invaders might enter. Instead, he watched me sleep. I would wake up to heavy breathing and find the dog staring at me with murder on his mind, like Billy Bob Thornton in *Sling Blade*.

I was angry. Angry that I had this dog, angry that some

criminal was now using my laptop, angry that his family had failed to nurture in him a sense of rightness and hope, angry that I wished to hit him in the face with a brick, angry that I'd lost my library card, that it's so much work to get a library card, that the people who give out library cards are in many ways the real criminals of this story, and that if they came into my house, I would ask my dog to eat them. But he won't eat them. He won't do anything but get real close and breathe his hobo breath on them until they stop loving every dog they've ever cared about.

I woke up. The big black dog was staring at me.

"At least you're all okay," friends would say.

But I was not okay.

And then, a miracle.

I was reaching into my briefcase one night, this piece of luggage I'd found empty in the yard, this bag I'd cleaned like it was filled with radiation, and there it was, right there, just sitting there, in a pocket that I'd scoured a hundred times. My wallet.

Everything was in it.

What I felt was not so much elation as pure wonder. The discovery created a kind of euphoria, an empowering buzz that felt like righteousness and light. What was happening? Was this a gift, some eddy in space and time, a message? I put down the wallet and walked outside and looked up at the heavens. I paced. I prayed. I tripped the motion lights.

Peace returned, the invasion over. I stopped patrolling my house at night. When people came over for dinner, I did not ask if they wanted to see my gun. When I went for walks, I did not put it in my pants. It was too big, and would have made walking unpleasant.

I knew: I cannot live like this, patrolling my house at night with a loaded weapon, fully dressed, preparing to shoot the people who bring us gifts. And so I took the slugs out, and put the shotgun back under the bed, and I started sleeping naked again, and I got rid of the dog.

"Where did Gus go?" the children asked.

"To the gas chambers," I said.

What we did was, we returned him. I'd kept the receipt.

I tried not to pick sides between the Gun Nuts and the Non–Gun Nuts. I'd always tried to avoid extremism of any kind, as it was my understanding that passionate beliefs could lead to excessive voting and the alienation of people whose cooking I enjoy.

We moved the girls to a safer room of the house, and prayed more, and worried less, and slept better.

And then I heard a noise. This was no midnight Shiraz delivery noise. This was a thud, several thuds, at 4 a.m. I groped for the shotgun under the bed.

"This is it," I said.

They had come back for the other computer, the TV, the Apple products, our very lives. We were all going to die. I found the slugs. I pressed them into the chamber, one, two, quiet as Little Tommy Tittlemouse. I crouched in the hallway. Looking down, I considered the tactical advantages of my nakedness. Usually, when I enter a room naked, my wife runs out screaming. Would it scare a burglar, too? Perhaps. Still, I worried. It would not play well with a jury of my peers.

"What was Mr. Key wearing when he shot you?" the prosecutor asks.

"Nothing but, but—" the defendant says, choking up.

"It's okay, this is a safe place."

"Just—just the socks."

"You must have feared for your life."

Another thunk.

I squinted and noted, also, that my eyeglasses were in the very living room that was quietly being ransacked.

"Naked, Blind Man Shoots Wife in Living Room," the headline would read.

I inched forward, turned off the safety.

I pumped the gun, loudly, hoping to scare them back out the way they'd come, and then I heard more rustling, more knocking about, coming from a bedroom. My four-year-old opened her door, saw the gun, and started to cry. Cover blown, it was time to act. I ran into the living room, gun ready to blaze.

My wife woke, came out, turned on a light.

"What are you—" she said.

"I thought—" I said. I nodded to the four-year-old. "I guess she dropped a cup or something?"

The four-year-old cried harder, and I looked in the enormous mirror that hung on our living room wall and was shocked at what I saw: a real-live Angry White Man. In nothing but his socks. Holding a giant gun. Like some kind of nut.

When a man stares at his naked body in a giant mirror, it's hard to have illusions. About his safety, about his mental state, about what this world is capable of doing to his children and his wife.

"You need a pistol," Pop said.

And he was wrong. I just needed an alarm system, and a faith to remember that blessed were the peacemakers, that we had already conquered death, that our motion lights would sear the corneas of any invaders. And as they stumbled into our house, blinded and groping, there would be a new sound, a beeping, because I purchased an alarm system that I could not afford, which had the added benefit of ensuring there was no money in my home to steal, which seemed the ultimate defense.

I knew it could happen again, that someone might come into my house at night without knocking, even if only to look at my lovely spatulas, and that I might end up doing my best to ensure none of the invader's organs will be usable by any hospitals, that I might not stop to ask about how much love he needs or wants or never got, or if he liked my laptop and its superior functionality. I might have to shoot first and ask questions later.

"Why?" I will ask.

And if that guest is Our Lord and Savior Jesus Christ, and if he is only coming to take us all to heaven, and if I accidentally fire into his diaphanous form, I am sure he will forgive me. "I thought you were someone else," I will say.

And we will have some wine.

CHAPTER 20

·

The Leviathan Under the Table

—⚜ ✦ ✦ ⚜—

A gun: That was the manly thing, right? Whatever that meant.

In our modern age, a man can be almost anything. He needn't be a hunter or a farmer or a bush pilot. He needn't even really be a man. There are many men walking around today who are actually orangutans, according to their wives.

In the South of my childhood, men worked, sweated, ate fried chicken, and had heart attacks. Women worked, too, and sweated, and brought things to the men, such as their chicken, and their defibrillators, because of the heart attacks, because of the chicken.

If I had to describe what, exactly, men did, according to my father, it would be: Outside Things. I don't think I ever saw him clean a dish. He didn't even know where the sink was. If you had thrown his keys in it, he would not have been able to find them. He would think you had made them invisible, that you were a witch. I grew up believing men could not do housework, that if you did, something bad might happen. One might grow an ovary.

About the only thing that could make my father do house-work was a reliable tornado warning, which forced him inside and often led him to vacuum, although what he did wasn't so much vacuuming as attempting to hurt the carpet's feelings. Eventually, the weather would clear and Pop ordered us outside, to do our Manly Outside Things, burning and hammering and such. It was like Separate But Equal, except Pop did not really have a place in his head for things that sounded like math.

It wasn't just Pop. It was the whole family.

Every Sunday, we would gather at the farm in Coldwater. These Sunday dinners are one of the load-bearing pillars of the first decade of my life, and I didn't think anything odd about them until I left home and told others.

It wasn't the food that was odd, having been grown on land one could see from the table, every sort of bean and tuber and leafy thing and many delicious meats, always fried, boiled, burned, but never microwaved. I once had a two-hour conversation with my grandmother about what a microwave was and spent most of the time failing to explain how the device was not a bomb.

No, the food was normal, but the service was not, because the men ate first.

"You did *what*?" people would say, when I told them this story.

"The men," I'd repeat, "ate first."

"How did that happen?"

Mostly with forks, I'd explain.

I't's ready," Grandmother Key would say.

And there we'd go, Grandfather Key, Pop, uncles, boy cousins, nephews, Bird, me. We'd eat with great pleasure, while the women sat in the living room, waiting, starving, planning our deaths, except for the one or two who stayed near the table, to serve us.

"To do *what*?" people would say.

"To serve the men," I would say.

Pop's glass would be empty, and he would shake it, and the sound of the ice would bring one of the women running, usually his mother, sometimes his wife.

Occasionally, I'd look past the table and see a girl cousin staring at us from behind a piece of furniture, licking her lips while I ate my third pork chop. It was hard to know what she was thinking. Did she want some of this pork chop? Did she want to hurt me with it?

But there was never any complaint, nothing to suggest that this was not the habit of every American family in every home at that very moment.

There was a part of me that felt, yes, maybe it was weird.

And there was another part of me that felt, yes, maybe I would like some cake.

When I left home, this story about Sunday dinners was one of my favorites to tell to my progressive friends. It upset them greatly, but they also loved it, for it confirmed what most of them already believed about certain parts of America. They always wondered how I could come from such a simian world and yet be so egalitarian and kind, which made me wonder how I'd ever given them that impression. After all, it was me, not my father, who'd met a coquettish redhead in my first semester of college and, within thirty minutes of knowing her, asked her to do my laundry.

She actually said yes. We even made a date for the weekend.

"And I need some things ironed, too," I said, as she pushed her bicycle home, my laundry in a sack on her handlebars.

Two days later, she called.

"I'm not going to do your laundry," she said, outraged.

What had happened to the sweet girl? Had she been studying Marxism? She explained that it was presumptuous of me to expect her to put a crease in my khakis. How dare you, was her tone. I could hear a woman in the background, feeding her lines.

She explained that my whites would be in the lobby of my dormitory, unwashed, and hung up the phone. Wow. I'd learned my lesson. From now on, I vowed, I would only ask female relatives to do my laundry.

Two months later, I met the woman I'd marry.

She was fifteen, and I was eighteen, and she was visiting my school, a placed called Belhaven, where since the nineteenth century, Presbyterian youth have gone to feel bad about lusting for other Presbyterian youth. I had a few classes with her older sister, who was about as warm to me as Vladimir Putin to a wounded elk, but I liked the looks of the younger one.

So, we met, and nothing happened for ten years.

She did not speak to me because, according to her, I was "weird."

I did not speak to her because, according to bystanders, she kept "running away."

Word on the street was, she liked soccer players, which I felt was a cry for help. She also cried for help when I would try to speak to her, which was another cry for help.

Then, a decade later, I came home from graduate school one weekend to find her sharing an apartment with a good friend. There we were, my friend and me, sitting on the porch, and this young woman just walks up, bums a cigarette, gives me a little grin, and goes inside.

"I'm going to marry her," I said to my friend. I could not explain why I'd said that.

A few days later, I saw her at a wedding.

At the reception, we talked.

At the party after the reception, we talked more.

My plan was to talk to her until her brain stopped working properly and then ask her to marry me. We did a lot of laughing. Nobody had told me how funny she was. How could somebody that gorgeous be so funny? She had clearly been exposed to gamma rays in her youth. It wasn't fair.

I told her about all my failures in writing, and she told me about all her failures with soccer players, and by the time I took her home, I was in love. I'd always thought I'd fall for a tortured poetess, but she was my opposite in every way. Unlike me, she had no interest in books or canoes or live music or talking about her every psychological state until those around her fell asleep or attempted to escape through a window. On paper, this was not going to work.

When fall came, I knew it was time to do something I'd never done with a girlfriend: take her to Coldwater for Thanksgiving. On the way there, our first real road trip, she taught me a great way to pass the time in the car called the Penis Game, where you replace any word in a traffic sign or billboard with *penis*.

"Do Not Block Penis!" she said, pointing to a traffic sign.

"Are you okay?"

"Penis Parking Only!" she said.

We spent the next two hours this way, laughing, dying.

"Penis Five Miles Ahead!"

"Number One Penis in Mississippi!"

Soon we laughed ourselves out. I could live forever with a woman who understood the value of a word like *penis*. As we got closer to Coldwater, I decided it was time to explain how we did things at Thanksgiving.

"The thing is," I said, "the men eat first."

"I don't get it."

"You know, we'll say a blessing, and then you go to the living room and wait."

"Wait for what?"

"To eat."

"And what are you doing while I'm waiting?" she said.

"Eating," I said.

I tried to explain that it had something to do with farming, the men needing to eat quickly so as to excuse themselves to see to the few chores, the Outside Things, but this explanation had no legs.

"That's the stupidest thing I've ever heard," she said.

"It is," I said. "It is so stupid."

Silence. Quiet.

"Penis for Senate!" I said, pointing, but she didn't laugh.

A few minutes after we arrived, all the men took their places around the table, and so did I. And my girlfriend followed me to the table.

"What are you doing?" I said.

"Sitting down."

She pulled out a chair.

"Maybe you'd like to sit in the living room?" I said.

She gave me a little grin and sat down.

My grandfather and my father looked at her, and then looked at me, while I looked into the mashed potatoes, to see if Jesus was in there.

A clearing of the throat.

"Let's pray," Grandfather Key said.

And we ate. That's when I knew I would marry her. And of course, I did. You know that already.

The first time I remember our discussing who should do what, the cooking and the cleaning and the housework, we were in the kitchen of our first apartment.

"Why haven't you taken the garbage out?" she asked.

She pointed to an unfamiliar canlike object in the corner. It was in a part of the kitchen where I had often seen my wife, but I paid no attention to what she did there. She had all sorts of hobbies that I felt were not my business, such as collecting empty milk jugs, which I made sure to save for her.

"Stop it!" she said, as I put an empty jug into the fridge. "Why do you do that?"

"Is this a trick question?" I said.

She just stood there.

It was a game! The name of this game was "Where Does My Wife Want the Empty Milk Jug to Be?"

"What about the sink?" I said. "So you can clean it."

"Why would I want to clean that?"

"You could fill it with rocks and make a shaker."

I made a shaking motion with the empty jug, and she made a motion that seemed like she was going to kick my face through my brain.

She explained that what you do is, you throw it away.

"But the can is full," I said.

And she explained what you do is, you empty the garbage.

She held up the bag with one hand and told me to take it out, which is what I did, hurrying back to the kitchen, eager to see her pull more fun things out of the can.

"Where'd you put it?" she said, of the garbage bag.

"The porch."

"No."

The bag of garbage, she explained, had to be transported to a larger can.

The beautiful woman with the shoulders and almond eyes, my own Sophia Loren, had become a garbage Nero. How had this happened? I felt the sting of a moral conviction deep in my young and ignorant heart, some friction between the way I thought of the world and how it actually worked. The sting was minor, almost forgettable, the kind of pain you can drown out with a beer and a good eight hours of sleep. It was nothing, I hoped.

That night, I thought about all the world's garbage being moved from smaller cans, to larger cans, to ever larger cans, until it got to the biggest can of all. Where was this can? Who emptied it? God? Does God have a wife? Or a husband? Or at least a maid?

The years, they roll on. You grow, you have children, maybe you fight about small things, like bath toys, which apparently are grown in the uterus when you have children. Like all our fights, the bath toy fight was really about the quality of our marriage, but saying, "I want to fight about our marriage!" is a silly way to start. It's better to begin with something provocative, like, "If you don't get rid of those bath toys, I am going to start peeing on them in the shower."

Happy Meal toys, landfill fodder, Popsicle sticks gnawed into barbed lances, the rubber ducks and turtles that retain water for several hundred years, I hated them. They lived on the floor of our only bathroom, where, in olden times, homeowners were expected to stand.

"Do we really need all these toys?" I asked my wife.

"Do we really need *you*?" she said.

She still wasn't very good at expressing her feelings in words, but I deduced, through a complicated series of door- and cabinet-slammings, that her position was this: The toys

represented the necessary messiness of family life, the frag-
ments of joy that she worked hard to provide for our children,
and that my hatred of the toys was really a hatred of our life,
and her efforts to make it a happy one.

And again, there came the old sting, rising up from down
under, and I pushed it back down. They were just bath toys. I
would've thrown them away myself, but bath toys are an Inside
Thing, and men, as we all know, only do Outside Things. Besides, if I'd thrown them away, she'd only have fished them back
out of the garbage, further confusing me about what should
and should not be thrown away. The way the fight ended was,
a special task force determined that I should insert my head
into my rectum and die.

Sometimes, we fought about sex, which we had to stop calling
a meeting, because our children had a gift for metaphor, so we
started calling it "the budget," which made it sound so much
more fun.

"Do you want to work on the budget?" I'd ask, while the
TV hypnotized our children.

"We did the budget already this week," my wife would say.

"We should review the spreadsheets."

"I've seen the spreadsheets."

"Some people make new spreadsheets every day."

"Those people are not doing their budget right," she said.

And then, if I decided to be hurt by this, we'd have a fight,
and our kids would think it was about money, but it was never
about money, unless it was about money, because sometimes it
was about money. Like any healthy marriage, we both made
gently terroristic demands of the other, and sometimes these
demands resulted in fights, and sometimes they merely resulted
in a quiet, respectful hatred. My wife's demands included:

Being "helpful"
Closing "drawers"
Reading her "mind"
Never touching her anywhere unless I have written
     permission
Not chewing or drinking or talking so loudly
Not making sounds ever out of my face

My demands of her included:

Taking a chill pill
Turning that frown upside down
Allowing me to talk during movies and TV shows and
     also when she is talking
Acknowledging my presence when I am declaring great
     ideas for novels into the air
Not checking her phone while I explain how great this
     salad was that I had this one time

When our fights got really good, I'd start bellowing like a
bull elk in rut, which frightened the children, but did nothing
for my wife.

"Oh, you're such a big man," she would say, when I got
loud. "SOOOO big! SOOOO important!"

I found this unfair, for two reasons: First, I had always attempted to be more progressive than my father, a man who indeed would have agreed that he was a very big man and should
be obeyed, and second, because secretly, I believed myself to be
a very big man who should be obeyed. That was the sting of it.

Is this what marriage was supposed to be?

You hear a lot about marriage in church. The Bible was

full of many exemplary unions, such as Adam and Eve's, who created original sin and gave birth to children who murdered one another and soiled creation with the blood of all humanity. Then there was Abraham and Sarah. Sarah was quite old, so God told Abraham to make a baby with the maid, Hagar, which he did, because when God tells you to make sex with the maid, you don't ask questions, even if she is named after a Viking.

There are more marriages in the Bible, but these two are the most normal.

Then there's the Book of Ephesians, which suggests that men ought "to love their wives as their own bodies," which perhaps meant the Lord wanted us to get our wives drunk and take them to the gym?

Most important, it is recommended that husbands are to love their wives "even as Christ also loved the church," which, if the simile was to be believed, meant that at some point my wife might demand I be tortured and then killed by the government, which, during some of our fights, did not seem unlikely. It's funny now, but at the time, it was not funny. At the time, it was a terrifying thought to think that much of our fighting was fated because my wife and I might have married the wrong person.

We passed the milestones: Year One, Five, Ten. We had babies. We bought a house. It got robbed. It was a life.

I took on new responsibilities at work, and she took on more at home, mostly with the children, who, according to a book she read, needed to be fed at least weekly, which required more groceries, which required regular trips to Walmart, which made her violent.

We did things happy families do. Cookouts, vacations,

birthdays with ponies. When we fought about things like bath toys, I brought flowers home, which she appreciated. Sure, we had problems. Maybe she didn't dance with me at bars, and maybe I didn't get excited about going to Disney World, and maybe I could feel the tremors of my conscience telling me I was doing this all wrong, and that if I kept it up, Something Bad might happen, but still, we laughed, we cried, we lived, we put the children down at a reasonable hour, so we could eat dinner in peace, just sitting there, watching television from different pieces of furniture, not saying a word.

Men over here, women over there.

Sometimes, out of the corner of my eye, not wanting her to see me seeing her, I'd look at my wife on the couch, and something sort of sickening would make itself known in my intestines, the shadow of some terrible monster circling under the water of our home.

Is she happy, I wondered?

Would she ever have an affair?

What would it be like to be divorced?

None of the insidious hurricanes that destroy marriages battered the roof: no addictions, no adultery, save what I'm sure was the mutual daydreaming of what life might be like with other people, as her body bore the marks of three children and I went from looking decent shirtless to being required by most city ordinances to be carried in a horse trailer. But on the worst days, I'd find myself wondering: Is this marriage dead? There was no hatred, no anger, just a blank space where love should be.

So you push the terror down with the heel of a boot and tell yourself you're happy, because you've got a career and a family and a life that you love and sometimes don't, and you find yourself standing in church and hearing a chord change in a hymn that hits you like a memory and the place inside you where the feelings live splits wide open and you get a little weepy.

It's a beautiful life, you tell yourself.

And later that day, standing in the kitchen with a beer, surrounded by your wife and children, you find yourself thinking that these are the salad days.

And then you finish that beer, and your wife puts the kids to bed, and you have a discussion about a few things, work, money, the future, and something comes out of your wife's mouth that ends the salad days forever.

Before I tell you what my wife said, it's important to know that all week, we'd been having an ongoing discussion about money and time. We had a big decision to make, which was: Should I work more, and make more money, which seemed impossible, since I was already working too much? Or should I work about the same, and make the same money, which had turned out to seem like not enough money, having three daughters who were required by oppressive governments to wear clothes and shoes to school?

My wife said, Yes, I should make more money.

And I said, Maybe we just *think* we need the money.

And she said, Do you know how much milk costs?

And I said, Time is more precious than stuff.

And she said, You're never here anyway.

And I said, That's not true.

And that's when she said the thing:

"If you're not going to be a part of our lives, at least we can have some money."

It hit me square in the tender part of my aorta, a dagger of a razor-tipped sentence. The room turned like the Gravitron, that ride at the fair that pins you to the wall until your organs slide out your earholes, and that's what happened. My organs slid out my earholes.

My wife did not usually talk about her feelings like that, and was as surprised as me that this thing she'd kept secret was out.

And what was the secret?

That she didn't really like me much anymore.

I asked her to explain, and it all came pouring out, that I was too focused on work, not there *physically*, that she felt like she was parenting alone, doing all the housework, all the childrearing, while I tried to remind her how money was made, that it required people being places for long periods of time, and that besides, *she* was not there emotionally, that the funny woman I'd married had long since been replaced by a deadness in the eyes, a joyless sighing in my presence, the sudden destruction of all general mirth in her vicinity.

The word *divorce* came up a few times over the next week, not in the form of a threat, but just a grenade, a pin pulled on a word to see what would happen.

I was pretty sure she hated our life, and maybe I did, too, and was it even really our life? It was two halves of a life. A divorce? It sort of seemed like we already were.

And then, a week after she'd said the thing she couldn't unsay, after all fighting and slugging, exhausted, our best punches thrown, what seemed like the last leg of the pub crawl of our marriage, she mentioned she might take the kids and leave.

"Where?" I said.

"Away."

I couldn't tell if it was a promise, or a threat.

That night, I marshaled all evidence against her, and there was no shortage: Her gloom, the way she winced like she'd smelled something rancid when I tried to touch her, how she refused to talk about anything, ever, until it was too late.

I tried to make her coldness the common denominator of our worst moments, her refusal even to try to enjoy what she knew I loved: dancing, jalapeños, videos of interspecies love between cats and dogs, the most hilarious passages of *A Confederacy of Dunces.*

But then, last I checked, all that stuff didn't mean I was not also a jackass. When I looked at the leviathan, all I could see was my face, and questions about toilet seats, and leaving them up, and drawers, and leaving them open, and giving the children tortilla chips to eat in the living room after she'd cleaned, and how I tried to hug her after a workout, knowing she would hate it, and how I left the lamp on late into the night, reading books, while she with her translucent eyelids tried and failed to go to sleep next to me, exhausted from the long day of doing all the Inside Things that my rearing told me were her responsibility.

I had inherited my father's sham dichotomy: men over here, women over there. And maybe that worked in olden times, or maybe not. Maybe that's not history. Maybe that's just a bad idea, a story someone told. Maybe everything I knew about women was wrong.

I got up, couldn't sleep, walked across the hall to my office.

I got so upset at the idea of my wife at some point in the future actually not being my wife that my heart began to beat hard, too fast, so fast I could feel it in my knees, in my ears. My heart dropped three stories into my kidneys, and I could feel it beating there, where it clearly had no business being, and my back began to spasm. I got down on the floor.

Is this what a broken heart felt like? It felt a lot like diabetes.

I saw clearly that there was one thing I needed to stop doing, and that was behaving like my father. He'd had three wives. Just because he could be an idiot about women didn't mean I got to do it, too. Besides, he'd finally figured it out. He'd been married to my mother for about forty years. He'd clearly learned something.

What a gift, to learn, and change.

I looked around my office, as I lay dying on the floor.

On the wall, two pairs of antlers, formerly attached to the heads of deer my grandfather killed many years ago, representative, perhaps, of the Manly Outside Things I didn't really do anymore. On another wall, books, representative of what I did now, which, let's be honest, were very much Inside Things.

My father had no interest in reading, or in the art on the wall, the fountain pens on the desk, the music on the shelf. There was a gun, but it was hidden, like a relative with a facial deformity. I was unlike him in every way. Why had I chosen to be precisely like him in the way I treated my wife?

I closed my eyes, tried to sleep on the bare floor. It would be a pitiful sight. I pictured my wife finding me there in the morning, covering me with a blanket. No, she would ignore me. You couldn't extract pity from the woman if you used an industrial centrifuge. Pity was not the solution.

I tried to remember why I'd married her, how funny and weird she was, how she smelled cups before using them, how lovely it had been, once, to see her at a wedding. And I remembered the Penis Game. A woman who will teach you the Penis Game comes along only once in a lifetime.

I loved that she didn't want to dance with me, and I loved that she tried anyway. She had something you couldn't get at, a fire in her that nobody could touch. I loved that. I tried touching it many times, and she always hit me when I tried to touch it, and I loved that, too.

Here was a woman who just sat down at a tableful of men and ate and didn't care, a woman who held my hand, grabbed my arm, seized my shirtsleeve, wailed to the high heavens when the tiny humanoid screamers we'd made together emerged from history, naked souls wailing. These were ours: We'd made them. She taught me to love these children, showed me how to do it with shit on your hands—and I'd taught her some things, too, like how to talk about her feelings using words and not doors.

That night, I dreamt about the garbage can, and even the larger garbage can, and even the city dump, where, one day, I could take my daughters to show them where I would bury the bodies of their boyfriends if they reminded me too much of the idiot I used to be.

Day came, the sun did rise.

I went on a walk. I sweated, I wondered.

What is a marriage?

It's not an economy, because spreadsheets cannot explain who should take out the garbage, and it's not a logic problem, because an equation can't tell you when to come home from the office, and it's not a zero-sum game, because love only makes more love, and it's not a hostage negotiation, where you make demands in exchange for what you want, because that's called terrorism. No, Jesus was right. The only good metaphor for marriage is death, and man, I felt like I'd died.

I finished my walk, sat on the back porch, removing my shoes.

She came out, stood there.

I was supposed to love this woman like my own body,

which was starting to make sense, because when I took a bath, I didn't expect my body to thank me, because that would be weird, because my body had no mouth, except for the one on my face, which I employed, in that moment on the porch when our life together could have been swallowed up by the monster, by saying these words to her.

"I'm sorry for being an idiot," I said.

And we talked.

"You have to stop working twelve hours a day," she said.

"Sometimes, I might have to," I said.

"Sometimes."

"You have to stop not telling me how you feel," I said.

"It's hard for me."

And we talked some more.

And I knew, as we talked, that I'd have to make my wife want me around again.

And that I'd have to work on the budget, the real one, not the sex one.

And that maybe we could work on the sex one, too, later.

But I didn't say it out loud, which was an improvement.

It had been a difficult season. The rains came, washed things away, exposed bones. It would take a while for us to laugh together like before, but we could get there. All it took was getting back in the car and holding hands and moving on down that road, trying to pay attention to the signs.

Penis Construction Ahead.

Why had she ever married me? I have no idea. Whatever it was, I was hoping she remembered. I think she did.

I stood up.

"I love you," I said, all hot, all sweaty, and she closed her eyes, and I touched her, and she didn't wince.

CHAPTER 21

·

The Old Man in My House

—≡⟨ ✦ ✦ ⟩≡—

It took a little time, but with great effort and prayer and love, the salad days returned, and I understood my family in a rich and profound new way, had seen the innermost wonders of my wife's tender and tangled heart. There were stories in that heart I had not known, and I knew them now. I listened. I learned. I ironed. She made me iron. My own slacks. My own shirts. My children's smocked dresses, which turned out to have more folds and pleats than an origami croissant, and I ironed the hell out of those dresses, often while cursing aloud.

I had been so terribly humbled, everything that mattered to me put into a bag and dangled in the air over a bridge over a river that would never give it back.

My wife was a riddle. I think all women are. Men are not riddles, even the smart ones. We are independent clauses, such as:

"I like meat."

"Water feel good."

But a woman is a sentence eighty yards long with no commas, a cryptogram, a *Finnegans Wake*, and a man is holding the book, and he is trying to read it, and he is confused.

"Women are funny," Pop said, on the phone.

"They sure are," I said.

These Sunday afternoon phone calls were reserved almost exclusively for expurgating the mysteries of women and football, but I had another motive, trying to convince my parents to move to Savannah by making Pop think it was his idea. He was getting no younger, and so were his grandchildren.

"Aw, boy, I don't know," he said.

"They have ESPN over here, too."

"Mm-hm."

"And you know Mom wants to come."

"Oh, she's about crazy over it."

We had been reveling in what we believed were the emotional eccentricities of women for many years, but these phone calls took on a new dynamic after the apocalyptic thundercloud had covered my own marriage for a time. I'd always thought it was mocking we were doing, but I saw now that we were only admitting to our own fumbling of the various balls we'd been handed to carry, much like our beloved Rebels, and that it was hard.

It had been a year since we'd talked of divorce, but it seemed a hundred years ago. We laughed, and even danced. My wife loved me. The way I knew was, she started mocking me in public again, which is how she expresses love. In the previous year, I'd learned to remember the best parts of our marriage, so that I could draw on those memories if things ever got bad again, so I could stop myself from believing it had never been good, which is so easy to do when you're enraged and wish to run over your spouse with heavy machinery.

Pretty soon we were looking at another wedding anniversary, and that got me to thinking once again about the strange covenant of marriage.

What had we said back then, a decade ago, in front of the church? I tried to remember our vows. I didn't recall much from that day, owing to fatigue and the residual effects of enough English beer to have tanned three or four beaver pelts. There were several cakes, I remember, and roses the color of butter, and my wife looked prettier than Grace Kelly. I found this quite disturbing, as it occurred to me that women who looked like Grace Kelly generally did not stay married to men who looked like me, unless we owned small aircraft.

Yet I did recall our uttering something about sickness and health. Which was good, because something had happened to my health, and I soon found myself lying on the couch and taking abuse from my wife.

"You're not sick," Princess Grace said.

"I am," I said. "I might die."

"Your back hurts," she said. "It's not like you have *cancer*."

I reminded her about our vows. "You promised to tend my infirmities," I said.

"Yeah, well, try giving birth to three children."

There was that irony I so deeply loved. My little shrew.

Princess Grace was always doing this, reminding me that she thrust three live human people through a hole in her crotch. She seemed angry about it, reminding me that I was the one who put them there.

"You didn't seem to mind at the time," I said.

"Vomit," she said.

Apparently, the very fact of childbirth trumps all pain-related complaining by all men for all time. I could have my arms ripped off by the world's largest gorilla and she would say, "At least it was quick. Try taking thirty hours to pass a watermelon out of your birth canal with no medication." But I would not be able to hear her, because the gorilla is beating me to death with my own arms.

I don't know how it happened: I simply woke one morning and was unable to stand fully upright. It felt as though the brisket of my lower back had been broiled in a still-warm oven. I pulled myself to a hunched position and hobbled to the kitchen, leading with my head.

"Oh, please," my wife said. "You're so weak."

"No, it *really* hurts this time," I said.

I cataloged my most ambitious movements of the day before. There was the small box (lifted), the flight of stairs (climbed), and the BMX bike that I appropriated from a neighborhood boy in order to demonstrate for the crowd of curious children how legends are made (ramped). Sensations rushed back, of this moment when I launched from the homemade ramp's zenith amid dropped jaws and willed my body and the bike into flight. Yet, just as my rear wheel left the earth, I received a message from my lower back that indicated caution and horror, a neural communiqué hushed by the endorphins of ramp glory and the cheers of neighborhood children—until now, the following morning, when I received a new message from my back, in the form of a letter of resignation.

I did not remind my wife of the bicycle incident, as it would only be cataloged in the evidence room of her memory for future depositions and prosecutions. Instead, I lowered myself to a supine position in hopes of having gravity collaborate with the wood flooring to help straighten me out.

"Don't be so dramatic," she said, stepping over me to fetch her coffee. "You'll be fine."

"All I am to you is a speed bump."

I lay there for the remainder of the morning, until she and the children departed for school. They mostly ignored me, although one of my daughters used me as a sort of park bench, sitting on me to eat her breakfast.

Finally alone, I pulled myself to a hunchbacked position, dressed in great agony the way I imagine Yoda must have, and mounted the Vespa for what turned out to be a torturous commute through the midcentury neighborhoods of Savannah that were nicer than my own. I moved slowly, feebly throughout Arnold Hall, the building where I work, and no one said a thing, except for a colleague who noticed my limping. He sidled up, smiling, had a secret.

"I've got two words for you," he said. "Horse liniment."

I thanked him and made a mental note to start bringing a handgun to work. I limped on, until something worse happened during my afternoon lecture, as I rhapsodized to a classroom about Aristotle's use of the topography metaphor in his *Rhetoric.*

"Think of the human mind as a map," I said, arms outstretched. Then something snapped, as though a distant bridge were slowly giving way, and it struck me that the bridge was nearby, and that it was the meat and bones and cartilaginous substances of my back, and that I was going to die.

"Oh, no," I said, falling to my knees in a dramatic flourish. The students, or at least those who remained awake, yawned, returned to studying the inside of their eyelid skin.

W hat seems to be the problem?" my internist asked as he settled himself onto a stool.

He had the build and disposition of a gentle, unassuming superhero: broad shoulders and thick arms and trim waist of a man who would probably look entirely normal driving a Jeep without a shirt. He was not a large man, but everything about him screamed fitness, protein shakes, and the dedicated consumption of legumes. He was in his late forties, I'd bet, with a model-worthy head of silvery hair that seemed to have no plans for retreating into the interior of his scalp. He was, in short, exactly the kind of man you hoped would be your doctor, if you were an emotionally scarred woman between the ages of twenty and seventy who had no qualms about removing her clothes in front of Captain America.

As for me, I didn't mind disrobing in front of him, because I liked to believe he had a tortured inner life that the horror of my nakedness could not match.

"It's my back, Doc."

"Take off your shirt for me."

The next few minutes progressed like many of my best high school dates, with a great deal of touching and bending and whimpering. It was awkward, also, because Dr. America and I frequented the same café, where I was usually in the corner, brooding, thinking of myself as a visage of controlled existentiality, as though I were prefiguring the dark Kierkegaardian voids of my own and many other possible lives. And perhaps I appeared to be that. But when Dr. America entered the café and saw me there, he knew about things that others did not, like my rash. This was the reason for my last visit, before the back thing. And so, when others observed me at the café, they might've thought: *Writer* or *Thinker* or *Chess Master*. But when he saw me, what he must've thought was: *Ointment*.

"What's wrong with me?" I said.

I secretly hoped it was something debilitating. A simple back injury would be enfeebling, emasculating, but there could be great glory in a disease requiring a wheelchair. Something permanent, but not terminal, a malady that might lead to a career in motivational speechmaking and the lucrative field of disease memoirs.

"I don't know how to say it," Dr. America said. "You need to strengthen your core." He swept his hand across the snug, tailored waist of his shirt, where his carbon-fiber abs lay dormant for weekend display on various beaches. He explained, as gently as he could, that my only malady was frailty. "You need to work out. Nothing too rigorous. Just the occasional crunch. Do you know the crunch?"

I explained that I was the kind of man who prefers to use *crunch* as a verb, but he only smiled the smug smile of those who feast on ambrosia from the navels of Polynesian virgins.

"I'm going to give you some exercises. Very basic," he said. "It won't even feel like you're working out."

He handed me a printout of an illustrated elderly man in various postures, mostly on his back and mostly looking dead.

A man doesn't like being told his body is too weak to stand upright, especially when standing upright is such an important part of his life. It's something I did almost every day, such as when I needed to walk from one place I had been sitting to a different sitting place. A moment like this makes a man wonder if he spends too much time sitting, and so I sat down, so I could think, mostly how men in my family did not generally complain about lower back pain or dental pain or whatever they call the sort of pain you have when an organ bursts.

Organ pain.

When Pop invariably lodged a barbed fishing hook somewhere inconvenient, like an eyelid or a nostril, he did what manly men do: He took out his pliers and did things that reminded you exactly where you'd left your sphincter. I have no memories of him going to the doctor for everyday complaints, although I am sure he did, to have his eyelid sewn back on.

This one time, when I was six, he had a heart attack.

It happened while he was duck hunting near the Mississippi River. As his heart exploded, he dragged a boat through a river bottom, loaded it onto a trailer, and drove himself an hour north to the hospital.

"Your father's had an episode," Mom said.

They were going to have to put him on the table, cleaving his chest open like an animal's, and saw through his sternum and reroute his arterial interstate.

It was difficult to imagine my monstrously vital father on a table like an animal, sawed practically in half, his holiest parts exposed, the very mechanisms of life laid bare for all to see and steal and ruin and wreck.

"He's going to be okay," Mom said, but she was not the same after that.

He didn't complain. Never complained. Never asked for anyone's pity about the long fat scar running from navel to neck.

I pictured him pulling a boat with one hand, heavy Red Ball waders dragging him down, a gun on his back, hitting his chest hard to keep the motor running, the fist coming down like a hammer, and getting to the truck, and getting to the highway, and getting himself to the hospital, his eyes going dark, the light fading, and marching into the hospital an hour away to tell the doctors he was about to die and to make sure his wife got the keys to his truck and his boys got his guns.

I told myself this story, and then I told others, and it was frightening and funny, and I kept getting new stories to add to the routine, and everybody laughed: The man could not be real.

"He's very real," I promised them.

And people would ask me to tell the story again, any of the stories, all of them, and that is how he became a legend, a man in a book.

Pop was a man's man, and I was a man's child, or a child's man, a hobbled man-child.

"What'd he say?" my wife asked.

"What'd *who* say?"

She rolled her eyes. My wife had elevated eye-rolling to an art that can only be practiced by the demon-possessed and various dark wizards of irony. The iris goes up and all but disappears under a lid that flutters like a windblown sheet of paper under the burden of a commemorative paperweight. I tried to imitate this maneuver, to show her how attractive it made her look, and came near to severing my optic nerve.

"Are you crippled? Is it a *disease*?" she said.

I wanted to lie, to invent something, a rare ailment not yet searchable on WebMD, but I decided not to deceive my wife. It would be too much work and might require the remembering of conversations, a responsibility I long ago delegated to her.

"It's my muscles," I said.

"What's wrong with them?"

"Apparently I don't have any."

"Where?"

"Anywhere."

"So I guess you have to start working out."

"I already walk."

"Walking is *not* hard," she said.

"It is if you don't have any muscles."

You could tell she did not think any of this was very serious, that it was nothing compared to having an angry biped scraping the inner walls of one's pelvis.

"I have a prescription," I said, holding it up as evidence.

She took it. "This is just Aleve," she said.

"I have to get physical therapy," I said. This was no joke, I explained. There might be war veterans there, and others who have overcome impossible odds and been featured in local newspapers for their demonstrations of courage. She gave me a look that suggested the newspaper industry had no interest in my story.

I went to physical therapy and believed myself to be in the

wrong location, as the room looked like something from the earlier scenes of *Awakenings*, when everyone is drooling, and I noted that many of the patients were old enough to have been veterans in any number of nineteenth-century wars. My therapy consisted of being rolled around like a ball of frozen dough, after which they attached me to a car battery.

"I didn't know we still electrocuted people like this," I said to my therapist, who said nothing. As the energy pinched and washed through my core, I thought of how emasculating it was, needing to be electrified so that I might regain the ability to walk upright.

I guess we all knew that Pop would eventually get old and stop being so big and strong and start being very small and weak, and it happened. One day you look up and the legend really is a legend, meaning: not really true. Something shut down, and he went into the hospital one way and came out another. He was shorter, it seemed, feeble. You see something like that, you just want to go into the backyard and heave for a while. It's life's way of reminding you that the man will die one day, and so will you, and it will be nothing but sad.

Mom became his nurse, with her diary of his sodium intake and medications and the procedural steps, written in her sweet schoolteacher's cursive, for the transtelephonic monitoring of the defibrillator that lived somewhere under his collarbone.

"Your father's old," she whispered to me, when he had trouble keeping up with us while we did some Christmas shopping.

"I'll stay with him," she said, and they sat down on a bench together, and she patted him on his leg, while he stared at his feet. There was still fire in the old eyes, though. He could still worry her, and he liked knowing it. He still fished, alone. Got on a boat. Fell into Pelahatchie Bay. Barely got out.

"Your father fell into the lake again," she said on the phone.

"Oh, good," I said, thinking, Oh, bad.

"It took his defibrillator a good minute to get him going," she said.

It's maybe the last manly thing he's got left, his ability to make his wife crazy, to worry her. And it made me feel better, knowing he still could. She was right: He was old. She was old, too. It was good, watching them be old together, watching the love get stronger when the body got weaker.

When my own electroshock therapy was done, I put my clothes on and hobbled out to my scooter and drove home.

"How was it?" my wife asked, as I positioned myself on all fours on the bed, attempting to practice one of the therapeutic poses suggested by Dr. America. The wrinkled man in the picture appeared to be imitating a male dog in the act of urination, and I could not get it right.

"They electrocuted me," I said, lifting my right leg into the air.

"Oh, I used to get that done all the time in ballet," she said. "It always felt good. Warm, like a massage."

"Of course."

The woman gave no quarter to any of my disease-based fantasies, and demanded to know why I was acting like a dog.

"I'm strengthening my core," I said.

"Please, not on the bed."

In time, after I suggested having her bathe me, she assented that yes, it was possible, perhaps, that I might be in something resembling pain. She did her duty, opening my beers for me, assisting me into the rocking chair, as though I were a tribal elder, where the children poked me with wooden spoons to see if I was alive. She even presented me with a gift.

"What's that?" I said.

"A cane."

"How sweet."

"You're an old-timer now!" my five-year-old said, taking the cane from my lap and wielding it like a broadsword. She held it high over my head, about to put me out of my misery.

"Yeah," the three-year-old said. "You're our grandfather now."

I watched Princess Grace going about her day, preparing dinner, carrying out the garbage I could no longer carry, seeing to the needs of the younglings. The woman has looked twenty years old since she was fifteen and still did. I always seemed much too old for her, with my premature baldness and high Gold Toe socks and love of pudding. And now, as in all May-September marriages that last, she had become my nurse.

"She's a good old gal, I reckon," Pop would say about Mom, and he said it more and more as he got older and fell into many lakes and waterways across the southeastern United States, and you could see a gratitude in him that you hadn't seen before, that had been dormant. "She takes care of me," he'd say, in front of her, smiling, and I thought: Yes, that is what you need. Someone who keeps a covenant made ten or forty years ago, even when we are old. My wife was my nurse now, and I'd have my turn to be hers, when a plague of migraines descended and would not leave. I'd bring her warm rags and keep the lights low and duct-tape the children to the walls to keep them from making too much noise. Yes, those days would come, but for now, it was me who suffered, hobbling through the days.

It's difficult to know how long this would go on, whether my core would ever be strengthened by the Congress of the Urinating Dog. But I did not care. It was pleasing to watch my child bride make good on her promises.

"Is this what it will be like when we're old?" I asked.

"You *are* old," she said, as the grandchildren flogged one another with my cane.

"Tell me you love me," I said.

"You love me," my wife said.

"I do, I do."

CHAPTER 22

.

The World's Largest Man

—⋇ ✦ ✦ ⋇—

Call me, 911," my wife's text said.

I checked my email.

"Call me, 911," said her email.

I was at the college, in a meeting.

Also, a missed call from my mother.

"Hello?"

"Your dad's unresponsive," my wife said. "Come home."

I hung up, turned to the people in my meeting.

"I'm leaving."

"You're leaving?"

"I'm leaving."

I left.

Unresponsive. What a strange word. My father had been unresponsive for seventy-one years. He responded to nothing, because nothing impressed him—not spaceflight, nor magic, nor Bach chorales, nor the Olympic Games, nor social media platforms.

"Pop, when are you going to get on Facebook?" I said, often.

"Face who?"

"Book."

"Book?"

He did not respond to books, either, unless they were being read during church, to which he responded by taking my arm in the vise grip of his earthmover hands and squeezing hard enough to weaken my vocabulary.

He was responsive to food and women and babies, whom he rocked with a mighty gift, and he was responsive to the acting of Charles Bronson, because he responded to the idea of a man shooting whatever he wanted to, and he responded to innovations in fishing lure technology, but not really any other kind of technology, such as the iPhone.

"You seen what this thang can do?" he said, when he got it.

I expected he'd show me some app that would tell him the location of the nearest escaped convict or Red Lobster. He pushed a button.

"Looka here," he said.

It was the compass feature. That impressed him. He liked knowing where he was.

He was unresponsive in other ways, too, such as the time when I was five and he fell into his raisin bran. I was sitting on the floor of the bathroom, putting on my tennis shoes for school, when I heard my mother cry out. I dashed to the kitchen, and saw Pop facedown on the table while Bird looked on with sleepy eyes and Mom lifted his head out of the bowl.

The ambulance arrived.

He woke up.

"I ain't going to no damn hospital," he said.

The next year, he had his heart attack.

Mom, fearing as she did another family member being

ripped from her arms and swept up to heaven, called these moments "episodes," as though Pop were a really great television
show. Over the next thirty years, he had many episodes, with
great reviews, many cliffhangers. I found him on deer stands,
looking dead. Was he asleep? Should I wake him? Fire a warning shot? Would it frighten him, and send him plummeting off
the high stand to the earth, killing him? I was too young to be
killing my father. It wasn't time for that, not yet.

"Pop," I'd whisper, from the ground below.

I'd have to get a stick, throw it at his face.

This long-running TV drama remained captivating, terrifying. He kept leaving, and kept almost dying, and kept coming back. He'd black out, run his truck off the road, nearly die,
which was fine, according to him.

"It was time to sell that truck anyhow," he'd say.

He was very responsive to new trucks.

"Goddang, boy," he said on the phone last deer season. "I
fell out the dang deer stand."

"Maybe you should stop hunting by yourself," I said.

To this, he was unresponsive.

Those blackouts were a rehearsal for his last great performance,
the one he wouldn't wake up from. And frankly, we were all a
little surprised that he'd lived this long, given how many times
he told women he was pretty sure they'd gained weight. He
had always been so big himself, and now he was shrunken,
withered.

There'd been an especially bad episode not long ago, back
in Mississippi, when he'd been unresponsive in his big chair
while Mom screamed and hit and slapped and cried at him to
wake up, which he finally did.

"What the hell is wrong with you, woman?" he said.

"I thought you were—" Mom said.

"Tired."

"Yes."

It was time to get them to Savannah, I knew. Mom could not scream at him all by herself. The show seemed to be in its final season, moving toward a final memorable episode that could really only end in one way. It would not be easy, asking Pop to leave the only land he'd ever loved, the lakes and rivers and woods he knew so well, his heart's terrain. He would wilt. The very move might kill him. They said his heart was at 20 percent.

"The girls sure would like you to come to their Christmas program," I said on the phone, hoping to convince him that there was no longer anything for him in his ancestral homeland, even though it was a lie. Everything was there, except his three granddaughters.

"We'll see," he said.

I couldn't say the thing I wanted to say, which was: I'd spent a life leaving him and had finally decided I wanted him back. I wanted to turn corners in my own town and see him.

It wasn't just his health that kept him from coming. It was money. Lucre was his tragic flaw, specifically his inability to not be an idiot with it. Sometimes his idiocy was selfish, such as buying a fishing rod that would've paid for that crown Mom needed, or perhaps forty fishing rods, and sometimes his idiocy was unselfish, such as giving a mortgage payment to a home for orphaned children. Nothing put him in a good mood like having money and nothing put him in a foul mood like sitting in his big chair wondering what in the hell he'd spent it on. He'd never had a budget. It was all in his head, he said, except when it wasn't.

"Hey, where's check number two thirty-seven?" he'd say.

"I don't know," Mom would say.

"Well you better damn well remember," he'd say, trying to reconcile various bank statements with the tale of magical realism told in the checkbook ledger. This was back before online banking, when the only way to tell how much money you had in the bank was to send a peregrine falcon to town and then wait two weeks for it to come back.

And they would fight.

"You think you can just buy anything!" Mom would say, her voice yodeling and high. "We don't need another lawn mower!" She would keep on and on about the new lawn mower, or the new rifle, the new rod, the new anything, until, growing tremulous, she would collapse, low and pitiful. "All I need is a perm," she would say, weeping now, her sad hair losing its curl in front of our eyes.

I prayed hardest on these days, when I was a young boy, kept my eyes closed tight until it was daylight. When I grew up, I vowed, I would have a job that paid for things. I would be master of my money. I would not have two lawn mowers, or one lawn mower, or even a lawn. I would have no hobbies, which required checks, and I would have a wife who did not require perms, even if it meant she had no hair.

Lawsuits. Bankruptcies. Repossessions. Boats he didn't need, because he already had other boats he didn't need, because he'd already won a boat in a bass tournament, which he sold, to use that money for a bigger boat. The bigger boats needed bigger garages, and bigger garages are always attached to bigger houses, because they almost never attach them to smaller houses, and so the mortgages grew in size and number, which meant the banks grew in size and number, and so did his blood pressure, especially when the banks came and took some of the boats away.

"Can't win for losing," he'd say.

"Stop buying things you don't need," I wanted to say, and often did, as I got older.

I wanted to move him to a place where his days could be occupied by his granddaughters, who did not require large garages. The move would call his bluff. He'd have to sell everything: the lawn mowers, the boats, the gun safe, the four-wheeler. They wouldn't fit in the apartment I had found.

"I found you a place here," I said.

But he did not want to die in a city, you could tell. He wanted to die somewhere quiet, somewhere you could drown alone, fall out of a tree, be gored in peace. And he didn't have the money, and this embarrassed him. He'd worked like a mule all his life, and all he had to show for it was a few guns, a few rods, and sixteen lawn mowers.

"Listen, Pop," I said. "I'll pay for it."

Money: He always responded to that.

The day they moved in, I stood with him outside his new apartment. It was a little sad, knowing he would never again live in a freestanding house, this born homesteader. But there was a nice lagoon he could see from his little porch. It wasn't Mississippi, but it was hot and green, like home.

There was great beauty in Savannah, of course, the Spanish moss that visitors gathered like the hair of Jesus, but there were also men in ponytails walking little poodles, and it made me even sadder knowing I had made my father live near men with such dogs.

"Would you ever get a tiny dog like that?" I said.

"And watch it shit all day?" he said. "Shit no."

The man with the ponytail waved at us. He seemed nice. Savannah had more than small dogs. We had big oceans, and he sort of liked that.

We got them moved in, got them settled, got them on a budget. Pop got him a bank in town, made friends with the tellers.

"I might would like to do some deep-sea fishing," he said, that first day.

A month later, he'd be dead.

There we were, driving to the hospital at unsafe speeds. Savannah had always seemed a little foreign to me, more East Coast than Deep South, but so many of the great stories of my life were happening right here, including this hospital, where two of my children had been born, where I'd carried my wife when her migraines had reduced her to cursing at people, where the man who made me would die. This was home now.

We parked. We heard sirens.

Had we beaten the ambulance here?

It screamed in. We ran to it, but were stopped by a cyclone fence, some sort of construction barrier. I grabbed the fence, wanted to jump it.

"Stop," my wife said.

"It's him," I said.

The ambulance doors opened. It was twenty yards away. They pulled someone out.

"It's him."

"No."

"It's him."

The thing on the gurney looked dead. White as a winter sky.

"It's not him," she said, and dragged me inside.

I looked back.

It was him.

Why all of human history is so concerned with its fathers, I'll never know. The mothers are so much nicer. The mothers cook us food and mail us brownies and fold our underwear. A mother quest, that would be nice. Where are our mothers? They are at home, waiting for us to call. They made spaghetti. Our favorite. So we go home, and we eat the spaghetti, and let them wash our underwear, and then it's over. Mother quest. So nice.

A cousin quest would be fun. Where are our cousins? They are down by the river, and they've got beer!

Or a wife quest. Where is my wife? She is probably at the Walmart. She hates it so much.

Moms, cousins, uncles, wives, sisters, teachers, lovers, these are all fine things to write about, but it seems like so many of us are always coming back to our fathers—who don't really excel in folding underwear. What they excel in is the Fine Art of Being a Real Sonofabitch. Even the good ones. Sometimes the good ones are the best at being a sonofabitch. It's like being a sonofabitch is what they think fathers are supposed to be. The Bible is full of sonofabitch dads, and so is Faulkner and *Star Wars* and Shakespeare. You know Shakespeare's dad was a real piece of work. And so was yours, probably.

If this story's really a Father Quest, then it started in kindergarten, on one of those days where all the dads are invited to eat lunch with their children and endure the humiliation of sitting in chairs that would ensure they could never again reproduce.

Pop said he'd be there.

I was pretty excited, because I'd been telling stories about him all year: How he was a big hunter and killed things and would soon allow me to kill things. How he fished the Red Man Tournament Trail and would soon allow me to put Red Man in my mouth, too. How he was generally Bigger and Better than Any Dad Anywhere and could probably beat up all the other dads.

"Yeah, but my dad has a tattoo of a dragon," one boy said.

"My dad could beat up a dragon," I said.

I have never, to this day, been so excited to see another human. My heart grows a size every time I think about how much I wanted to see him on that day, so they would know, so everyone would know how great he was.

Other fathers and grandfathers arrived. I was not impressed. These men were small. None of them would be carrying a knife, for example. Pop would have a knife. He would show it to everybody, if I asked. This was back when you could take a knife to a school, before people forgot that knives were not for stabbing people.

"Where's your dad?" my friends asked.

"Ha ha, he's not coming," they said.

"He's coming," I said.

Could they tell I was worried? I was worried.

The growing crowd of fathers spoke in kindly, vaguely in-terested tones to their offspring, in baby voices, not at all the way Pop talked to me, one man to another.

Soon, it was time to walk to lunch, and he was still not there.

Everyone lined up, but not me. I would wait.

He would come, I knew it. He must.

And I did what any little boy would do. I cried.

There was a knock on the classroom door.

It's him, I thought.

It wasn't him.

Our mothers, most of them, tell us who they are. They tell everything. Their hearts live on the outside of their bodies, because we are their hearts, and we are no longer inside their uteruses. But our fathers are always aliens. We were never inside them. Or maybe it's just me.

After that day in kindergarten, my relationship with Pop only got harder. He was just too large to be anything other than the Everest out before me, something to be scaled, conquered, known. I was not an untalented child, was blessed with modest intelligence and curiosity and a gift for making some people laugh, even my sister-in-law, this one time. But if you have read even half the stories in this book, you know there was one thing I could not do, and that was to love what my father loved. I quested, on woods and water and fields of play and farms of work. I did. I quested like a real sonofabitch, and could not find him in those places, or even myself.

It took many years before I realized I must have baffled him as much as he confused me. What must he have made of me, with my love of baking and books and bow ties? What a riddling abyss I must have seemed to him, when I announced that when I grew up, I desired very much to be a ventriloquist? Mom made sure I got a Bozo the Clown dummy that Christmas, and the only real trick I learned was to create a sense of shame and dread in my father. As I got older, I was no longer allowed to go grocery shopping with Mom, or to help her in the kitchen, because any boy who liked to cook was a sodomite.

Then, when I was twelve, I overheard a conversation between my parents, where Pop described some horrible thing he'd caught me doing the day before. Mom didn't want to hear it, was afraid, but he insisted she know.

"You know what I found him doing?" Pop said, his voice hushed at the horror of it.

"I don't want to know," she said. "He's a good boy, he's a good son."

"He was in our closet," he said.

"Doing what?" Mom said, moaning, covering her ears.

"Sewing a goddamn pot holder."

It was a Father's Day present.

Here was this boy, who he'd been told was his boy, and whom he resembled from certain angles, but who must've seemed like he'd been fathered by extraterrestrials, as when I came home from college and made the grave announcement that I was going to be in a play.

"A *play*?" he said.

"*Romeo and Juliet*!" I said. "I'm playing Mercutio!"

I knew he'd be upset to see his boy wearing tights, but I hoped they were similar enough to baseball leggings that he might not notice the difference. Perhaps he would not see that they were purple and festooned with gold sequins.

Mercutio has some great lines, and I did all my speeches in an acting style that could best be described as "speaking very loudly." Mom said they were going to bring the video camera, so the night they were there, I made sure to be extra loud.

In Act III, Mercutio dies. It is perhaps the greatest death scene in all of dramatic literature. Mercutio is stabbed, wounded, dying, but he rages.

"I AM HURT!" I screamed. "A PLAGUE ON BOTH YOUR HOUSES!"

By the time I was finished dying, I knew my father was going to love Elizabethan drama.

A few years later, I was at home with Mom and found the videotape they made that night. I watched it. It may have been the worst production of Shakespeare in the history of higher education. I fast-forwarded to my death scene. It was as loud and long as I remembered. As soon as I was dead, the tape cut off.

"Where's the rest of the play?" I said to Mom. "Didn't you tape it?"

"Oh, well," she said, a little embarrassed. "Your father thought that since you were dead, we should probably go ahead and leave."

I wanted to be offended, but of course was flattered. He had no interest in supporting the arts. For him, *Romeo and Juliet* was not about star-crossed lovers. It was about a young man in purple tights who seemed to have a hearing problem and then got stabbed, probably because he went around screaming at everyone.

His being there was merely a part of his own journey. Call it a Son Quest.

Maybe all this time, maybe what I've wanted to know is this:

Was I a good son?

I did everything he'd ever asked me to do. Shot things, hooked things, cleaned and hit and tackled and mauled and murdered and burned so much flesh and flora, worlds of blood and dirt. When I was little, I thought I'd love this stuff, and when I was a little older, I thought I could learn to love it, and when I was old enough to be a young man, I knew: no.

I know it hurt him, to see me quit football, then baseball, then the church he'd raised me in, to bury everything he'd given me, the hunting and fishing and fighting and foolish ways of a certain kind of Southern Man that I both am and am not.

And I wanted to hate him for it. And guess what: I did.

Like so many boys, I found myself believing my father to be a monster, an ignorant, hateful, bigoted wastrel who refused to respond and change and grow. That's why I left home, and left him.

Screw the Father Quest, is what I said.

And so he became the one waiting on me to show up: To church. To the deer camp. To the football game. To come home.

The phone would ring.

"Is that him?" Pop would say.

"It's not him," Mom would say.

I know it must hurt when your children reject the things that make you more human. I put a deep sadness inside him, for a time. But a funny thing happened a few years after I left. I'd come home to visit and find him gone.

"Where's Pop?"

"Fishing," Mom would say.

"With who?"

"A boy from our church," she'd say. "He's adopted. His daddy doesn't really take him anywhere."

He was drawn to young men with no fathers, or bad fathers, or absentee ones. He hired these boys, brought them to the house to work, paid them, fed them, spoke to them in virile tones about What a Man Is and Should Do and Not Do. He coached them, clothed them. He took whole trucks full of children out to lakes, to show them how to cast. I'd come home and find him out back, sitting with three black boys from up the road, him trying to be a father and them not snickering at all, but listening, talking, laughing.

"Them boys ain't got daddies," he'd say, after he'd paid them and taken them home.

He was a born father, and he was going to do it with or without me. His Son Quest was over. I was what I was. And what I was, was a writer and a teacher. One thing I can say for him: He never made fun of my wanting to do something as silly as writing. Never once. I was his boy. He still believed I was as much of a badass as I'd believed he was. If I wanted to write, shoot: It must be a good thing to want.

"My boy's writing a book," he'd started telling people, with pride.

And then I finally came back, and I came with a beautiful woman and a family of my own, and guess what? Those three little girls were better than any number of animal heads. Animal heads don't climb in your lap and hug you. Not unless they're still attached to their animal bodies.

When my parents would visit, my daughters would run to Pop, climb him like a tree. I watched them climb and wondered: Would they be so different from me, that I would not understand them? Will they reject what I love, those things that make me human?

We found Mom in the ER, sitting, worried.

"Come with me," someone said, and we went. I held my wife's hand, and my mother's, and couldn't shake the feeling that wherever we were going, nobody would be there. They

took us to a small room deep in the gray half-light of the hospital, and we waited.

The door opened, the team came in: a doctor, a nurse or
two, and a retinue of medical students and residents who were
getting their lesson in How to Tell a Family That a Loved
One Did Not Make It. The attending physician, a pleasant,
competent-seeming man about my age in wintergreen scrubs,
began to speak, offering a brief medical history of what had
happened in the previous hour, much of it originating from
what mother had told the EMTs: Pop's climbing the few steps
to his new apartment, how he'd fallen back onto Mom, the
CPR, the paddles, the intubation, and so on, and so on; the
story was too long.

The doctor kept talking, and I stood in front of my mother,
maybe hoping to keep her from the news she was about to hear.

"We pronounced him dead at four fifty-nine p.m.," the
doctor said.

And they left us alone, to cry.

People came in and out, asked questions. Did we want to
see him, one last time?

Mom nodded.

"Yes," I said.

It will happen to all of us, at some point, someone asking us
if we want to walk down a hall to see a dead man.

The last time I saw him—really saw him, not just the tank that
had been his terrestrial habitation, the color of cigarette ash and
laid out on a steel table, mouth open wide, as though violently
asleep, but him, the man, in his body, alive—was four days
prior. It was Mother's Day. We'd had Sunday dinner. We ate,
we talked. He was quiet.

I was happy to have them here, finally, all of us together,

Pop and me and five women we loved, eating on a Sunday. It was almost like Coldwater.

At lunch, his hands shook a little. Mom looked at me and made a face and motioned with her eyes to look at his hands, which I did. Despite the havoc that a dying heart had done to his body, bending, breaking him, the hands remained enormous, square, two fleshy earthmovers.

"That's what toting eighty-pound milk cans will do," Bird would say, a week later, at the funeral, when Pop's hands lay folded across his body. They would not fit together, were too big.

When dinner was over, Mom and Pop got ready to leave, and I walked out first, with my father.

"We need to get you a cane, old man," I said.

Normally, he would not have said a word to something like that, a remark meant to question his strength, but this time, he responded.

"I don't know what happened," he said. "I don't know what happened."

It was an odd thing to say, but I knew what he meant: He had gone and gotten old and was about to die. He was as shocked as anybody.

It was May, hot. He wore a camouflage jacket, because his dying heart could not keep him warm. He walked away from me, toward the car. I reached out, touched him on his back. The man had grown small, but when my hand touched his big broad back, I could feel no weakness there.

He was an Army Corps of Engineers spillway project, his head the outlet tower, his outspread arms like two granite weirs, his back the wall of stone that confined an awful power. I ran my hand along the sweeping granite of his back and marveled. He still felt a mile thick. He was my spillway, and I had come through the mass of him and out the other side, a man.

I wanted to tell him what he meant to me, but that would've been admitting he was leaving us. I hoped he knew what I didn't say. I hoped he could feel it in my hand.

"See you later, Pop," I said.

"See you, boy."

A week later, Bird and me and four other good men would carry his body to a little piece of land beside the Bull River, and if I told you how heavy that casket was, you might not believe me.

Often, these days, when I am sad and thinking of my father, I go back in my mind to that elementary school, that day in kindergarten, when I longed for him, back to a time when I was not trying to outrun him, to escape his habits and affections.

I was a tiny boy, shuffling down the hall at the end of the line. He hadn't come, and now I felt silly for crying, for letting everyone see my feelings. And then, when I rounded the last corner before the cafeteria, I saw something I'll never forget: Him.

He stood there in front of the cafeteria doors, waiting, so tall, so big. I looked up at him, wiped my face, sucked back any evidence of feelings.

His greatest lesson was the one he never said out loud, the thing a father should do, which is this: Be there. Always be there. And never stop being there, until you can't be there anymore.

"Hey, boy," he said, smiling, jangling the change in his pocket. "You ready to eat?"

"Yessir," I said.

I felt silly, crying there in the cafeteria line, and trying not to cry.

But now, I don't feel silly. I just feel a rush of something up through my heart, wide and deep as a river of light, and it rushes over the banks, and up through the throat and into the mouth and out my eyes, a great big surge of something that for so long had no name, a fugitive animal in a wood, and I know the name of it now, and what it is, is love.

Acknowledgments

—⚜ ✦ ✦ ⚜—

Thank you to God, who made trees, so we could have books and napkins.

Thank you to my wife, who did so much to help make this book, such as nod and smile when I was talking about it every day for the last six hundred years like that was normal. I love you even though you say I breathe too much when I eat, but I have a reason for breathing like that, like I said.

Thank you to my children, who insist on climbing me like a tree. Whenever I need to smile, all I have to do is think about holding you and kissing you and then needing to put you down because something happened to my back because of holding you, but I hold you anyway and will keep holding you until I have no back and possibly no front.

Thank you to my parents, who gave all of themselves to their children, and who gave us so many stories, the only real inheritance worth anything in this cosmic economy. And also thanks to my brother and sister, who taught me about love in ways not immediately obvious until I was older and much less stupid. Thank you all for not drowning me in the bathtub.

Thank you to Deborah Grosvenor, my agent, whose guidance turned this book from a flaccid beast into a healthy, energetic sprite with many life goals. You are a sorceress.

Thank you to Cal Morgan, my editor, who does this thing called "editing," which is similar to falconry in so many ways, including the fancy glove that he wears to meetings.

Thank you to Paula Wallace, SCAD president, friend, mentor, and maker of delicious soups, who showed me how to do something again, then do it again, then do it again, until it was perfect, then do it some more until I was pretty sure I was losing my mind, at which time it was almost right. Thank you for being brilliantly insane about getting it right, and thank you for hiring me, so I can help teach others to be insane, too. On that note, thank you to everyone at SCAD and the SCAD School of Liberal Arts, and also the good people at the Edward Albee Foundation for giving me money/love/space/time to help me write this book.

Thank you to Eliza Borné and others at the *Oxford American*, who gave me a place to test-pilot some of these stories and turn them into machines that would fly without killing too many people.

And, finally, I want to thank those aunts, uncles, cousins, nephews, ex-girlfriends, ex-roommates, ex-bandmates, and others I'm fortunate enough to call friend or family, many of whom show up in a story with a different name and a severe facial deformity to protect their identities. Thanks for not hating me for changing your name to Cheryl, especially if your name is something like Bill or Walter.

Word Search Featuring More People Who Helped Me Do Things

```
M  C  C  C  Z  X  M  A  R  K  B  L  A  N  T  O  N  S  I  O
H  C  Y  J  A  M  E  S  L  O  U  G  H  C  I  O  L  P  L  S
Y  H  Z  W  A  U  T  H  V  L  J  D  U  A  S  T  O  L  B  R
M  N  K  L  T  Q  X  P  S  U  E  R  N  R  X  Y  I  V  U  E
D  A  V  I  D  R  U  S  H  V  T  W  E  O  L  T  R  I  O  N
K  I  H  O  P  Q  Q  L  N  I  O  D  X  L  S  J  B  I  F  N
J  L  W  N  T  M  C  C  S  W  N  D  I  A  E  S  X  F  S  A
L  G  J  U  O  M  R  W  Y  A  E  E  C  N  M  R  O  S  H  H
E  I  R  N  T  B  I  N  R  T  R  L  O  N  V  N  J  A  Y  N
E  B  H  A  X  L  N  E  I  S  E  I  T  F  R  P  H  G  K  H
G  R  D  G  K  K  L  H  U  F  C  G  N  I  O  B  Y  O  T  O
U  I  O  E  E  Y  W  I  O  C  P  N  M  T  S  Y  S  I  J  J
T  B  W  N  T  L  T  S  U  J  A  S  D  Z  X  D  F  W  Z  H
K  E  Y  M  I  A  N  G  N  Q  C  F  E  G  M  F  C  D  F  D
I  O  I  E  N  E  B  S  Y  R  Y  S  C  E  I  O  B  I  Q  D
N  J  N  G  Z  O  D  N  A  S  E  N  I  R  E  H  T  A  K  P
D  U  I  I  B  K  U  M  Z  V  X  S  G  A  J  O  N  T  H  N
B  E  T  H  A  N  N  F  E  N  N  E  L  L  Y  F  B  F  O  G
B  I  L  L  M  U  R  R  A  Y  E  R  C  D  C  Z  S  I  Q  B
C  Y  D  J  T  R  O  Y  B  L  O  U  N  T  J  R  E  E  S  V
```

BETH ANN FENNELLY

BILL MURRAY

BOB GUCCIONE JR.

BOTTOM

CAROL ANN FITZGERALD

CURTIS WILKE

DAVID RUSH

EL CASTILLO RESIDENTS

IGNATIUS REILLY

JAMES LOUGH

JIM TYLER ANDERSON

JOE BIRBIGLIA

JOHN BONHAM

JOHN HANNERS

JOHN MAXWELL

KATHERINE SANDOZ

LEE GRIFFITH

LEE GUTKIND

MARC SMIRNOFF

MARK BLANTON

NEIL WHITE

ROY BLOUNT JR.

WYNN KENYON

Word Search Answer Key

```
M  C  C  C  Z  X  M  A  R  K  B  L  A  N  T  O  N  S  I  O
H  C  Y  J  A  M  E  S  L  O  U  G  H  C  I  O  L  P  L  S
Y  H  Z  W  A  U  T  H  V  L  J  D  U  A  S  T  O  L  B  R
M  N  K  L  T  Q  X  P  S  U  E  R  N  R  X  Y  I  V  U  E
D  A  V  I  D  R  U  S  H  V  T  W  E  O  L  T  R  I  O  N
K  I  H  O  P  Q  Q  L  N  I  O  D  X  L  S  J  B  I  F  N
J  L  W  N  T  M  C  C  S  W  N  D  I  A  E  S  X  F  S  A
L  G  J  U  O  M  R  W  Y  A  E  E  C  N  M  R  O  S  H  H
E  I  R  N  T  B  I  N  R  T  R  L  O  N  V  N  J  A  Y  N
E  B  H  A  X  L  N  E  I  S  E  I  T  F  R  P  H  G  K  H
G  R  D  G  K  K  L  H  U  F  C  G  N  I  O  B  Y  O  T  O
U  I  O  E  E  Y  W  I  O  C  P  N  M  T  S  Y  S  I  J  J
T  B  W  N  T  L  T  S  U  J  A  S  D  Z  X  D  F  W  Z  H
K  E  Y  M  I  A  N  G  N  Q  C  F  E  G  M  F  C  D  F  D
I  O  I  E  N  E  B  S  Y  R  Y  S  C  E  I  O  B  I  Q  D
N  J  N  G  Z  O  D  N  A  S  E  N  I  R  E  H  T  A  K  P
D  U  I  I  B  K  U  M  Z  V  X  S  G  A  J  O  N  T  H  N
B  E  T  H  A  N  N  F  E  N  N  E  L  L  Y  F  B  F  O  G
B  I  L  L  M  U  R  R  A  Y  E  R  C  D  C  Z  S  I  Q  B
C  Y  D  J  T  R  O  Y  B  L  O  U  N  T  J  R  E  E  S  V
```

About the Author

Harrison Scott Key is a contributing editor for the *Oxford American* and a professor of English at the Savannah College of Art and Design in Savannah, Georgia, where he lives with his wife and three children. His work has been featured in *The Best American Travel Writing* and numerous magazines. Find him at www.HarrisonScottKey.com or @HarrisonKey on Twitter.